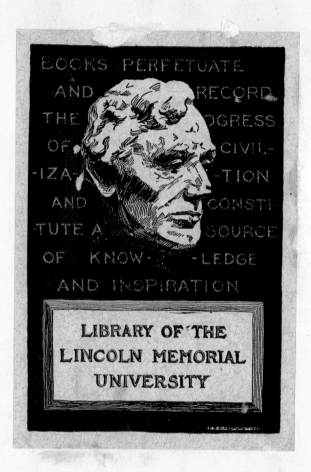

MARION NICHOLL RAWSON

has also written:

LITTLE OLD MILLS

"It is a volume to thrill all who are devoted to Americana and especially all who would get close to the beginnings of our great industrial enterprises of today."
—John Clair Minot, in *The Boston Herald*

SING, OLD HOUSE

"I can think of nothing finer or more valuable than these adventures into the American past."
—Herschel Brickell, in *The New York Post*

"A thoroughgoing guide of profound interest."
—*The Baltimore Sun*

"A woman who seems to know more about how early Americans lived than the most profound historians."
—Harry Hansen, in *The New York World-Telegram*

FROM HERE TO YENDER

"The whole book is abundantly conceived and keeps well the unhurried measure and observational tone of old journeys throughout the country."—*The New Republic*

"A happy mixture of knowledge, experience and human interest, co-ordinated by clear and limpid writing."
—*The Boston Evening Transcript*

WHEN ANTIQUES WERE YOUNG

"A charming exposition of the social customs of old New England."—*The American Mercury*

"A collection of vivid details of the actualities of living."
—*The New York Post*

COUNTRY AUCTION

"To the lover of the antiques of the early American style, the book may act as a guide, but to the lover of real American home life the book is a treasure."
—*The Buffalo Evening News*

"A book of beautiful spirit."—*The New York Times*

CANDLE DAYS

HANDWROUGHT ANCESTORS

The old Beckwith blacksmith shop at Drewsville,
New Hampshire — standing on the tip of a
hundred foot drop to Cold River

MARION NICHOLL RAWSON

HANDWROUGHT ANCESTORS

ANCESTORS

THE STORY OF
EARLY AMERICAN SHOPS
AND THOSE
WHO WORKED
THEREIN

ILLUSTRATED BY THE AUTHOR

E. P. DUTTON & COMPANY, INC.

*Typography arranged and prepared by
S. A. Jacobs, The Golden Eagle Press
Mount Vernon, N. Y.*

DEDICATED TO
THE EARLY AMERICAN
INDUSTRIES ASSOCIATION
BETTER KNOWN AS
The Pick and Shovel Club
❧❦❧

Some of this material has already appeared in
the "Antiques" section of *The New York Sun*

TABLE OF CONTENTS

CONTENTS

HANDWROUGHT ANCESTORS

❦ I ❧

"The deed is to the doer and comes back most to him;
The song is to the singer and comes back most to him,
It cannot fail . . . " — WALT WHITMAN

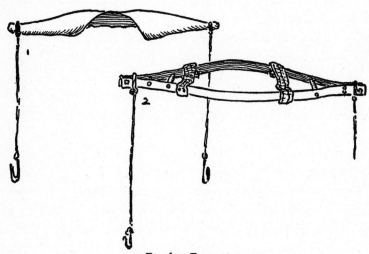

Burden Bearers
1. Red painted yoke, leather thongs and natural
wooden hooks
2. Stick yoke with shoulder posts and braid bands

Work

NOT so much what the workman made in his shop, as what the shop made of the workman, is our concern. Many a tiny tinkerin'-shop turned a botcher into a skilled workman, and a mere tinkerer into a man. Those ancestors of ours who did not work, were, in the language of their day, candlewasters, or spendthrifts of life, while those who labored at large or small became through their labors more worthwhile and handwrought than their finest output, be it polished highboy or soft-singing pewter porringer. To be sure, they knew neither that they were achieving "highboys" nor themselves becoming "handwrought," for these words of today's favor were not accredited a hundred years ago. They would have told us that all things were perforce made by hand (how else, and call it handwrought if you will) and that the high chest on slender legs was but one of many kinds of chests, a little more delicately set up, but much less commodious than those which ran full of drawers from baseboard to girt.

There is much which we do not know about the lives of our ancestors, and much which we would like to know; of how words common to us were unknown to them and yet grew out of their living; of the depth of vexation of soul from failure and lack, and the swing to uplift, as they stood at spinning-wheel, bench or forge and knew the joy of creation; and of how art developed all unconsciously under their fingers when the purifiers among them had cast Beauty and her snare behind them in the Old World, and even those who would have wooed her were apparently bereft of the means whereby to beguile her. The long look back, the treasured work of their hands and hearts and shops, and the memory of their staunch, ingenious souls, give us this one great knowledge and assurance, that cause and effect worked side by side to make them handwrought men and women.

Characteristically they gave the meaning of their lives in a nutshell, using words which had significance for all who should hear: "Them as sets on two chairs will likely set on the floor." There was no time for currying favor in two camps, for there was but one camp, and that was work. Like the lonely but upright chimneys left standing in the cotton fields, which have burned the cabins from off their backs and made themselves isolated but eloquent figures of independence and endurance, the early settler gave up his neighbors, and staked off for himself in a lonely tract — what? Except for a few landed Southern gentlemen of wealth, not one of them planned a hunting preserve or a summer camp for idle hours, but merely a part of the earth's surface where he might work without distraction on his land or in his shop, from dawn until dark, and on and on until the cows came lowing to the bars at dusk on the last day of his life. A chance to work was what most of our ancestors wanted and won for themselves, until work became a habit so strong that to be deprived of the daily stint was to suffer unhappiness. Work does not merely keep one from unhappiness but creates an active happiness, which makes us "highblest."

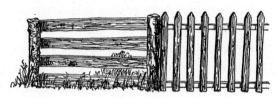

Rainy-day knittin' work in the shop
The moonlight seat

"I just run down to the line fence and visited awhile with Clary, and to hear her tell it, her day hadn't amounted to anything at all, just putter, putter, putter and trot, trot, trot. But I know Clary. It's really just work, work, work and scrub, scrub, scrub, every minute from the time she steps her foot on the floor at four in the morning 'til she crawls back into her bed again at night."

HANDWROUGHT ANCESTORS

A Man's Calling

Why did some men build blacksmith-shops and some build tinkerin'-shops, some whack up a shelter for baking bread and another hang out his sign for barbaring the neighbors? While the local soil and the climate and the nature of the forests and winds had much to do with what a man would choose as his life work, there was yet that indefinable something, that hidden inner urge which "called" him to shopboard, anvil or forge. "Callings" should never be denied and the nice thing about them is that they do their best to disentangle the misfit from his entanglement and set him on the right road. "Calling" is a lovely word to express delight in or tendency toward or natural "leaning" for a certain life work. To many, the choice of a trade or craft for our ancestors seems to have been the merest chance, or perhaps inheritance. There were few laws to regulate a man's craft and he was free to do his own work, and yet he was free only as a bird is free, free to follow his inward call.

There are those who think that the birds are free to fly where they will at all times, and yet a crested phebe-bird will build her nest on the same beam year after year, and if she be disturbed in its construction, will continue to fight for a home in just that one spot, and finally build one there even though the mating season is passed. Her persistence is more than desire — in the face of brooms and hoehandles — it bespeaks an uncontrollable must. Her flight from the water-spring where she must dip for the cementing of her mud lining, is an unvarying low arc over the same weeds, missing the same branches by just so much each trip, clearing the chimney by half a foot, covering always the identical shingles and swooping beneath the eaves between the same vine tendrils. A quick slap of her bill against the growing ball of grass and moss, and she is off again over the same air trail to volplane once more down to her private brick yard. If then, a denizen of the air, hatched with an urge for nests, and circumstanced by shape and size of wing, by the chance proximity of a broad porch beam, and the location of a tree-branch or red brick chimney, not only can, but seemingly must, wear a path of shadow across a hardhack pasture and cut a tunnel through summer air by persistent flight there-in, it should not be difficult for us to realize how natural bent and native surroundings determined the choice of work, the habits and ultimate successes of our earth-bound and much circumstanced forebears.

The steps were easy. A man loved the feel of his adz and saw, and built him a carpenter shop. He loved the glow of the charcoal fire in his forge and the ring of the hammer on the steel-true anvil, and a blacksmith shop grew up under the shading boughs of a chestnut tree — or an elm.

Farm Tinkerin' Shops

Old and deserted farms have their remaining rock designs scattered through the grass, foundations of buildings which once stood there, and among these there will be the ground-floor pattern of the "old shop," which perhaps joined humble shoulder with the big hay barn, or sided with the wagon-house. It was usually within a hop, skip and a jump of the house — which it usually pre-dated since within it the nails of the larger building had been pounded out — for easy reaching on rainy days which were sacred to shop-work. It mattered not that drifts blew high, or rain spattered against the small windows, that the gutters gurgled with full throats and ploughing had stopped, within the four walls of the old shop there was peace and plenty — of work. On busy outdoor days the shop door stood always open, ready for that quick want of a bolt to replace a lost one, a hammer to pound back the cast shoe, or a "crow" for hefting a timber too heavy for man's muscles. All could be found within the shop. A tinker is a mender of kettles and pots, but a tinker-er is a different sort of soul. He may be young or very old, but always he loves to tinker things into shape, mend this and try out that, and the shop is the place for tinkerin'.

Farm shop at North Easton, N.Y. Built in 1786 and autographed with a jackknife by John Wilbur

Perhaps typical of all old tinkerin' shops, or farm shops which have been the battle-field of much exploit, there stands in the dooryard of a farm home in North Easton, New York, an old shop built about 1786 and still doing business. Three and a half feet up from the ground it bears upon one side the cut name of "John Wilbur." It measures about ten by fourteen feet and is but eight feet high at the corners. Door and window are narrow and hugging close together, and the door rock is proportionately small. To show that once upon a time it sheltered curing cheeses, there are great shelves paralleling each other down one side of the interior, while across the way the great bench and vise hold the fort. Nails and tools, hoops and boxes, iron shoes and bootjacks are here in force but there is always room about the tiny stove for more and more things and the bench has its perfect equipment of orderly tools for every purpose. Outside, the barnyard brothers it on one side, and on the other it is sistered by the dooryard and the great stone wall which curves up from the highway far down the lane, and is hung with posies and perfumes.

Through the narrow old door the sun has shone upon a long line of workers of the same family. Forrest Pratt, the present owner, says: "Old shops are always a curiosity to me. I spend a great many happy hours in mine. Probably my heritage is greater than many, anyway I feel I have more to strive for. The sixth generation on this homestead must not fail."

Expansion

The metamorphosis of old shops followed along perfectly natural lines, changing in character whenever a new need arose in the neighborhood. As we have seen, they were at first purely a necessity for the carrying on of the home, but later when more clearings were made, or the next generation had inherited its farm with the hardest work done by its forebears, there was time and inclination for turning a skillful hand and an ingenious mind into broader usefulness, and the man who could whittle or gouge wood or bend it into many forms, spent much of his winter in his little shop, making articles which he knew the neighbors or the less ingenious folks in the nearest village or town, would gladly barter for. A Connecticut Valley farmer reminisces thus:

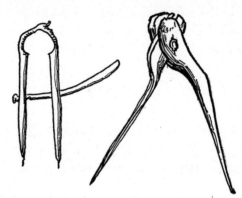

Compasses of twisted and natural-bent wood

"I knew a man what made wooden trays all winter, then come spring he'd go a' peddlin' of 'em. Get him an old hoss and start out. I remember he'd take a pople tree just as wide as he wanted it, then dig it out. He made 'em rounded. Had a cloth against his knee and he'd put his knee into the tray, then hack one end, and then th'other." Another man spent his time peeling and thinning and twisting and steaming slender branches of trees, to be bent into pairs of wooden compasses, and the hoop or hinge of a flail, or the bales of wooden butter tubs and other useful things. Some men whittled toys for children, for fun at first, then for a few pennies. Tops there were with finely pointed ends and a flaring skirt, topped with a slender upright rod to be held in the fingers for twisting, or they cut great lengths of wooden chains from a single piece of wood, each link a free and separate part of the whole. There was the great feat of whittling a little peaked house, like a covered well-curb, with a

18

ball turning within it, and all of one block of wood; and there were little wooden dolls with hinges, and paper knives and wooden spoons, and many another useful article which would take to the road when the frogs began to sing and "mud-time" passed, and "barefoot-time" had come.

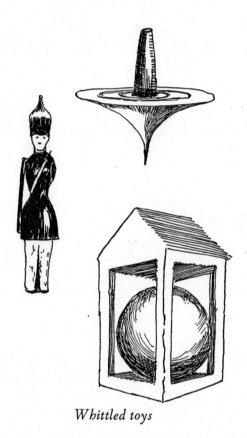

Whittled toys

The Shakers in their communities of the 1700s made their shop work a specialty and fine furniture was made along with the daintier things, such as horsehair tea-strainers, the hairs of a horse tail forming the interwoven bottom, and

19

some of these works of art measuring but an inch across. Snowshoes grew in some shops, and of various sorts. Only sixty years ago some of New Hampshire's snowshoes were nothing but thin pieces of wood with the leather footpiece or "shoe" working on a hinge, winning for themselves the name of "clapper boards,"—a good idea too. These little old shops were useless after the sun went down, for daylight meant work and darkness meant rest, before the coming of our great white lights of science. When a man gathered up his unfinished work and took it into the house before the chimneyplace and its spreading light, it became nothing but knittin' work to pass the minutes before the candle preceded the worker to his kitchen bedchamber.

Wooden pin used in braiding corn-husk mats
Process not known by author

If many folks wanted his wares the workman was warranted in hanging up a sign, and soon, if all went well, a little shop with a counter was undertaken in the same locality or in the nearest village "on the street," and over this counter the retailing of home goods began. Soon these farm beginnings would be but a shadowy reflection or memory.

THE WRIGHT WHO WROUGHT

One of the strange prohibitions of the past was that which kept women or perhaps "ladies," from entering these little shops of men. There were plenty of dame shops where one might trade and yet wear a petticoat, but no lady would go into a cobbler's shop or a blacksmith shop without an escort, while a cigar store was as taboo as a saloon. There are still many women who hesitate to enter these spheres of men where the unknown is carried on, and for this reason men alone have seen the blacksmith swing his great hammers and had the joy of seeing beauty grow under his skillful strokes, of seeing the breathing bellows as the smith leaned his great arm upon the long handle and fanned the forge flame into rosy flowers, or heard the quiet philosophy which slipped from the lips of many a workman who worked alone and found truths of life and time to con them. It is no wonder that women, cut off from so many of life's big, broadening influences, grew circumscribed in interest and gossipy in thought, for only through creation do we ourselves grow and baby creation was limiting.

The Cradles of American Art

When East Jersey began a division of her land into ranges and lots the first of these lots were set apart as "tradesmen's lotts." Newark gave out one of these six-acre lots to the first man of each trade who came for permanent settlement. In 1684 an appeal was sent to London by Governor Lawrence, that tradesmen be sent over to the colony which needed them for swifter growth. Send us a brewer, some carpenters, a baker, a mason and bricklayers, a cooper to make our barrels and casks for our cider, and a smith to make us plows for this rich new soil, was their cry, and until such as these had settled in to any settlement, its

21

growth could not but be retarded. Even though many good farms came in time to include their own mills and shops — the first for grinding and tearing down, and the second for building up — the home cider-mill, saw-mill, shoe-shop and blacksmith-shop of scattered men could not supply the needs of a growing town or bring hope of outside trade. What the authorities wanted was the hum of wheels and the echo from the anvil, an open door on a village street, a Monmouth cap bent over some piece of work, a red-bound green jacket topped with a linen handkerchief, and stout knee-breeches under a leather apron, and homespun legs which moved hither and yon at the town's work. They wanted ingenuity caught in wood and iron, steadiness and thrift, a fair toll, ready-cash, and a few "scores" or chargings, set down in the shopbook — if need be.

Wood-Johnson Farm Shop, Acworth, N. H.

And so the wright wrought in his little shop. Only recently have we come to realize that these humble wrights were sometimes artists and that in their primitive shops, where men sawed and carved and painted and welded and forged, hammered and settled world problems, sometimes crudely, sometimes with an exquisite art, the beginnings of American art were being born. Few masters from across the waters were needed for the laying of this foundation after things had been put under way, and few for its development. Hobby-horses were carved, hinges wrought from iron, block-front furniture hewn and rubbed into loveliness, and many a portrait, now called the "American Primitive," was brushed into the light of day by the hand of a wagon-painter or a preacher, who was native-born and worked in a native shop.

≈§ II §≈

"Good wine needs no bush."

Solid iron shoe sign of 1825
Hanging sign of wood

Pre ABC Days

A MERE alphabet is a stupid thing for all its quarry-like capacity of supplying us with words for every thought and every feeling. It is stupid, like all stupid things, because although potentially productive it has yet no vital spark of its own. Perhaps it is better to liken it to a great black pot which has boiled down to its last essences with the flavor and color of those essences long since gone up in vapor. Our far-back ancestors would have none of it, or them, and did very nicely without, finding the picture or image of the thing to be expressed much more alive and inviting, especially when it was something to be swapped with a neighbor. Back of

24

our alphabets glow the color and body of those early devices which were hung out to catch the eye of the possible swapper, who like the advertiser himself, had no ABCs.

Think of the simplicity of hanging out a provocative replica of one's stock in trade and knowing that the item thus advertised had its advertising taken care of forever, no bills from daily papers or national magazines, no clever copy to be written up — since no man could read. Anyone seeing a boot or shoe hanging from a pole, or beside a door, would easily guess that within the door more boots and shoes might be found, and a wooden hand would suggest gloves, while a mortar and pestle would hardly fail to beckon to the passerby who was in need of epicack or minced frog. Up then with the boot and the glove, and all of the clever symbols which needed neither specs nor larnin' to point the way!

The ancient vintner, whose business was to retail wines, seems to have been the first big advertising man, the first to hang out a shingle, and his was but a branch or "bush" of ivy, the plant supposed to be sacred to Bacchus. The "bush" took many forms, a twig of evergreen, a bunch of ivy, a bundle of brush tied to the end of a pole, broomlike grass hanging before the door; and the quaint and wise saying that "good wine needs no bush," is thus easily explained.

It was but a step from the vintner who retailed wine, to the vintner who added an extra bed or two to his home and became a tavernkeeper. The tavern sign then became the bush. In 1591 they said: "Women's beauty is like vnto a Iuy bush, that cals men to the tauern, but hangs itselfe without to winde and wether." Later, a bunch of vintner's bottles took the place of the bush, or a bunch of wooden grapes, and we were off on the long trail of solid objects which, although not bushes at all, retained that name until the end of the 1600s, not only at tavern and wine cellar doors, but wherever a public notice was necessary. Later we see the wooden frame bearing a picture of vines and grapes or bottles, and wearing upon its head a crown, gentle suggestion that here royalty wined and dined.

The wooden mariner who has shot the sun with his sextant in front of "Riggs & Bro" — watch shop, Philadelphia, for nearly 100 years. Now a landmark rather than a sign

Having been proven successful before places of good fellowship, the sign began to appear before the doors of tiny shops. While the majority of old signs still speak plainly to us today, there were some which have us puzzled. Just why an alligator or a tortoise should have been adopted as a sign for a chemist or apothecary shop, can be understood only after some research, but later, when we enter the shop of the apothecary, we shall know why. The mortar and pestle followed the alligator, and then came the more pretentious glass bottles placed within the shop window, safely protected from stone-throwing boys. These bottles were double and triple affairs with the cork a bottle as well as the body, and they were filled with highly colored waters, suggestive of we know not what, unless it were poison. Then with alligators, mortars and bottles all relegated to the dark lofts, the simple word sign — evolved from the alphabet — came to tell us where to go for drugs, and now for nearly everything which one may require. Man was now an alphabet-wise creature, a reading prodigy.

The Significant Sign

In the villages or on country roads it was really not necessary to hang up a sign, for the neighbors knew what everyone was doing without sign or symbol, and if there had not come the occasional stranger on horseback or by coach, little shops would doubtless have gone on forever with no mark or sign. Some which did appear caused as much merriment as a punch-and-judy show. Rural New York had one shop whose output is utterly forgotten but the firm name of "Crooked and Straight" is ever remembered. Another New York country road had a little cooper's shop with the sign:

I. HAIT THE COOPER

and children passing by to school never forgot to shout, "I hate the cooper, I hate the cooper!" until the cooper began to answer back: "So do I hate thee."

In Brooklyn there was KICK, THE PRINTER. With such startling names no picture or legend was necessary to attract the eye.

A little New Hampshire town, settled by both English and Irish, was rather unique in its stand for absolute democracy among its members. A lawyer among them in all good faith hung out his shingle. It took no time at all for the neighbors to go into a huddle for his banishment. He was given until the next Saturday night to leave the town for this offense, the town fathers decreeing that "We will have none who is best among us; if there be any such let him go elsewhere and among others." A sign which became famous a few miles away hung over the door of the crossroads store and read: "This store will not be open on Sunday, except in case of sickness and death." At Bennington, Vermont, there was a sign before the "Green Mountain Tavern," during the time of the boundary dispute between that State and New York, which has not been forgotten. It was of the prealphabet type. Upon a twenty-foot pole a great stuffed catamount sat "with his large teeth grinning toward New York."

Long, thin signs to nail against each barn rafter or store ceiling timber. "Cure for spavins, ring bones, splints, Pink-Eye, Epizootic and heaves"

Following the Revolution, Samuel Dyer, miller, of Albemarle, Virginia, nailed above the door of his combined store, stagecoach and postoffice, the little sign, PLAIN DEALING. The name came to mean not only the store but the whole estate therabouts. Towns were settled and paths broadened into roads before names were thought of to designate them, but the shop-signs hanging on high acted as guides and even came to mean whole neighborhoods. "Near the sign of the Black Horse" was direction enough to bring you to the locksmith you were seeking, and friends met and goods were traded and money passed hands at The Sign of this and that.

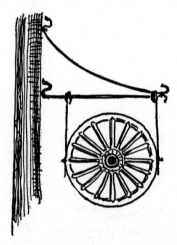

Sign before a Pennsylvania wheelwright's shop

While signs were for many years merely homemade articles and delightfully unique, the same crafts kept rather closely to the same type of symbols. Briefly:

The Music Shop — *A Harp, hautboy* or *fiddle*
Baker Shop — *Wooden peel* or *sheaf of wheat*
Brewer's Sign — *Dray and Horses*
Shoemaker — *A Last*
Cobbler — *Boot* or *Shoe*
Tailor — *Shears*
Undertaking Shop — *Coffin or deathhead*
Tooth Puller — *Huge Wooden tooth*
Spectacle Maker — *Wooden Specs*
Jeweler — *Watch* or *clock*

29

HANDWROUGHT ANCESTORS

Wheelwright Shop — *Suspended Cart Wheel*
Blacksmith — *Supersized horseshoe*
Tobacco Shop — *Human figure,* generally *an Indian* and
  sometimes *a trapper*

Pawn Broker — *Three Balls*
Glove Maker — *Wooden Hand*
Ironmongery — *Handsaw*
Dairy — Picture of *Goat*
Cutler Shop — *A Knife*

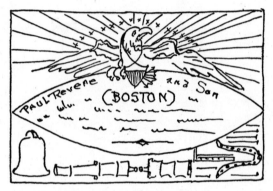

Business card of Paul Revere

The spread eagle was hovering over the commercial world
long before the United States claimed him as a symbol of isola-
tion and strength, for in 1659 he was hung as a sign before
a bookshop in England. When Paul Revere designed his
business card he took the spread eagle to carry his message
to the world, with a striped shield hung about his neck, and
a flare of arrows, stars and rays of glory. Some of the early
American school-marsters hung signs before their doors to
entice youth to a life of learning, and upon these signs were
pictures of boys being switched with the birch-rod. An
inviting lure, surely. Many of the signs were printed "every
which way," the letters turned backwards and badly mis-

shapen. One in Gloucester, Massachusetts, read: "HORSES BAITED & CARPETS BEAT" and the letters showed the handwrought penmanship of some of our ancestors who kept a livery stable.

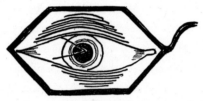

Half of a sign that watches through storm and shine

Persisting Signs

The die-hards among the famous old signs may still be discovered at their old stands in both city and country. In fact, the old signs are being restored wherever resurrected, and starting upon a new era of usefulness and effectiveness. The great spectacles which hang before an optician's shop are still in place, although perhaps electrically bedizened; the solid wooden shoe still swings over quite elegant shoe-shops; huge wheels which once advertised the simon pure wheelwright now point the way to the shop of the handy-man; molars tell us yet of tooth-pullers behind office doors, three balls where the pawnbroker hangs out, wooden watches where we can purchase a new spring, and the striped pole of the barber where we may get a bob or a haircut. There is a six foot monolith of coal in Westfield, New Jersey, which has there marked the coal dealer's tiny shop for more than half a century. Sadly gone, however, from the sidewalks of our towns is the beloved wooden Indian. One old shop sign which used to be seen Down East, read: "God helps them that help themselves, but God help them that I catch help-ing themselves around here."

31

HANDWROUGHT ANCESTORS

Famous Sign Painters

Many a painter who started his art by painting signs for shops, became famous as a portrait painter after the years of youthful potboiling were over. Some of these were Benjamin West, Gilbert Stuart, Charles Willson Peale, Mathew Pratt, and there were others of the same period. These humble beginnings were natural in the face of the fact that the man born to be an artist in the early days of America had a hard row to hoe. There were no wealthy patrons saving their souls by vicariously decorating our churches through the hands of the poor artists — as was so often attempted in the Old World — and often the price of a piece of canvas was more than the would-be artist could afford. A good piece of wood, however, was a splendid medium for painting George Washington upon his prancing white steed, and it were better to have one's pictures swinging high in the clear air of day than never to be swinging at all.

Where all who run may read

SHOP SIGNS

There is a story from Cambridge, Massachusetts, of a huge leather shoe which hung before a shoemaker's door, as a sign of his trade. Over it was this sign: "If it fits you, it's yours." It hung for some time and then one day an express-man dropped in to enquire the size of the shoe hanging above and finding it fitted him perfectly, asked for the mate and walked off with a gift from the skies. Somewhere, they say, there's an answer to every question and a man for every need.

THE TAN YARD

~§ III §~

1 . THE TANNERY

"Neighboring tan pits scent the passing gale."

Country shoe of leather — New York State

Source Materials

IF one may divert the usual meaning of a common phrase, leather and wood may be called the "source material" of the early American settler. Both were used for shelter and clothing, for the making of utensils, and even for food, the cattle surviving on brouse when fodder ran short, and men "eating their boots" when in a similar dilemma. The great usefulness and need of leather is perhaps not as generally recognized as that of wood, and a glimpse at the workableness of

34

this material leads to far fields of interest. When a drinking vessel was needed, wood would make a capacious tankard of slender staves and whittled cover, or yield itself to the gouging shave of the noggin-maker, while leather went into the formation of the "black jack" drinking mugs, so that the Englishman laughed at the colonist for drinking out of his boot; both materials made excellent sieves, the one by criss-crossing its slats close together, the other by being punched with numerous holes placed rather for profusion than for order and symmetry; but when it came to the matter of breeches, wood made a bad falling off and left the field to leather, the former being a flat failure when it came to wrapping itself about the human form for reasons of modesty, protection or adornment. So, while possessed of an amazing sturdiness for lasting wear, leather's greatest asset was its ability to lend itself gracefully to the needs of the human frame, while wood refused to yield an inch and remained unbending and stiff-necked. To the trees and the animals, then, our ancestors went for their chief materials of everyday living.

Move On, Poor Tanner

Among the little shops of our ancestors are those where leather was cut and formed into various articles, and among these the best known were the shoemaker, cobbler, harness and saddler shops; but behind these lay the places where hides were brought from their native state into the durability and usefulness of leather, and these places were called tan yards or tanneries. The tannery with its broad spread of running waters and vats, various sheds and buildings, may perhaps be challenged as a legitimate "shop," but shop it was, or included, for without the currier and his manipulations, leather would have had few of those yielding graces which distinguish it from wood, and the currier worked in his own "shop."

Poor tanner! He seems to have been doomed by his trade to "move on" at the call of his neighbors whenever his yard lay within or too close to the confines of a village or town, for in the manipulation of his hides and their curative dressings he was forced to the use of combinations which smelled to heaven, so that almost invariably storms of protest arose and swarmed about his honest head like swamp mosquitoes. It was no uncommon thing for a tanner to be suddenly invited to take himself and his wares and equipment farther afield from sensitive noses. In 1739 Philadelphia drove all of its six tanners outside the town, and then settled the trouble with a compromise when the tanners promised not to "burn their tan" on the premises. In 1674 New York City found its four tanners entirely necessary to their living but utterly impossible as near neighbors, and pronounced their trade a nuisance and compelled them all to move beyond the city wall, or the Wall Street of today. These tanners were in reality shoemakers who did their own tanning, so one may imagine the inconvenience of having to travel away out to the Van Tienhoven Grant, the present Maiden Lane, to prepare their hides when their shops were back within the distant city walls. Within two years the tanning center, or "shoemaker's land" was at the "Old Swamp," in the vicinity of John and Frankfort streets, near the Brooklyn Bridge, and to this day the leather industry is largely centered there.

The tanner was usually also a currier as well as a shoemaker, since there was less division of labor in those days, and a man who knew leather at all knew it from the ground up in all of its possibilities. A tanner who lived in Philadelphia and doubtless spent much of his time in his tan yard, went by the happy name of "a skinner."

Bay Tanner

Toward the end of the 1700s Jonathan Bass Rawson arriving in New Hampshire from Massachusetts was put down in the county records of his newly chosen state as a "bay tanner." This name had nothing to do with the color of his hides nor the horse he may wish to have owned but did not; it had to do only with the fact that he came from the ancient colony and state which curled about Massachusetts Bay and chose always to be marked and known by its lapping waters. This bay tanner raised four sons on the proceeds of his tanning carried on "down the path" from the dooryard of his new farm in Alstead, the "East Part." Close to the brook he placed his simple first shelters, "put down his tan yard," built a capable chimney of brick, installed a sturdy pump as one of his few mechanical helpers, dug and lined vats or pits, saw that the stonewall which surrounded his new yard was stout and solid everywhere except where it must be left open to the highroad — really a stump-filled trail — for the entrance of farmers coming to him with their yearly supply of hides for home use, and then got down to his smelly but honest trade.

Today there remain to mark the old tannery only a row of silent and remembering maples, a rock-climbing brook, a sinking pile of bricks where the old chimney long ago gave up the ghost and fell in an untidy tumble, the clearing so arduously won in the beginning — which still fights back the onrush of thieving alders but yields to the touch of beauty when the season brings the sunny blossoms of the elecampane — and, last but not least, the slumbering row

of four remaining vat hollows which although slowly filling
with the years, still refuse to grow quite up to the level of
what is no longer the tan yard but a rough and neglected
cow pasture, thus proving its loyalty to an honorable past.
Up in the old farmhouse the old "corn chamber" is still
pointed out on the second floor, where the bay tanner
stacked his sheep skins through the winter for the refrigera-
tion which Mother Nature would give at thirty or forty
below zero.

This Jonathan was wise, for he eschewed proximity to a
settlement from which he might one day be asked to "move
on." Three generations of his family worked in the old tannery, and a son of the third "when he came to his majority"
went five miles from home and built himself a tannery which
is now also a vine-bound ruin, after having served its tanner
for a long life time. This grandson bettered his grandfather's
location by choosing the banks of the lovely but wild
Ashuelot River rather than the side of a simple farm stream.

Beginnings

Experience Mitchell, arriving on the ship *Ann* in
1623, was the first American tanner, although the first
known date of his establishing a tannery was in 1650 at
East Bridgewater. It is claimed that the first tan yard "put
down" in America was achieved by Francis Ingalls at
Swampscott, Massachusetts, in 1630 or 1632. Ingalls'
house, built in 1629, was a log cabin and close to this, in
the dooryard, one might say, he sank two vats with raised
plank siding, and set up three rough frames made of sticks
crossed at each end with a pole laid across the top, sawhorse
style, where he hung his skins to dry. His quantity achievement may have been small, but it was from these incredibly

simple equipments that we get some feeling of how little our ancestors needed to work with, to accomplish great conveniences in living.

Nicholas Easton established a tannery in Ipswich in 1634, and a tanner was dressing goatskins and hides at Salem in 1639. It is difficult to ascertain just when the tannery business began in Elizabeth Towne, New Jersey, but this place was called "the mother of tanners" for many years, and the Ogden family, responsible for its carrying on, sent its trained workers into other nearby colonies.

Virginia, in 1662, acted legislatively to have tan houses erected in each county at county expense, with the provision that tanners, curriers and shoemakers be provided as well. The pay for each hide brought to these public tanneries was two pounds of tobacco for every pound of hide, while the shoes produced from the hides were sold for thirty and thirty-five pounds for the six largest sizes. The price of the daintier sizes seems to have been forgotten. Perhaps the counties encouraged small feet by shoeing them gratis. It is well to remember always that when a colony or group made a point of legislatively encouraging a certain industry, that industry had not been a popular one.

In 1693 the plantation of Samuel Mathews had its retinue of servants and slaves busy in the various shops, some of them working in the tannery where enough leather was tanned to keep eight shoemakers busy at their trade. We have already seen that New York had early turned to tanning and its tanneries soon made up the outstanding tanning center of the country for that period. While tanneries did not spring up wherever hemlock and oak grew, there was never a tannery for bark tanning unless these trees grew in the vicinity and in abundance.

*Tannery of Matthias Smith and Peter Doremus
West Bloomfield, New Jersey, 1807
Currier house built by David Riker — twenty by
seventeen feet. Site at 38 Church Street,
Montclair, today*

Tannery Layout

Although there were many processes carried on there, a tannery might be entirely in the open or have but one real building or shop within its enclosure of stonewall or board fence, and that would be the dry house and currier's shop where the leather was dressed and perhaps colored. For the rest there was the brook, the pond or pool, the barkmill, the tanyard and the vats — time brought further shelters and buildings. New Jersey histories show that after nearly two hundred years of tanning in this country, Matthias Smith and Peter Doremus built just such a primitive tannery in the environs of Newark at West Bloomfield, in 1807, and the sum of $190 covered the cost of material for the shop twenty by seventeen feet, and the building of it by David Riker. This Jersey tannery was not a one-horse affair but important in supplying leather to the growing business of shoemaking nearby in Newark, and run by men of importance. As another sidelight, history in the same State records the fact that fifty-seven years before this, or in 1750, Benjamin Biles had a tannery in Trenton, which covered over two acres and included a bark house, mill house, beam house, bark mill, stone currying shop, leather house, a hay house, stable and chaise house, and vats enough to tan calfskins and eight hundred hides a year. This may stand as a record of how many buildings were really needed, or could have been used in those old tanneries which got along with so few, and impresses us still further with the ingenuity of our forebears who could make something out of nothing with remarkable ease.

In spite of the elegance of this Trenton tannery and the improvements entered upon by a certain Colonel William Edwards remembered in this connection about 1794, the primitive layout was retained generally until well into the 1800s. Bishop, the historian of early industrial development says: "Rude appointments of a tannery before 1794. A number of oblong boxes or hogsheads sunk in the earth near a small stream without cover or outlet below, to serve as vats and leeches. A few similar boxes above ground for lime vats and pools, an open shed for a beam house, and a circular trough fifteen feet in diameter in which bark was crushed by alternate wooden and stone wheels, turned by two old or blind horses, at the rate of one half cord a day." The Edwards improvements were in the line of vat construction which were to lead to easier ways. Trunks of plank were laid down and made tight beneath his vats to carry off the spent liquor, and there was a junk to receive it. Next, leeches above ground were built in tiers one above another, the liquor raised by a suction pump worked by two or four men. Incidentally, there are men alive today who remember the great envy they had, as little boys, of those friends of theirs who worked the pumps in their father's tanneries, the latter probably suppressing from their envious friends the hatred which each carried in his young heart for those tedious, hardworking, play-forbidding pumps.

A Remembered Tannery

Howard Slocum of Easton, New York, sat on his doorstep one sunny June morning and remembered back to the days of his boyhood when a tannery had been a part of the lovely white cottage in which he was now living. It may be well to set down briefly his rememberings as a preliminary resume of the art of tanning by the simple methods of the latter half of the 1800s, before taking up the various steps in greater detail. He pointed back under the tall locust trees which shaded his grassplat and cooled the garden as far as the high bushes and trees which have now buried and absorbed the old tanyard:

*A. The "beam" for holding hide while scraping
down to remove hair. Early. Ten feet
B. Later "standard" — straight surface of yellow
glass fastened to wood*

THE TAN YARD

"The farmers brought their hides into the basement of the finishing room, and there was the office too. There was a vat six feet deep and about six or eight feet across the top. Folks used to bring their hen manure by the barrel to sell for the hen lye, and this went into the vats and they'd throw the green hides in and let them stay all winter or for months. This took off the hair. Yes, these are all cowhides I'm talking about. There was a leanto on the west and when the hides were taken out they were carried there and split down the backbone and beamed. The beam was a great thing — rounded slablike — hewed out of something, with a yard long board three inches thick that took off the stuff, rubbing against the beam. This was called beaming the hides.

"Then I remember there was a haybarn, and a horsestable down underneath.

"Oh, yes, after that they put the hides into hemlock vats and let 'em lay there for months. The vats were ten feet long and six feet deep and lined with hemlock four by sixes. You see they had to have hemlock bark for the tanning and the farmers brought it in by the cord. It was ground in a monstrous old building to keep it dry, and after it was ground it was put into these vats. There was a big iron grinder or hopper three foot round, and we boys helped break up the hemlock bark and throw it into the hopper. Up above, the old horse-shaft run up through the floor — you see the second floor was right off the ground on this hill slope — and the horse walked round in a fifty foot circle and ground it. The curing was done back in a long narrow building called the bark shed. After sometime it was carried into the office and put on a marble slab ten by four foot and three inches thick, and set table height. See that porch floor back yonder by the kitchen

43

door? That's part of the marble slab. They cut it off to make it fit the porch after the old tannery was gone. The man that crushed the hide had a piece of heavy glass four by three inches set in a black walnut handle and he'd rub that across the leather with both hands until he'd smoothed it out just as slick. Then he worked in the oil, and the piece was ready for market — as soon as it was rolled up. I suppose I don't remember maybe all of it for it was all back when I was a boy. I'm all boogered up now — not much good." Then, "We're still ploughing up hair and bricks and tan bark."

The Beaming House

A "green hide" was not a hide with green pigments, but simply a fresh, new hide brought from the slaughter-house or the home killing without preservative, and better than a salted and dried hide because it would not crack in the later drying as the latter often did. The first thought of the tanner was that the hide of whatever nature be trimmed of its poorer parts, cleansed, dehaired and defleshed for later tanning. If the hide were green and unsalted it needed only to have its blood and dirt removed, and if the hide were dried and hard it needed softening and swelling. There was the clear running brook ready to give a limitless number of needed baths, and where necessary, make ready for the softening bath in lime water, after which the harder hides were kneaded with wooden rollers. When the brook came to be considered too primitive a cleansing vat, casks were resorted to, great tubs measuring fifty-four inches across and standing four feet and a half high. Still later a "tub wheel" or rotating drum was devised in which hides were tumbled about to loosen their blood and dirt. This initial bath filled two purposes, that of loosening the hair and of softening the hide by loosening its fibres to make it more pliable as well as more vulnerable to the later application of tanning substances.

When it was found that the innocent looking droppings found beneath the branches where the hens roosted, when dissolved in water would remove the lime and alkali as well as loosening the hair, another step from earlier tanning had been taken, a step which could not have been depended upon by the earlier settlers since hens in quantity were not among their belongings. A new means of making money had come to the farmer. In 1862 the tanners in Florida were removing hair with lye leeched from oak ashes.

The "beam" which gave the name to the beaming house, was often nothing but a tree split in two lengthwise, measuring sometimes ten feet long, generally shorter, and raised on one end to working height or between three and four feet high. It was over this beam that the softened skins were laid. The beamsman, holding a double handled knife which stretched beyond the width of the beam, scraped away from his body down the incline of the beam, thus removing the loosened hair, the horny and rough excresences. When this was accomplished he turned the hide and with a sharper knife removed any remaining portions of flesh or fat. In this part of the tannery he also split the hide "down the backbone" and rescraped it, trimming off the less perfect ends and edges, and sometimes wasting much good material in the light of today's knowledge of the trade. The hides were then again washed in clear water mixed with barley or some acid ingredient, and were now called "butts."

The Bark House

"Tanning" means turning the hides of animals into leather, apparently coming from the same derivative as does

45

the word "tawny." During the 1700s and earlier these two words were used interchangably, although the latter was more correctly applied to tanning leather white. It is generally believed that it was in the attempt to color, or taw, or tan skins, that the process of preservation was discovered, and that the word "tan" which meant "to turn brown," came, after this, to mean curing and preservation as well. In other words, the natural coloring agents such as tree barks and plants which were used for dyeing leather, began to ward off rot in the hides and give them a degree of permanent usefulness. When this discovery had been made there was still no attempt to make the pliable leather of today, but simply to administer enough dye and preservative liquid to give some pliability to the animal skins remaining after the flesh had been devoured. It was for later generations to discover that the fermentation which took place when these coloring barks were left in water, developed a substance which was given the name of "tannin," and the lexicographers of the late 1700s did not know the word.

The oak was the usual bark of earlier tanning days, but was followed by other barks, and after 1800 the hemlock became the great favorite. While oak tanning continued in oak abundant sections, it now had a rival where the hemlock flourished. The wood, nuts and leaves as well as the bark of the chestnut tree were also found successful for tanning, as well as gall nuts and the leaves of the sumach for lighter skins. The farmers found it a lucrative task to furnish these needed barks for "tawing" for they brought three or four dollars a cord in 1792, a large sum for that day but pitifully inadequate if the matter of time had entered into the price, which it seldom did with the old fashioned farmer.

"Oh, time? I wasn't doing nothing else, might as well been doing that as anything."

Tan mill for grinding bark by man-power, 1866

Those who brought hemlock found that during June the bark most easily separates from its parent stem and so, their trees having been felled, they would "peel, pile and let it lay till winter and then sled it off" to the tannery. The tanner was known not only as a tanner of leather but also as a grinder of bark. We have already found the hopper method of the 1800s, but before this the crushing with a great stone disk seems to have been called the likeliest way. A great revolving post was fastened between floor and ceiling of the shop, with a great wooden sweep projecting from one side. At the end of the beam was the horse, but half way between the two the shaft passed through the eye of a great stone disk like a millstone but with its edges corrugated and roughened. When the horse began his circling course around the central post, the stone moved in a smaller circle over the bark scattered on the ground. Sometimes post and stone were at the same end of the sweep, and against the other end two or four men pushed to keep the stone revolving, this time in a more restricted circle. In Newark, New Jersey, in 1676 "the tannery was planted above a meadow where tan vats were placed on a hillside convenient to a water-fall. On the oak floor a huge wooden cogged wheel slowly revolved, crushing the black and red oak bark." Sometimes there were two wheels, one of wood and one of stone, which alternated in crushing the bark in a great fifteen foot, circular trough, or "pool." These crushing stones are described also as acting like the grinding stones of a grist mill, which were placed one above the other, with the bark crushing in between upper and nether stones.

The "bark house" in time became the "bark mill" with its great wooden water wheel which did away with the bent backs of men and the circling of the blind horses around the central post. Where bark was exposed to the weather in the outdoor type of tannery, it soon became evident that it was of prime importance to keep it covered and dry that it might retain in fullest measure its dyeing and tanning properties, and the bark house and later the bark mill became buildings of considerable size and used both for grinding and packing away.

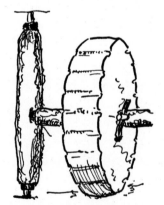

Tanbark mill run by horse-power

THE TAN YARD

Vermont did away with an old horse-mill at Johnson where was set up a large overshot wheel which turned the great crushing wheels, and we find that there too the great wheel of the Bacon tannery, mounted about 1830 and surviving until the 1900s, became then a hillside relic of quaint loveliness. It was an undershot wheel twelve feet in diameter with blades eighteen inches wide, on which were set pockets for catching water from the brook below.

Tan House

"I made me a trough out of a big pine-tree, into which I put the hides of any cattle that died among us. I used ashes for tanning them, instead of lime, and bear's grease for oil. The thickest served for sole leather and the thinner ones, dressed with a drawing knife, for upper leather; and thus I made shoes for myself and neighbors." This is signed by Benj. Birt, Potter County, Pennsylvania, and dated 1811.

The primitive tan vat was perhaps only a sunken hogshead, but more often a six foot rectangular pit dug in the ground and lined with spruce or hemlock planking, this lining protruding above the earth. The early tanneries seem to have had somewhat smaller pits than those which were used later, for pits varied in size from five to more feet with plenty of room for easy packing and later turning of hides. From the little picture left to us of the first New World tan yard at Swampscott, we find only two pits. Vats increased in number until there were at least four, making it possible for the hides to pass through a series of liquors starting with a very weak one and ending with the strongest.

Bark tanning was unknown to the American Indian who was yet the most skilled of tanners when the white man arrived. He worked his skins with fat and oils and the brains

and livers of animals, and his white buckskins were of such
high quality that they have never been bettered by later
processes. It was the Indian, working with the sharp foreleg
bone of an animal who did the real "tawing" or tanning
leather white, soft and weatherproof. Elk and deer skins were
made "soft and plume and as white as milk" and this was
said of the white man's work after he had been taught by
the Indian how to turn fresh hides into untanned leather.
Hair was left on the skins for winter warmth, the garment
into which they were made being worn with the soft hair
next the skin.

The principle of bark tanning was that beneath the re-
movable epidermis and an under tissue of the hide there
remained the corium, a fibrous material with an albuminoid
secretion, which, upon immersion in tannin or a tannic acid,
had its fibres brought together into a hard and stiff mass,
which remained solid when put into clear water, but became
soluble in lime water. This process was sometimes spoken of
as "fulling" the hides, in the first half of the 1700s, and
gave the name of "fulling mill" to some of the tanneries,
since fulling meant both to whiten and to thicken, as with
cloth.

A sort of club sandwich of several stories was built up in
the vats when the tanning proper was to begin, a layer of
bark about an inch thick being sprinkled between each layer
of leather, and then this was covered with water and started
on its leeching of many months. With a long wooden pole,
with a hook on the end which measured over a foot, the tanner turned and rearranged the hides from time to time so
that the liquor might permeate the different butts evenly.
By looks and by "feel" he knew when they were ready to
be removed. The tanner of today, lacking this more intimate

knowledge, trusts a mechanical test at this point. A half year or more was generally necessary, especially if the hides were heavy and thick, since tanning was about as rapid a process as the making of the old hasty puddings, which took at least an hour and a half when done in a pot, and four and twenty hours when entrusted to the oven.

After the tan bark had served for a half year or so it was called "spent tan" and pressed into lumps,—"the Bark cast out of Tan-pits, wrought into Turfes and dried — good fuel."

Drying frame for skins

The Dry House

With the actual tanning accomplished the leather was washed, oiled and hung up to dry. The magnified sawhorse in the open did service for the original tanyards for both the first period when some drying was allowed in order that the tan might set, and for the long after drying. The next manual work was the "striking," or rubbing with a stone set in a block of wood. Later years brought the "striking pin," a two handled, three edged tool which removed the greyish gloss or "bloom" assumed during the long leeching in the vats. Another washing was now due and this might easily be in a bath of sumach, with another dripping and setting period before the drying began. Old tales tell of tanners, situated just outside a city gate, spreading their wet skins out across the paths so that people passing in and out would tread them, both drying and toughening them.

HANDWROUGHT ANCESTORS

Great drying houses were gradually acquired, or the drying was done in the loft of the beaming house or other building. Hides which had been dried when brought to the tanners were given extra attention at this point, dried a little and then sweated in a heap on the floor, to make them more pliable, and less likely to crack; but this method was finally abandoned for while it increased pliability and thus lightened the "lether dresser's" work, it often went further and achieved a fatal rot. A cowhide is a heavy piece of material when it is stone dry, but considerably heavier when it is wet, and so, long carts were built for hauling them from vat to drying rack or house, drawn by the patient blind horse when he was not circling his sweep-pole.

By and large, the work of tanning a hide, including the cleansings, scrapings, tawings and curings, its dryings and brushings, took a good part of a year.

THE TAN YARD

2. THE CURRY SHOP

Leather Dresser

ONE ox or one cow must be marked each year for fatting, killing, tanning and dressing for a family's needed supply of leather. There must be at least one spoken for, but in addition to this all skins of all animals which fell by the wayside would be saved and in time carried to the tanner, if not tanned at home. This was the rule for the farms of America during its first two centuries, and longer. If the family ran on toward twenty in numbers it goes without saying that shoes for the entire outfit could not be squeezed out of just one hide, no matter how carefully the farmer shoemaker or the tarrying shoemaker might cut his leather or save his tag ends. There were the breeches and the harnesses, the hats, and often the skirts of the women folks, not to speak of all the straps and hinges and shoe thongs and binding thongs and numberless other articles which must be supplied by "Old Star" or "Old Buck," or the milder Sukeys, after their flesh and bones had been salted down in brine, hung up to freeze for winter use, been smoked for days in the smoke-closet, or fried and boiled and stewed, or jerked and dried for food.

While hide and skin may be one and the same thing to the layman, to the worker in leathers, the "hide" is the skin of the larger animals, the fullgrown ox, the horse and buffalo, while the "skin" is the covering of the smaller animals, such as calves, goats, deer and sheep. In other words there are not, and were not for our forefather shoemakers and leather dressers, any such thing as "cow skin" or "goat hide," but

53

rather cowhide and goatskin. There were also the "kips," or kip skin, leather prepared from the skin of young cattle or other larger animals. Naturally sole leather came from the first group which supplied heavy hides, while shoe uppers, gloves and breeches came from the lighter skins, and the skin of the sheep was good only for still lighter needs, such as pocket-books and book covers. The currier or "lether dresser" must know all hides and all skins and their various possibilities, and how to make them tough and stiff or soft and pliable.

We have already learned that the corium is that part of the hide buried below two coverings, and it is this part which becomes the leather proper. The outer part on which the hair has grown, called the "grain" of the leather, is fine and close, while the "offal" is naturally the under part which comes in closest contact with the perishable flesh of the animal, and is therefore loose and coarse. The worker on the "corium" became the "currier," the one who "drubbed" and beat and struck and pounded, then smoothed and oiled and brushed and polished — if necessary — the leather for its many uses. The stableman curries his horse's fine coat, which means to rub and comb and smooth and make beautiful.

Undressed leather, after it had been tanned, needed only to be smoothed and softened and fulled with a small stone-inserted instrument, and then brushed for a finish. Dressed leather, on the other hand, needed "stuffing"— a tanner word — with oils and fats to make it stronger, more impervious to water and while more solidified, yet flexible.

Massachusetts took a deep interest in her leather output in the 1640s, and she had her "leather sealer" or "marker of leather" who saw to it that State tanning laws were ob-

served. A law of 1642 required the tanner not to curry any
sole leather with anything but good hard tallow, nor with
less than the leather would receive, nor dress nor curry any
upper leather (shoe uppers) but with good and sufficient
stuff — not salt — and should thoroughly liquor it until
it would receive no more. They were not to burn or scald
any leather in currying.

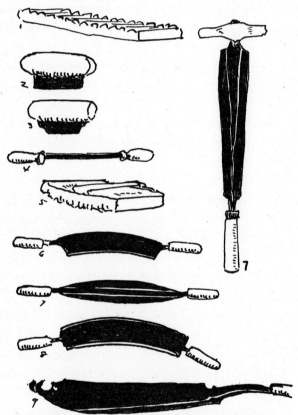

1. Pommel 2. Scraper 3. Slicker 4. Roller
5. Raising board 6. Unhairing knife, 17 inches
7. Tanner's pin—to remove bloom 8. Fleshing knife
9. Iron sciver for cleaning hides, 15 inches

HANDWROUGHT ANCESTORS

It is good to know that the currier was entirely independent of other men, even the blacksmith, in the matter of his tools. His best friends were the wood of the nearby trees and the stones beneath his feet. For years before there were knives for his easier laboring, he removed the hair from the grain of the hide with a sharp edged narrow stone set in a handhold of wood; with a board he removed fleshy parts left below, and did all of the nicer scraping and smoothing and polishing with stones of various edges and widths. The beam upon which he accomplished the former was but a split tree trunk, or puncheon, and the slab for the latter was either a block of wood faced with stone, or a smooth stone of the right height and inclination.

Many settlers took care of their own hides and knew how to tan and curry and finish leather. It was a matter of learning how to soften by stretching and rolling, with hands and simple tools while the leather was caught across a "stand" or laid flat upon a stone slab. Then again the leather must be scraped smooth of its bumps and excrescences, lose its wrinkles and natural crinkles. In 1802 Joseph Condit, Junior, of Bloomfield, New Jersey, found that the resultant shavings from this process had a value all their own, and won a patent for the exclusive right to use these "currier's shavings" in the manufacture of certain kinds of paper.

Stuffing With Oil

There is a vitality about the hides and skins of animals which is remarkable. Long after they have become leather, centuries after in fact, they still not only want to be given their victuals and drink, or sup and bite, but insist upon it, threatening and achieving a fadeaway if the want is not filled. Old leather on ancient books which crumbles in dry

56

red rot against one's clothes at the slightest handling, will spruce up and grow smooth and crumbless — for a while at least — when oiled and caressed back into happiness. The currier knew this need for food or fuel or grease and supplied it according to his circumstances or his pet theories. That some curriers were careless in this matter may be inferred from the making of laws to prevent carelessness, but we have ample evidence on all sides that as a rule our handwrought ancestors did not begrudge labor or fine care in their work, whether it was with leather or lumber or whatnot.

The Indians, knowing nothing of bark tanning, worked their hides and skins into a leather perfection by simply taking the brains and livers of their animals and smearing them over and into the skins which had once covered and protected them. Old "Leather Stocking," of James Fennimore Cooper fame, kept his tanned leather leggings in good condition for their lasting service by stretching them, every few months, on his roof, nailing them at the corners and giving them a good dose of well rubbed in salt, which substance we have previously seen had been forbidden by law in early Massachusetts Bay Colony. Some tanners used "Liver Oil," or a combination of oil and homemade soft-soap; some used an ordinary "fat liquor" from the dripping pans set upon their hearths to catch the drip of juices from their roasts of spare-ribs, hanging and twisting about before the flames; some used lard tried out at the winter killings.

In the 1880s, almost at our own threshold of time, tanners were using whale oil, preferably that which had had its "try-out" at sea, or the "winter pressed," — the "summer strained" oil being less potent. Herman Melville described the odor of the smoke which came from this trying-out of whale oil, thus: "It smells like the left wing of the day of judgment, it is an argument for the pit." So we find one more smell to be jotted down to the credit of the tanning world.

Stuffing was not applied lightly with a cloth or brush as a general rule, but was hammered in with a mallet, no loopholes being left where it had not entered into the body of the grain.

Since the color prescribed by economy and style for all shoes of earlier days was black, the currier included the coloring of his leather with the rest of its dressing. The leather had acquired its tan or tawn in the tan vats, but this tended toward a brown, and so lamp-black was resorted to as the deadliest black and was made applicable when mixed with tallow and oil, or with linseed oil to which tallow and wax and a little soap were added. Copperas water — green vitriol — came to be one of the blackeners of the grain side of leather, and even after official sealers and markers of leather were a thing of the past, tanners continued to mark their leather with a "G" for good, or a "B" for bad, through the first quarter of the 1800s.

Unlike the tan-yard proper, the currier's shop was a pleasant place to linger, for the odor of leather may be as sweet and wholesome as a June rose, if one cares for it.

SHOEMAKER – COBBLER SHOP

"Nay, if a Schoonmaker me wed,
his Shop-Thread I can spin."

To mill or to meetin'

Backgrounds

IT is evident from the above remark that the life of a shoe-maker's wife was made difficult by having her family spinning stints augmented by the spinning of thread for the making of the schoon of the entire neighborhood, a good bit of a task for a colonial mother, and testing her hand-wrought character rather well. The wife of the "cobbler" was probably no less busy, for a mender of shoes must have needed quite as much thread as a maker of them.

59

HANDWROUGHT ANCESTORS

The shops of both of these tradesmen and craftsmen must come within the circle of our interests, for both were among the most conspicuous and necessary of their day.

The earliest tanneries presupposed a shoemaker's shop, since the initial reason for tanning leather and dressing it in the first quarter of the 1600s, was for the purpose of supplying shoes to the neighborhood, and a man was a tanner in the summer and a shoemaker in the winter. We find the names of the first shoemakers synonymous with those of the first tanners, some of whom we have already discovered. We know Experience Mitchell, the tanner who arrived in 1623; and in 1628-9 there was Thomas Beard sent out by the Plymouth Company in London, who "hath in the Shipp May Flower divers hydes, both for soles and vpp leathers, wc hee intends to make vpp in botes and shoes there in the country." Lynn, a later citadel of shoes, welcomed its first shoemakers, Philip Kertland and Edmund Bridges in 1635. Newark, New Jersey, with a tannery running since 1676 and a perfectly good deacon for a leather sealer, put herself on record in 1680 as "willing that Sam'l White-head should settle among us provided he will supply the town with shoes." Newark was apparently somewhat chosey in her welcome to newcomers, but illustrates fairly well the supervision which local governments were keeping over their industries.

The difference between the northern and southern sections of the New World — the former producing largely for itself, and the latter, with greater fortunes, buying abroad — is well known, but this revealing statement has a place here, and Charles Town, South Carolina, was probably typical of the South in 1731:

"Most of the shoes are brought from England and generally sell for forty shillings per pair. Not but that they have Hides enough and very cheap — an Ox's Hide being sold for thirty shillings, neither are they destitute of the Means to Tan them: for they make very good Lime with Oyster-shells, and the Bark of the Oak trees is so plentiful, that it costs nothing but the trouble of gathering: They want therefore only a sufficient number of good Tanners and Shoemakers. I might say the same of Leather Dressers since they send every Year to England above 200,000 Deer-Skins undrest. Yet Carolina produces Oker naturally and good Fish-oyl may be had from New York or New England very cheap: So that they might be drest and made up into Breeches in the country, for which those skins are very proper being warm in Winter and cool in Summer."

Cobbler's kit, New Jersey
Hole made in cobbler's arm-chair by throwing the
awl between punches

What was his Name

Today the words "shoemaker" and "cobbler" are synonymous as applied to the old fashioned workman who sat on a low bench and made or mended shoes. To our ancestors there was a distinction, the former being known as a maker of shoes from the rough hide through to the finished boot, and the other the mender of boots and shoes. There were probably many shoemakers who were also cobblers, but the cobbler was not necessarily a shoemaker, although many may have been so dubbed. Even today one seldom hears a New Englander speak of a "cobbler." A cobbler, in the late 1700s, was a "mender of shoes, a botcher." A "botcher" was a mender of old clothes. In the early 1800s the word-books said that a cobbler was a mender of shoes, and "a bungler," and in the middle of the century they had defined the word cobbler more definitely as "a clumsy workman." St. Crispin, the shoemaker's god, must have writhed a little to hear even his repair children so named. So it is probable that our ancestral shoemakers did not relish being called cobblers, if indeed their patrons ever erred so flagrantly as do we today. Side by side these two artisans may be placed and treated together, for it is little likely that the first settlements had two separate shops, one where their footwear was made and another where it was mended. With the coming of shoemaking machinery in the middle 1800s, the shoemaker was the large manufacturer and the cobbler the man who still sat on his bench and made or mended shoes.

Before either of these names were used the maker of shoes was a "cordwainer" or cordwinder, the former persisting to within a few years, and the latter being a corruption of it. Even the old spelling of "shoe," which was "schon" and "schoon'" in the 1200s and 1300s in England, and sometimes even inviting a "k," showed an occasional hangover in this country, and "shoomaker" was not unknown. Some say that England learned the word "Cordovan" when some

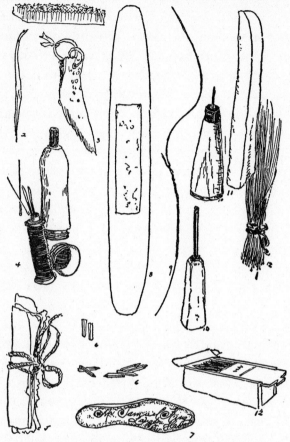

1. *Sheet of wooden pegs* 2. *Forked awl point*
3. *Leather-covered instep-form against which eye-*
lets were cut. (See circular marks)
4. *Awl handle with points and thread inside*
5. *Roll of left-over linen pieces from linings*
6. *Wooden pegs*
7. *Peg-dented last bearing owner's name*
8. *Polished wood with stone insert*
9. *"Waxed End" hogs' brustles twisted with waxed*
linen thread
10. *Awls* 11. *Whitebone rasp* 12. *Hogs' brustles*

63

of Spain's fine goat and horse leathers were imported for dress shoes, but seemed to have found the word "cordwain" better fitted to her northern tongue, for "cordwain" soon came to mean a fine grade of Spanish leather, and "cordwainer" the man who worked with it. Others claim that before Cordovan leather was known in England the word "cordwane" was in use.

Whatever his nomenclature, the shoemaker or cordwainer was a man of no mean standing in the community, and credited with having a mind able to weigh and balance the philosophies of life, and of spending hours of quiet sewing or pegging on most abtruse matters. "Old Man Cable could think and peg at the same time." Many a knotty problem has been solved for a customer through talking it over with the cobbler of his shoes. Henry Wilson, "the cobbler of Natick," Massachusetts, became vice-president of the United States, serving during U. S. Grant's second term.

Like his brother shoer, the blacksmith, the cordwainer wore always a heavy leathern apron, not cleft far up since he did not need to hold his patron's feet between his knees like the blacksmith, but left whole to provide a lap for his "lapstone" and other tools and equipment. One New Hampshire shoemaker was so wed to this badge of office that after he had wed his bride he flatly refused to accompany her to Meeting on the Sabbath unless he could wear his beloved apron.

Very Smart, Once on a Time

The adopted Indian moccasin was one of the first shoes which the white man was glad to wear and in time to make, after his arrival here. By 1650 he had learned its manufacture and was exporting it for sale. For over two hundred and fifty years moccasins were worn by some of our farmers, the father of a man still living in New York being partial to his "wool sheepskin moccasins" for ordinary wear. The first shoes made in Lynn for women were of woolen cloth or neat's leather, with white silk for weddings. In 1670 men's shoes with straps and buckles made their appearance and were smart throughout the country until after the Revolution, at which time pantalloons arrived from France and brought their own boots.

The usual shoe made here toward the end of the 1600s was a heavy coarse affair which made clumpers of our forefathers and mothers, no matter how hard they might try to step lightly and with grace. These shoes were square-toed and adorned with the aforesaid buckle. For the servant when he was dressed up, there was the shoe of coarse neat's leather, and bare feet for the rest of the time. At one early period the gentry wore calfskin with a sole flaunting a rind of sheepskin stitched into the upper layer of sole, whose whiteness was stanchly retained. There was the shoe of neat's leather with the wooden heel in 1719, and the cowhide or "kip boots," and the buckskins for those who chopped in the deep snow or were much in the open. The clog was a wooden boat like those worn in Holland, or it was made with the whole lower part of inch-thick clumping wood, with a duck or linen top for lacing and drawing close. This until the late 1700s.

In 1676 Connecticut settled upon "five pence halfe penny a size for all playne and wooden heeld shoes, for all sizes above the men's sevens, three soles shoes well made and wrought, nor above seven pence halfe penny a size for well wrought French fall." This brought the sizing of shoes back in our first century. About 1750 finer shoes were concocted of white and russet rands (borders) closely stitched with white waxed thread. The toes were sharp and the heels of wood covered with leather, and measuring anywhere from a half inch to two in height. There were three grades of shoes which bespoke their own station in life, the "crosscut," the "common," and the "court."

Since the majority of people in the New World were country men and country women who were not able to follow styles even if they had wished to, it is not to be supposed that our little shops turned out the flowery types used in the cities by the minority. For two hundred years it was, for many, bare feet until the snow blew, and when snow did blow there were many who depended upon their socks rather than upon their shoes for staving off a deadly freeze. Many never did achieve boots but plunged their feet into pair after pair of home spun and knitted socks, or feetings, drew on their clogs or heavy low shoes, reached for more socks and ended up by wrapping the resulting bundles in cloth, soaked in neat's foot oil, a sure preventive against freeze. Men lost toes and parts of their feet by changing from heavy clods and greased wrappings to tight, badly fitting "Meetin' boots," in which they felt compelled to go courting even though the tempstick were down below zero.

In the early 1700s a Reverend preacher and tanner of the North supplied Georgia with two hundred pairs of sealskin shoes. About 1870 the rubber boot made its important arrival into human life and thereafter the great-leather-boot wearing style slipped slowly into oblivion. Old gentlemen, who could not change to modern styles, wore leather boots until the 1900s had arrived, the half way to the knee type, but made of calfskin which was kept polished until it shone like patent leather. "Congress boots" helped out those who wanted the high leather covering but hid it beneath a discreet pantleg. But it is useless to try here to tell of many styles in footwear of the past, for they were many, and strange in the isolated sections. Our aim is to find the humble makers of shoes at work in their humble but popular shops, where the boot-jack also became a part of the output, enabling the stiff boots to be pryed off of feet where hands and arm-muscles availed little.

Shoemaking at Home

There were various types of shoe which could be made at home with but a modicum of skill, with a little wood carving, some spinning and weaving, a good "waxed-end," or a cupful of pegs. Home shoemaking was done during the winter when the land released its owners from constant attention, but cobbling was done throughout the year whenever a "wet day" presented itself. "We all done our own peggin," the average farmer who has lived in the last seventy or eighty years will tell us "Peggin" meant "mendin' " or "tappin," and while many made no attempt to make a shoe outright, it generally simmered down to the case of the famous old knife, which although its blades and its handle had all been renewed or replaced from time to time, was yet the same old knife. Many a shoe and boot has lived on under the same name and ownership which was entirely unacquainted with its birth-day equipment.

Naturally a shoe was a hard earned treasure to be preserved and respected when it had been so intimate an object as to have been seen grazing in the meadow and lowing to the bars each evening, for as long as one could remember. A man with a pair of real boots might expect to have them last him a lifetime, properly cared for. If one were a child and really owned one's shoes, they must not be allowed to wear

67

out, for at least two years. In order to accomplish this feat there were certain expedients to which a child resorted; one was arranged by the shoemaker himself, when he made both shoes exactly alike, straight ahead shapes, so that they might be swapped from foot to foot each day and thus save undue wear in any one spot — their wearers becoming what might be termed ambidextrous if only they had worn their shoes upon their hands. Since feet will grow when one is young, shoes were made large enough for children so that they would still fit at the end of two or three years. This made the wearing of the shoes a matter of rubbings and blisters for the first few months unless one were ingenious. Many boys and girls have wrapped their feet about with "baize" to keep them from slipping about in the new shoes, reducing the wrappings of this open coarse cloth, a kind of flannel, as the months went by and feet grew larger. This of course applied to the country child whose lot was the common lot and not the exceptional, as was that of the city born. To "run and slide" was a sin, even on the smooth field ice on the way crosslots to school, for one's sole was much more important than one's soul's happiness. One woman who is in her sixties remembers very well having to show her father her upturned shoes each evening that he might look for signs of slidin' on the ice. She remembers too his switch hanging by the door. Another device warranted to assist in long life to a shoe was to hammer the soles full of large headed tack-nails, or even small nails, which made practically an extra layer of metal to scuff upon. Heel irons and toe irons came early, heated and bent by the local blacksmith and applied to the soles of young and old, or brought into crude shape on the home forge in the tinkerin' shop.

68

SHOEMAKER — COBBLER SHOP

Traveling and Journeyman Shoemakers

Two very different workmen were these two. A journey-man was one skilled in some trade who yet worked for hire under someone else, and thus did "journey-work." A journey-man shoemaker was one who had learned his trade as an apprentice, that is, been taught the "trade, art and mystery of the business," served probably his seven bound years, with a garret room, coarse clothing and three meals a day "found" by his master, come to the age of release when he was given a "store suit" and two or three dollars with which to start in the world of shoe-wearers; and suddenly found himself his own master. Those who were really masters at heart would in time open their own shops and become master workmen, probably passing through a period of doing day's work as a "journey-man" until they had money to start their own business. A journey-man did not necessarily journey, in fact he seldom went beyond a day's journey for a day's work, but he must understand "the stuff and silk branch." Those who were not master at heart became journeymen for life.

The itinerant or traveling shoemaker was a man of parts who made regular trips through the country to his various patrons, spending a fortnight or month with each one and shoeing the family. We have then the apprentice learning how, the graduated journey-man who was generally an employee, and the shoemaker who owned his shop and either worked alone or had "help." Naturally the last named resented the traveling colleague who kept trade from his shop. He scorned his work as inferior, calling him a "cat whipper." This wide spread "whipping the cat" was however popular with the farmers and their families who welcomed visitors at all times and looked forward to the news sure to be forthcoming from other farms. The kitchen became a shoe shop for the time of the traveling shoemaker's visit and every chick and child and grown up including the help, was measured for a boot or a shoe right by his own fireplace. The farmer "found" the leather for this wholesale cutting and sewing and was also able to watch that no waste enter into the process. If his own hides ran out he would go to the local tanner and invest in more hides from other farms which had been left in payment for others tanned and carried home. Many a cart wheel tire was saved wear and tear on the stump-punctuated roads by having the shoemaker come to the farm and save the farm's going to town.

Actually, the first itinerant or traveling shoemakers were the forerunners of the village shoemaker's shop from which later jealous comment arose against their methods. The settled man becomes at once the man of dependability, while the rolling stone is supposed to gather no moss, and so old-stay-at-home criticized his progenitor as an inferior race of men.

To his fortnight's or month's work at a farmhouse, the traveling shoemaker brought his lapstone, his lasts, his flat-headed hammers, his paste-horn, and whatever else a farm might lack to assist in his work, besides the beloved leathern apron. If he knew that the farm was equipped for such work he might come through with only a small knapsack of tools on his back, but if more must be carried he had recourse to the well-thought-of wheelbarrow, a sort of side-car motor cycle of those days, running under arm-power, which carried tools, leather and even the bulky cobbler's bench with wondrous ease. It was well too to have some sort of a conveyance handy to carry away one's wages, a setting of pumpkins, a peck of corn, a side of beef, or perhaps a cowhide for barter.

SHOEMAKER — COBBLER SHOP

In one section the charge for a pair of shoes was from one to three pecks of corn, according to its size. Anyone who has examined a child's tiny shoe will wonder how one peck of corn could ever have been accepted "in trade" for such a careful work of time and talent, surely a more difficult task than the making of a larger size. There is probably no old fashioned farm shop, or tinkerin' shop, where one may not find shoe lasts, awls and a scattering of pegs in some box, either tucked away for further usefulness or handy by for continued use today — barring the pegs.

Infant's shoe, "Brick End" Shop, Acworth, N. H.

Village Shoe Shops

Thirty-five years ago a New England boy wanted to be a shoemaker in his hill village, and so his people thought to send him to one of the shoe centers so that he might learn the trade thoroughly and come back a real workman rather than a pick-up-your-trade-at-home sort of chap. He entered one of the shoe factories and at the end of a few months came home again. In answer to the villagers' inquiries he said, sadly: "They've kept me making heels at one bench ever since I left home and it come to me finally that I was in the one place where I never would learn to make shoes."

It was the village shop after all where the young men learned to make a shoe from toe to heel, in all of its parts. Shoe machinery made its appearance before the middle of

71

the 1800s, but that did not mean that the village shops gave way before an influx of machine-made shoes. They continued to shoe our grandfathers in large part until several decades had passed.

We have already seen that the shoemaker of the 1600s started at the bottom of things. He saw a farmer on horseback ride into his tan yard, fling a great green hide from his saddle, proceed to give the ages and sizes of his offspring, the length of his wife's foot, stick his own out for measuring with a wooden rule, and then ride off again with a hope that all would be ready "before snow blows," the following year. Having "found" the hides the price of the shoes would be less than if the shoemaker had supplied them, and this was of course right, since the farmer had bred his shoes along with his sides of beef.

Mrs. Lucy Wyman of Meriden, New Hampshire, who died within a couple of years at the age of more than one hundred and one years, recalled once the shoemaking and leather production on her father's farm in nearby Cornish. "When the animals were slaughtered, the skins were taken to the tannery. The thickest leather was the cowhide and this was used for sole leather. Another grade made the uppers. The finest grade made from the cattle was called calfskin. The leather made from our sheep — they used to graze way off on the ledges — was used only for the shoes for the babies, and these were made by mother. It was pliable and soft and could be folded up like a piece of cloth. The traveling shoemakers that had used to come to the farm years ago had stopped coming by my time, but I have heard them tell how they appeared once a year and sat in the kitchen for a fortnight or more and made enough shoes for all to be well shod for the next year.

SHOEMAKER – COBBLER SHOP

" 'Home shoes' we used for the district school, and these were made by a shoemaker in the neighborhood. I used to go to have my foot measured and every year he would laugh and say it was a little bigger, until I got to be a great girl. The shoes came just above my ankle and were laced with leather strings of sheepskin." The village of Meriden assured itself of shoes in this way: The farmers raised the beeves which furnished the hides for Mr. Stephen Fifield to tan into leather which Messrs. Jesse Carter, Samuel Chapman and Abe Spaulding turned into boots and shoes.

The village shoemaker's shop was small, reminding one of the exterior of the old red school-house in a sparsely settled section. To stand at the door and look within one might feel that there was a great litter of many things strewn about, but a litter is perhaps only a litter when its master-mind is conquered by it, and no old cobbler ever seemed to hesitate when he reached for a certain piece of leather, a peg or a tool. A lone workman had of course but the one bench where he sat hour after hour, but when his business grew he added other "berths" or spaces for benches and their natural co'lat'ral, and many an eight berth shoeshop measured but ten by twelve feet. This meant that each man with his bench and water-bucket, jacks and all the rest, could be fitted into rather close quarters. If the outside of the building looked like a school-house, the inside carried out the idea as well, for benches were set in the same careful rows as were the unpainted wooden desks. Isaac Morris of Amsterdam, New York, had, in 1700, an "extensive shoe factory" with twelve workmen busy all day long.

It is a bit difficult to realize that until the middle of the 1800s and somewhat after, the small villages of the land still had their shoe shops turning out shoes to be sent to great

73

distances. The South depended upon the North largely for its footwear, and shoes were sent too from small eastern villages to the mid-western States. In many villages the shoe-making trade was the outstanding one, and the workers were just Tom, Dick and Harry, or Deacon Smith, elder Brown and any other well thought of man along the village street.

One central New York village shoemaker, around 1850, prospered to the point of having thirty-five shoemakers working for him and a salesman on the road, one of our early "drummers." The shop was not large and quartered in a loft above a grocery store at the crossroads where finished shoes could be sold with no effort. Later an offshoot for retail trade opened across the road, and the little white cottaged hamlet enlarged its business and yet kept its beauty, with no sign of factory anywhere about. Trouble began though when the salesman began to bring in orders — more orders than the shop could fill easily. There was therefore just one common sense thing to do, recall the salesman, which was done at once. The total monthly wage for these nearly three dozen workers was $600.

While all of this sounds like real prosperity for the 1800s in the North, what of the following will which disposed of the equipment of a shoe shop in Virginia in the 1660s:

          122 sides of leather
          72 pairs of shoes
          37 awls
          26 paring knives
          12 dozen lasts
          curriers' and tanners' tools
          shoemaker's thread
          gallons of train oil
          proper colorings for leather.

SHOEMAKER — COBBLER SHOP

While the South did not go in deeply for shoemaking, surely the early Virginians made an excellent start.

To return to those simple little shops where one might hear the bees humming in the honeysuckle vines between hammer taps, the nature of his work demanded that the shoemaker have plenty of light, which might fall through several broad but too high windows — placed high as a heritage of days when Indians were apt to pop your head off if the window did not hang high,— or stream through a "bay" or glazed box-affair attached somehow to the outside of the house like a sleeping bat. This big window of many small panes not only let in light but "gave upon" the village street where our good man seldom walked, for a cobbler's bench was seldom allowed to cool. One little old cobbler in New Jersey sat for half a century or more upon his leather seated bench at just such a window and upon just such a street. As far as the villagers knew he sat there all night as well as all day, for his light was burning when others were blowing their's out for bed, and when morning brought the red-hot coal to relight theirs, his was burning in a steady glow. Somehow, though, his work never won him the name of philosopher, for his eyes had a way of peering out suspiciously on the lovely world about him, upon hollyhocks and quaint and ancient houses across the road. It seems hardly logical to connect this little, old, bald-headed cobbler with night depredations, but the children in that village of little crime were startled one morning to find that their elders laid to his bent thumbs and horny palms the slaughter of a cow in a widder neighbor's pasture, some time between the blowing of their candles and their morning re-light. There lay the poor beast, once so lowing and friendly as they had passed it each day, but her tasty quarters both hind and

75

fore were quite gone. After that the little bent figure by the big window took on a new interest. His spectacled, near-sighted eyes still peered closely at the shoes strapped to his jack between his knees, and the few remaining hairs on his little bald head still stood up in the same confused, tangent angles, but he was now a person apart. A night candle-burner can come to no good. He was a thief, and thieves were marked objects in those days. His funny bent thumb, de-formed with much pulling and pushing through heavy leather, was now a mark of Satan. Before, he had gone by the name of his own, wily expression: "If you haint got the money, the shoes haint done," but now it were better not to name him at all, but hurry by until the tap, tap, tapping of his hammer had grown dim and distant in one's ears.

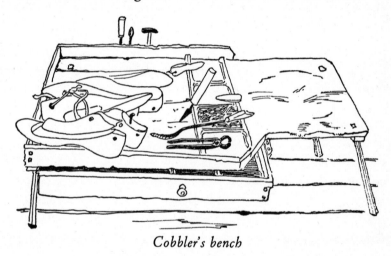

Cobbler's bench

Cobbler's Bench

Just what the reaction of an old fashioned cobbler or shoemaker would be if he saw his old bench used for a tea table, one can only surmise, but it is certain that he would be utterly unable to understand how anything so shabby and workaday as the base of his labors could thus find favor today. With a batter pitcher for a teapot, the tea service in many a summer home is now considered, perhaps not complete, but well started. These old benches are as fascinating as all pieces of furniture equipped with drawers and shelves and cubbyholes and possible secret hiding places, and no matter how much they may show their service of years, nor how crudely they may be made, they have their instant appeal to the lovers of the handwrought days. Cobbler's benches varied in their styles of seats. New England was pretty united in its preference for a shallow hollow gouged out of one end of its "shoemaker's bench." New Jersey and parts of New York went in for greater comfort and made the shallow cut into a real hole and then nailed cowhide across it.

The usual bench was on one plane, with the larger end given over to partitioned off spaces where pegs and tools and lasts might lie ready for the reaching hand. Below this was a drawer, also partitioned off into spaces for more pegs and nails, hogs' bristles and thread. The unusual bench was one which had across one end an upright, hooded and with receding curved brackets which was also full of drawers and cubby holes. These were ambitious benches, looking almost like a young Welsh china cabinet, or a Southern hunting sideboard, but they do not make such nice tea tables today, which is probably the reason why the old cobblers did not go in for them more. The cobbler's kit was his outfit of tools, and might be the flat bench well equipped or the bundle of equipment carried by the traveling workman. When cobblers grew old, they rarely, but sometimes, abandoned their backless benches which had made them bent and round-shouldered, and drew a comfortable rocker up before the bench for easing of the old back. There had to be a place where the wickedly pointed old awl could be jabbed quickly as soon as a thread hole had been pushed through, and from which it could be seized again as soon as the thread had been drawn through, so Grampy Isham of New Hampshire gradually wore his "awl hole" in the side of his rocker's handle, a hole which is cherished by the present generation.

Cobbler's Tools

At Essex Institute, Salem, Massachusetts, an old shoe-maker's shop has been saved to us, with its broad windows, its lines of wooden lasts hanging upon the walls, its odd pieces of leather here and there, the old benches — and here we find a note which was not usual — the front of the bench's seat scooped in to make it possible to draw the jack and vise close in between the worker's knees without having to sit forward precariously to reach them easily. There is the old cider pitcher for carrying water when leather needed softening up a bit, boxes of this and that, oil cans, receptacles full of tiny pegs, litterings and scraps just as they were left on the old shop floor years ago. Here we find the Windsor chair with broad seat and comfortable arms, braced in its legs with cross pieces of rough wood, probably the seat for that one who came, not for his shoes to be "half-soled and heeled while he waited" in his sock-feet, but for a quiet chat with the man who could think while he worked and philoso-phize while he blew the wooden pegs right side up from be-tween his teeth, at need, and gave each two raps home. One who "analyzed at night the thoughts which flitted through his brains in the day." Such men were bound to have visitors, for no matter how crude we may seem, we relish a thought

SHOEMAKER — COBBLER SHOP

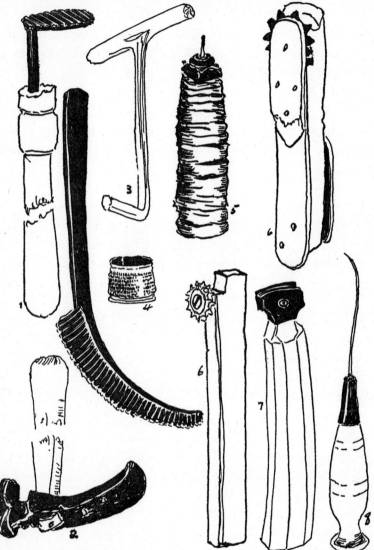

1: Nail rasp. 2: Shoemaker's hammer. 3: Last puller—for pulling
last from finished shoe. 4: Open top thimble. 5: Homemade awl
handle of leather layers. 6: Marking of wheels—to prick place for
even stitches. 7: Sole cutter. 8: Peg of awl — point fastened into
"chucks" of different handles—with wrench

which is more than passing drivel, and there is always something fascinating about the movement of hands turning this way and that in intelligent labor. To the old name "knight of the lapstone and pegging awl," might have been added "and the thoughtful mind." But not always.

"Yoo Skoomaker, have you all your tools . . . your hand-and-thumb-leathers and good Saint Hughs bones to smooth up your work?" Imagine the bone of a saint for smoothing up the shoes of our ancestors!

One from the swamp, one from the loft, one from the barn, one from the pasture

There seems to have been no end to the needs of these makers of shoes when it came to tools, to judge from the different lists of early times, and yet an old cobbler's bench found recently in a New England tinkerin' shop, while full of tools of many sorts, is yet simply equipped, or at least within the limit of a man's count. Perhaps the following is a typical list. There were nippers and pincers of different sorts, knives, bones for scraping (Saint Hugh's, doubtless) hobnails and pegs, lasts and lasting sticks, hammers and measuring tapes, marking wheels with pointed cogs on their peripheries for running around a sole and marking the line of the awl holes, patterns for sole and upper, wooden forms for leg fitting, hog's bristles, a ball of wax in a wax-cup, a lapstone, a paste horn, blacking pot, pegging awls, the thread box, and wooden jacks and vises.

Cobbler's Jack

The cobbler's jack is perhaps as interesting as any of the old tools. It was the wooden frame upon which the shoes were fastened upside down for pegging on soles. There seem to be no two of these old jacks which are exactly alike. The four which are pictured here were picked up at odd times, one from an old barn, one at an auction among the "junk," one from a rocky pasture where it had been tossed and forgotten years ago, and one from the edge of a little roadside swamp which had been supposed to swallow it with other rubbish but had resisted its indigestibility. Their day over, they were disposed of ruthlessly. Today we find them something to study. Each man had his own design for making something which must be sturdy, have two uprights upon which the shoe might be laid, and some sort of a device for pulling and holding tight a strap laid over the shoe. This meant two hollow topped uprights of oak coming to the height of the cobbler's knee. Some had cogged iron wheels half way down their length, which caught in corresponding ratchets and were pressed with a lever until the strap was tight and solid, while others found their power in a wooden contrivance of slightly different design. One trembles to think of the days ahead when individual ingenuity shall have been entirely supplanted by wholesale standardization, but those who prefer that day will chuckle over the fact that the jack was superseded by a simple clamp which was nothing more than a strap sewed end to end to make a loop which held the "last" firm across the cobbler's knees while his feet kept it taut below. A cobbler's knees were said to grow callous enough for him to hammer them at a vigorous pace and yet not feel the blows. Some of the old wooden lasts, both those which were hewn and whittled and those of smoother mold, show their bordering ring of tiny holes cut there by the ends of pegs or nails in many tappings.

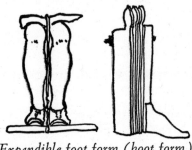

Expandible foot form (boot form)
Tough knees for a lasting-jack

Lasts

"All day long I have sought good beer,
And — at LAST — I have found it here."
— *Beneath a cobbler's sign.*

The wooden form which looks like the lower part and instep of a human foot was called a "last," from the Anglo Saxon "laest" which meant track or footstep. Lasts were clumsy affairs made by hand and when one examines them carefully one does not wonder that the saying "as easy as an old shoe" was a popular one, the inference being all too plain. Like the barber with his flowered cups and golden names belonging to his different patrons, so the cobbler or shoemaker or cordwainer had his special last made to fit his different customers, the names marked on with ink or the initials cut in the form itself. In spite of this we know that shoes made to fit a last rather than the foot itself, must have been hard taskmasters. Many an old last shows where the jackknife has gouged out a comfort spot for some sufferer, or shows a padding of layers of leather nailed on out of respect to a bunion.

Before the Revolution the lasts were one and the same for both feet, but after that they became more individual and were called "lefts" and "rights" the word "last" being somewhat forgotten in the new achievement. Old fashioned shoe-making is one of the few things which we do not wish to call back, although it must have "made character" through bitter suffering, and we could do with a little more character without hurt.

A "lasting jack," just another jack name, was also made to hold the "upper" securely while the shoe was being shaped, the shoemaker with lasting pincers, gripping the edges of the uppers and drawing them over the last. Lasts were made of various woods, but the shoemaker who used one kind had no use for any other. Some swore by black gum as the only good last wood, others liked aspen and poplar both for lasts and the heels of the shoes fitted upon them, and still others believed that rock maple was the only last wood. Whatever the wood, it was seasoned for a couple of years in the open. Their making was a skilled job and a man was supposed to get about 500 pairs out of a cord of wood — this, after the cruder home-whittled ones were improved upon. It is interesting to see that in 1696 in Philadelphia, last-makers received their sixteen shillings not for pairs but for single lasts, since there were no rights and lefts.

There are two old saws which fit in here, one suggesting that it is a man's job to mind his own business, and another quite as convincing that there is something beyond a man's nose which should have attention. "Stick to your last," and "The shoemaker must go beyond his last."

Pegs

Tucked far back under the rafters of an old barn loft an ancient "shoemaker's bench"— so we know that it was in New England — was brought to light. One incongruous thing about the equipment was a tall tin coffee pot, not young, but not old enough to hobnob with the bench. Upon having its cover tilted back, it showed full of shoe pegs, a new supply laid in and never used. The daughter of the old cobbler was not young either and she remembered her father's asking for something which would hold his new pegs. The coffee pot had sprung a leak and so went out to the shop. At the back of the bench a long leather strap had been nailed every so often to hold different small tools, and in two of the loose spaces hung two tiny pewter tea spoons, as delicate and lovely as those made of silver, and beautifully chased along the edges of the handles with finely cut vines. These, it seems, had been used to pick up the pegs, for "pa's hands got clumsy toward the end and he couldn't get the little things out of the pot handy with just his fingers."

It is a never ceasing wonderment that so many of our conveniences have come into existence only within the last hundred years or less. That our forefathers should have been compelled to whittle their own pegs, or set their boys at the job for "knittin' work," out of "the maples down in the swamp" or anywhere else, as late as the early 1800s seems a bit incredible, but in order to hasten matters they pointed them only one way, and yet found it possible to make them slip into the awl holes without much trouble.

The town of Acworth, New Hampshire, and nearby

"little Lynn" where its eight families made shoes, donated a generous share toward the problem of covering feet in New England, since not only shoes and pegs were made there but shoe boxes for sending them off as well. Until the second quarter of the 1800s shoes did not travel in separate boxes but in a great box or barrel. The older folks of today remember buying shoes which were always tied together in pairs, a custom which grew out of the wholesale shipping and packing and continued after the individual boxes had come into use. There are stories of shoes being sent by water to certain ports and being shipwrecked on some shore where the inhabitants gathered them up and spent days sorting out the pairs which had been shipped without even a cord to keep them together. Such a little while since much that is now usual was not even dreamed of. Finally Harley Bailey invented a plane which would "point the pegs both ways," and constructed "cards" of them about four inches square,

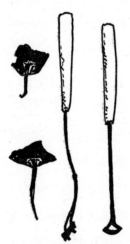

For cutting and smoothing off ends of wooden pegs protruding into shoe. Spanish boot-nails of 1600s

so that the cobbler could knock off a row or two and then crack the individual pegs apart. Bailey saw more light and improved his machinery so that it would also split the pegs off, after which he sold them in quarts or even bushels.

Heel-pegs were made from the trunk of a hard maple by sawing across the grain into sections one half inch thick. Parallel lines were then marked upon the broad surface in both directions, these lines were grooved and the pegs split off with a knife and mallet. Some heel-pegs came in cards of smaller circumference and were split off at need. The two Connecticut pegging tools here shown are of iron. One shows the single blade which called for twice as many strokes as the other, since the second one being sharp on both edges cut the peg off of the strip with the up-stroke and sharpened it with the down stroke. The names of Gabriel Thomas and better known Joseph Walker of Hopkinton, are associated with wood pegging in the first half of the 1800s but wooden pegs were apparently not used generally until later. Because wooden pegs no longer hold together the soles and uppers of our shoes, many of us have thought of them as an initial step in shoemaking, but the above dates will undeceive us. Sewed shoes were the usual shoes throughout the long past, with some use of iron and copper nails and even screws a few hundred years ago. In St. Augustine, shoe nails supposed to have come from the shoes of the early Spaniards, are being carefully preserved. These strange and crude nails must have served two purposes nicely, that of keeping the soles tied on with their long jagged shanks, and of actually surfacing the sole itself with their broadly spread heads, some of which measure over a half inch across. Handwrought and banged on the head while still hot, these old shoe nails are ugly looking weapons.

SHOEMAKER – COBBLER SHOP

Of course one would guess that pegs were used for the heavier shoe, more often for men than for women, but the latter sometimes wore what was known as a "bat" which had a heavy sole and a light calfskin upper. An old storekeeper of Duanesburg, New York, recalls vividly his days of including shoes with food and other merchandize in his stock, six pairs in a case and sizes from six to ten. He remembers the big nuisance of having to use his "boot and shoe float" for "rasping out wooden pegs" which had gone on through the sole and left a wicked point to injure the feelings of his customers at the trying-on. The "float" had a curved top set upon an upright arm, and over this top he must rub the shoes back and forth until he had rasped the wooden point away. When iron nails later showed their heads in the wrong places he must work them out on an "iron flat which resembled a heel" and then add a little pounding for good measure.

Cobbler's Thread

The old saw at the beginning of this chapter seems to have been apt and true for several centuries, for shoemakers' wives and daughters had the regular task of keeping a supply of homespun thread ready for use. A pair of shoes with "an oak-tanned sole sewed with well waxed homespun thread" was a real possession and one bound to stand by for years. While the hide of the cow and the skin of the calf might make up the shoe, it was the coat of the hog which supplied a most necessary gadget for sewing them together after the sole had first been glued down with glue from the "paste-horn." A needle was never used in hand shoemaking, for the four-inch bristle of the hog was found to be a perfect implement for drawing thread through the awl-punched holes. These bris-

87

tles or "brustles" as they came to be known by country folks, were saved after a killin', collected in bundles by the farmers and sold for around thirty cents a pound. They are still used by shoemakers today, a Florida cobbler pulling a bunch out from under his bench and then tossing them back again as though they were not an interesting relic of the old ingenious days. It is good to find even a hog's brustle lapping over from the pre-machine era.

The cobbler's thread was broken by rubbing it up his leg, and the usual length for working was from six to seven feet of good Irish flax or linen. Loosely spun, its strands could be easily pulled apart, and this was done when the hog's brustle was attached. When the cobbler had loosened the strands thus and rolled to a good point, the brustle was laid on at one end, with a good part of its length lying along the thread. The strands were then closed about it and it was waxed firmly into place with a button of bee's wax, or a wax made of pitch and rosin and about one tenth of tallow. The cobbler now had his famous "waxed end" ready for service. Great care had been taken that the brustle "might follow the awl the better." Here was a needle which could go through a very small hole and never unthread. When the sole was being made fast there were two waxed-ends at work, one being put through from each side and pulled up with a full-arm motion —"whipping the cat."

The making of the shoestring may be mentioned here since it seems allied because of its slender length. It was made from a piece of calfskin only about two or three inches square, in the following way: "Stick an awl in the center and cut a circle by drawing the leather against the edge of a knife which is stuck in a board. Then pull out the awl and cut a starting place and with a stick for a gauge draw out the string from the circle, a yard or more in length. Then moisten the string and roll it underfoot." Behold a leather shoe string!

Shoe Building

The construction of the shoe, even back in the days before division of labor had been instituted in factories, was often accomplished by several hands. Shoemaking near Eaton, New York, in the 1800s was a village affair and no one might claim to have made a whole shoe by himself. At Abington it is remembered that a few Irish immigrants began in a simple way. They cut the leather by hand in the open; their women "closed the uppers with waxed thread," or "bound the uppers together"; the children pasted in the linings; while in each dooryard there was a small shop where the men put on the soles. The sewing of uppers was quite commonly done away from the shop proper, the women of the neighborhood taking them home for sewing and finishing in readiness for the soles. This "home work" for women was done also when larger factories came into being, and for other articles than shoes, and where we read of early "factories" of whatever sort we may be sure that the women and children outside did much of the work. If a cobbler worked alone he might make a pair of shoes in three days' time.

An old cobbler still busy at his bench in Jacksonville, says that "any good shoemaker will try to make his leather better and firmer and more lasting by pounding it on his lapstone. It's full of fibres, little fibres, and you want to pound it to make it flexible and closer wove. The lapstone is just a cobblestone out of a brook, wore smooth and curved." In this "fulling" the leather is clamped to the lapstone which lies in the cobbler's lap — apron-made lap. This simple little lapstone has become symbolic of the cobbler and shoemaker, probably because it caused the most noise and kept the cobbler in the consciousness of the nearby citizens, while his waxed-ends worked so quietly that no one ever heard them. "Knight of the lapstone, indeed.

> Come hame to your lapstone,
> Come hame to your last,
> It' a bonny affair, that
> Your family maun fast."
> — TANNAHILL

When a sole was made of not one thick layer of cowhide but three, measuring an inch from the ground up, it meant much cutting and pruning of a heavy material and the cobbler's knife must have a keen edge all of the time. This was acquired by sharpening it on the edge of his kit or his own shoes perhaps, or upon a curved wooden whetstone covered with leather, while there was always the grindstone for extra special edges. If the sole did not dull his knife the heel surely would, for it was compacted of many layers of tough hide all of which needed cutting and shaping and trimming.

While queer old shoes of past years are always interesting they are often extremely ugly, but it would be hard to find a single little child's shoe of earlier days, which would not clutch at the heart with its insistent appeal. Why does a little shoe, stubbed and overrun, make us stop and caress it even though it was made by some country cobbler with few tools and less ingenuity in shaping and making comfortable? It is not only the thought of eager little feet running here and there in the new and great adventure of spying out the world, but there is something very lovely in the tiny proportions which make for beauty where an older's shoe would not please at all. The little copper-toed boots fitted to children from three years up and having all the proportions of their grandfather's boots, but finished with a bold little patch of red leather across the front top, are treasures to be kept well and long; even the clumsy little handsewn low shoes worn less than a hundred years ago on New Hampshire farms, and having not one iota of style and almost no shape, are precious to us. Purple leather was also an embellisher for these tiny boots and shoes, and an old "upstate" New York man who lived near a shoemaker's shop once upon a time, tried to recall just where his last piece of this royal old purple leather had disappeared. "It's been knockin' round for years. I swan, I believe I tied it round that young pear tree over yonder to keep it from rubbin!"

About seventy-five years ago "children cried for them," we are told, not soothing syrups but those little copper-toed shoes which were clumsy but also impervious to "kickin' out." At Turner, Maine, a farmer by the name of George A. Mitchell, began to wonder how he was ever going to keep his many children in shoes with the toes scuffing out in the first few rounds of service, and decided to cover these vulnerable parts with sheets of copper. Finding the scheme to be a great success and adding a threefold endurance to the shoes, he patented the idea and made his rights cover not only copper but other metals, including silver, for tips.

One of the "one man" work troubles, whether it was fulling cloth, tanning hides or making shoes from leather found by the farmer, was the keeping one man's property separate from that of all the others. It was an arduous task to make sure that the farmer received back the same material which he had brought, and did not carry home the wool, or broadcloth, or hides or shoes of some neighbor — always, of course, an inferior article! For years the shoemaker was supplied with the leather from which he was to shoe the family of Dobbin or Sykes or Monroe, and he spent more time keeping these leathers apart than the farmers had had in keeping the original stock apart in their home pastures before the killings.

There was also the trouble of having leather arrive in all kinds of shapes, from which it was hard to cut to advantage. At last the worm turned. Country shoemakers began to announce that they were through with "bespoke work" and that they would refuse any more "measures" or orders, until they could buy their own stock and cut it their own way, and be relieved from the penning off of one farm's leather from that of another. Clamor arose on lovely hilltop and in sheltered valleys, except in the tan yards where the tanners rejoiced that if the new threat held good they would no longer have to tan on shares. Folks declared that they would not use what was called "salework" nor buy "sale shoes" made from any old leather. There seemed a deadlock between shoemaker and consumer, but the former finally won his point by offering to pay for his relief from hap-hazard skins by a twenty-five percent cut in the price of the sale shoes.

When, from 1830 until 1870, shoemaking machinery came into use in the different sections of the country, the cobbler became the cobbler in undisputed right and in the truest meaning of the word, and he tapped for those who could not tap for themselves, heeled for those who "ran over" chronically, and sewed up broken harnesses now and then, since the harness-maker too had come on new days. In the 1880s the "high shoe" had a rival in the "low shoe" or oxford. For another decade when an elderly woman raised her trailing walking skirt from the dusty sidewalk, one might still see the high shoe, buttoned or laced, showing high and black and with an undulating curved top showing clearly against the exposed white cotton stocking.

Sunday Oiling

While the old tannery leather wore well and long, it did so by eating gluttonously of all sorts of oils, and to oil one's boots on a Sabbath morning was as usual as to take the weekly bath at that time, or the night before. "Good fish-oyl" from New England was satisfactory, as well as "train oil" from the whale, but cheaper than either of these was the grease tried out of home mutton and smeared on generously. They "greased 'em" with tallow in the village shops and set them aside to season for a year, and when the mold gathered they simply rubbed it off. Not only was it necessary to feed oil to shoes for their strength and longevity but to make them waterproof, for rubbers are fairly recent arrivals. When they did become procurable they were of pure rubber, and though strong, were heavy and awkward to manage, the original "gums."

A skillet was generally kept in farmhouses at the top of the cellar stairs on a convenient ledge. This skillet was a good three-legged black iron receptacle with a little strutting handle easy to find and catch hold of in the dark, and in this was a piece of wood, a "swab" with which the farmers and their sons scooped up the tallow and placed it on their boots to be rubbed in well with their bare hands, while they silently speculated on the chance of seeing so and so at Meeting or wondered whether there was any danger of a hot-box in the left hind wheel before they got there. In Gloucester, Massachusetts, they moistened the leather a little so that the neat's oil, which would open the pores and soften it, would not burn it, and then they used castor oil to keep the water out.

Always oil on leather will call a truce with Time.

❧ V ❧

1. THE APOTHECARY SHOP

"They diligently follow their labors, sweating whole days and nights by their furnaces —— they wear leather garments with a pouch, and an apron wherewith they wipe their hands."

— PARACELSUS, *Father of Chemistry*

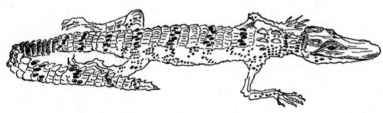

The sign of the apothecary

From Alchymy to Sundaes

THE alligator was perhaps the first of the signs to appear before the old apothecary shops, and the reason for this strange choice was this. The English apothecary shops became centers of social gathering, much like the club of today or the barroom of an old tavern, a place to foregather for comradely moments, and effort was therefore made to decorate them with as startlingly interesting exhibits as might be found. The Spanish word for lizard was "el lagarto," and this became fused into "alligator" in the 1600s by the English apothecaries who had begun to collect such strange sea monsters as were procurable from the sailors and travelers

95

who had already found Florida and Southern waters a mine of wonders and taken the names from the Spanish there before them. The tortoise ran a close second to the stuffed alligator in popularity as an ornament to be suspended from a chemist's shop, but never seems to have reached first place.

In the early 1800s the doctor man at Weston, Vermont, rode out each morning after breakfast on his horse's back, and as he rode he rang his handbell to tell the neighbors and those on the near farms that he was passing by. If someone were ill the doctor was hailed, and stopped the ringing of his bell until he had administered some simple or benefit. Our early country doctors were men apart, generous dispensers of medicine and comfort, father confessors, and physician and drugstore rolled into one, with saddle bags full of soothing herbs and liniments, and offices bristling with mortars and pestles, blood-suckers, bleeding cups and pill boards. During the few hours spent at home the tough roots gathered in the countryside must be ground and pounded, and herbs dried and powdered, until his home was as an apothecary or chemist's shop. Only the cities had the chemist handy for dispensing drugs, and his shop, even after it had become a place of retail and not a spot of divination and mysterious tubes, smacked only of its own reason of being, drugs and salves, simples and benefits. Some Southern drugstores today bear the same lean, business-like appearance of the early American shop, where the center of the room is empty, the walls covered with shelves filled with bottles and crocks, many behind glass doors, and on the counter only the paper and string for tying up a purchase, the weighing scales and a vial or two. Some day these too will probably be filled with soda fountain and chairs and tables, current libraries, and all the rest, the modern druggist apparently basing his idea of proper stock upon an advertisement which appeared in New York City in 1768, which read:

Early Manhattan building used by chemical industries

"The Medley of Goods Sold by G. Duyckinck at the Sign of the Looking-glass & Druggist pot." A farmer looking around a modern drugstore said recently: "You've got all the bottles and budgets above ground, I van!" From Paracelsus to a chocolate sundae!

At the beginning of the trail stands the alchemist or "alchymist" who, before the 1500s, was working diligently with mercury furnaces, crucibles and much hocus-pocus, from formula whose dates have been forgotten. His aim was to make gold from the baser metals and to this end he used most amazing devices, crooning mystical incantations over his concoctions of roasted lizards and dried toads. Fraud and villainy entered finally into what had once been an honest endeavor toward bettering the condition of mankind. During the 1600s Paracelsus entered the field and we find him turning the course of alchemy from the making of gold to the preparation of medicines for the human race. The following picture of one of these early shops gives us the taste of eeriness which surrounded early research, which to many meant a dabbling in the things of Satan.

"A gloomy, dimly lighted place, full of strange vessels and furnaces, melting pots, spheres and portions of skeletons hanging from the ceiling, and the floor littered with stone bottles, alembics, great parchment books — the bellows with its motto, "Spira Spera," (breath and hope), the hour glass, the astrolabe and over all, cobwebs, dust and ashes." How did all of this influence our little American shops with their mortars and pestles balancing on a ledge above the door?

Chymistry — act of separating bodies by fire
Alchymy — sublime chymistry
Pharmacy — the art of preparing medicines
Apothecary — a compounder of medicines
Druggist — one who sells drugs
Drug — a medicinal simple
Simple — a single ingredient, an herb

The word "benefit" may well have a place here, for, meaning to "advantage one," it came in time to be applied to simple remedies.

Mortars and pestles for pounding, ladles and wooden bowls for stirring. Lantern for night-cap calls

Apothecary shop of Dr. Seth Peck and his son, Dr. John Peck from 1832-87. Corner room in "Old Spanish Treasury" — built of coquina in 1690, in St. Augustine. Now called "Old Peck House" or "Burt House"

Reminders

The old apothecary shop left behind it several quaint and worthy articles, perhaps the most artistic being the old mortars and pestles. Whether of wood or stone or iron or bell metal or brass, they are sure to have finely shaped bodies, and should be saved wherever found. Many a drugstore has such an old keepsake of the days of hand-grinding of medicines, one which graced the outside of the shop as a sign or received its share of pounding within. There is an old apothecary shop which was in use from 1832 until 1887, still to be found in St. Augustine. It is within the ancient colonial Treasury Building of Spanish era and built in 1690 on the narrow and lovely street of St. George. A street corner room in the old coquina structure, it yet opens as well on the beautiful court in the rear, where, appropriately, the famous native spice tree of great rarity, grows in a grace all its own, and shows beneath the arches of the overhanging story.

In this pleasant old room Dr. Seth Peck opened a drugstore, and equipped it thoroughly. The old shelves and drawers which he installed remain today, having been used by his son after he was through.

Counter from Dr. Seth Peck's apothecary shop
Over a hundred years old

FOR-THE-SAKE-OF-THE-PERSON SHOP

2. THE BARBER SHOP

"His pole with pewter basons hung,
Black, rotten teeth in order strung,
Rang'd cups that in the window stood,
Lined with red rags to look like blood,
Did well his threefold trade explain,
Who shaved, drew teeth, and breathed a vein."

꒰ꆤ꒱ꆤ꒰ꆤ꒱ꆤ꒰ꆤ꒱ꆤ꒰ꆤ꒱ꆤ꒰ꆤ꒱ꆤ꒰ꆤ꒱ꆤ

Bloody Poles

QUITE the most personal shop which one entered in old days was that of the barber. It is surely personal enough to-day when "a shave and a haircut" are the most conspicuous of this artist's abilities, but when it came to the administering of the knife for bleeding, and the iron pincers or nail and hammer for doing away with one's teeth, the shop struck even nearer home, a little too much so for the unfortunate piddler, or squeamish one.

The famous old barber pole began its career back when phlebotomy was the rage, or physicians believed that blood-letting was the great cure-all for man's diseases. The method was to have the pole ready for the patient to grasp tightly — this making the blood flow more freely after it had been cupped and started through the skin. Having thus well blooded the pole it was hung outside to advise the passerby that here was the place to come for this delicate service. Finally, the aforesaid piddler being augmented in number, and finding the sight of the pole more than his stomach could stand, the barber decided to paint the pole red to begin with, and thus make the blood less conspicuous.

101

A. Old Connecticut pole
B. Old Lady Downs' Barber Shop pole,
Dummerston, Mass. (4½ ft. high)
C. Split barber pole at Charleston, South Carolina,
half at side of front and other half at side of rear
door. White and red — white and blue

Then, to make it more realistic as well as to have things handy, the white cloth which would be used in connection with the operation, was wound in readiness about the pole, making a spiral of white against the red. Whatever germs gathered from the outer world were left to care for themselves and bound in with the wound. In time, the barber's pole was painted with red and white, black and white, and even with red and white and blue, and a surgeon was required by law to show a blue and white striped pole with a red flag and a painted and glazed pot, or gallipot, in addition.

FOR-THE-SAKE-OF-THE-PERSON SHOP

This gallipot was symbolic of the cup which was placed over the spot where the scarification or incision was to be made for the blood-letting.

The signs for these old "shavers" have run the gamut of many designs, being poles set upright in the ground, hitched at an angle from the side of the door or corner of the shop, and cut lengthwise so that half a pole was fastened flat against the shop wall at each side of the door like a pilaster, with hemispheres topping each half.

Wig Maker and Perukier

If there had been no bald heads there would have been no wigs, but when royalty went bald and conceived a wig, the court must shave its hair and don a wig. Thus did the wig-maker and the wig-weaver come into existence. Cuthbert Hubbard of Williamsburg, Virginia, in 1771 added this N. B, postscript to a notice which he placed in the local newssheet: "The Subscriber still carries on his business of Peruke Making, shaving and Hair Dressing in a shop nearly opposite Mr. James Cocke's Store."

Tin shaving mug with hole between two compartments

One of the early definitions of barber was "he who shaves the head"— meaning of course the head of the other fellow

103

— and also, "one who dresses wigs or hair." "This gave him a double duty toward his customers, that of shaving off the hair and of replacing it with a wig of false hair made by himself. A good barber must have at least two or three wigs, or perukes or periwigs — a smaller style wig — arranged upon their wooden blocks shaped much like the human skull, and ready for the whim of his patrons. From the tales which have come down to us of the barber's loquacity with his patron under the blade and while he "accomodated gentlemen in the best manner," it is probable that if he wanted to turn a penny he could sell any or all of his wigs before the gentleman was allowed to arise from his chair. Certainly no tradesman ever had a better chance to put over a sales talk than the voluble barbers of the past.

There were styles in wigs as there have always been styles in haircuts; there was the wig of generous proportions well curled, sheltering and impressive; there was the periwig a shade less important in size and circumference; there was the peruke, still less cumbrous, and in the 1600s sometimes even made to imitate the natural hair of the head; while the Bob Wig was the one with which we are familiar upon the head of George Washington, cut quite short, with a ribbon hanging down behind. As late as 1836 there was a sign on lower Broadway which told of a "CURL AND WIG SHOP," surely the last gasp for this sort of shop, and evidently a wig-shop proper, quite separate from the more vulgar barber.

The ladies seem to have been more beautified by the wearing of wigs than their menfolks, for while the latter often looked peaked and strange beneath their curls, the ladies had a period when they all appeared beautiful, whether they were really blessed by nature or not. Put on a powdered wig, plenty of peach coloring beneath it, and a black patch or two, and there you were, beautiful! Wig-shops changed slowly into shops where switches were made of the combings of women who assiduously gathered up every hair which fell in combing, filling bandbox after bandbox that they might be carried to the switch-maker and turned into "an adornment of natural hair."

Equipment

Some of the wooden blocks which held the finished wigs were skull and face shaped, but fell off at the chin — also natural sometimes. Some were poles with the semblance of a human face painted on a block, so that the purchaser might see himself as others were to see him. A wig box was most important, and one with the owner's name upon it, for wigs must be frequently curled and taken to shop and left there for a time. With our great search for bandboxes and leather hat boxes it is strange that we find so few wig boxes, or perhaps we find them and do not recognize them.

The barber's chair was not the elaborate and easy cradle of today, but a mean sort of chair without grandeur or comfort, doing little for the victim of the razor or shears.

There was also the powdering of the wig to be remembered quite often. While this might be done at home, and powdering rooms were a part of the larger Southern homes and generally just off the ballroom, the barber must also do this. In the late 1600s the hair powders were imported and one small case of hair powder and "four dozen and a half Sweet hair powders," cost a pound and sixteen shillings. Later we ground our own hair powder in mills where grain was ground. Hair powder is made from deposits of talc found in

the Appalachian States and ground up, and near Shelburne
Falls, Massachusetts, there stood once long ago a talc mill.

*A barber pole at Cherry and Roosevelt Streets
Old New York. "Valentine's Manual"*

3. THE STAYMAKER'S SHOP

"Long, very long, was Mistress Dinah's waist,
The stiff stay high before."

Historic Corsets

THE staymaker's shop, like other shops, was an outcome of home work, except for those staymakers who came from England as full-fledged artists in the business of "trussing up the women." David Burnett was among our earliest stay-makers and he arrived in Boston in 1714. Sandwich had its staymaker, and a couple of years before the first guns threw us into the Revolution, one John Burchet, "stay and riding-habit maker from London and Paris," opened a deluxe shop in New York City and advertised as being at the "Sign of the Crown and Stays." Far from being a forerunner in this business he was but following in the footsteps of centuries of other trussers, for corsets or stays were being worn in the 900s and perhaps earlier. One of the most lasting and tor-turing enslavements to which women have submitted, we find that the first patterns were perhaps the worst of all, for instead of shaping the female form into the desired slenderness they were often successful in making it quite in-visible — in the grave. Many women have died as a result of our little stay-shops.

Historians of this delicate subject remember that after about six hundred years, the English decided that the bodice might do this work of slenderizing, and so began these lovely outer garments. But there was still the stomach to be dealt with, since that organ will not always down under direction. The "stomacher" was therefore introduced, made of a piece of wood, pointed at the lower edge and doing its best under its silken and lacey coverings, toward hiding the natural form and suffocating the wearer's lungs, by its tight side lacing. Some stomachers reached almost to the chin, and some seem to have been as useful practically as the slack carpenter's gump-wedge. Thus: "If a Tailour make your gown too little, yo couer his falt with a broad Stomacher."

Then came a ray of hope. In 1628 Harvey made his great discovery anent the circulation of blood through our bodies, and surprising as it may seem, style went down somewhat before science and the stays of women grew looser. Came Victoria, that great paragon of domestic virtues, and they tightened up once more, not to mention the hoopskirt planned by the worthy Queen for hiding her form during the carrying of her unborn children. Less than fifty years ago the tight waist style had not entirely disappeared in this country, and those who still "laced," having pushed their waists into their hips, wore great leather breechings about these noticeable parts beneath the shelter of their three petticoats. It is only the last two generations which may safely laugh.

We see from the above a difference between a pair of stays and a bodice, yet the original meaning of "stay" was "bodice," not to become static but to support. "A pair of stays is a laced underbodice stiffened by the insertion of strips of whalebone (sometimes of metal or wood) worn by women (sometimes by men) to give shape and support to the figure." Made in two parts, stays always came "in pairs." Other names for stays were "jumps," "gazzets," "caushets," and "coashets," the last three names verging closely upon our more familiar "corset, which of course came directly from the corselet, the light armor of battle which protected the front of the body.

Materials

To one who has seen an old handmade corset which has been handed down from several generations — not for further use as was done in the past with a slight refitting of the bones — but because it was too lovely to destroy, the word stays has lost all evil meaning. The most elaborate work was put into these under supports, for they were quilted, embroidered, shadow-worked, featherboned, hemstitched and put together with such rows of invisible stitches, that they are works of art in the needle-work world. The long slender runlets for the whalebone or whatnot which stiffened them were done with ironlike security, and the material itself was unbreakable and untearable. Special goods were woven for "stay tick." Such material as the best white water tabby, a sort of brindled silk, or white sattinet, was used for stay tick. This was stiffened to a boardlike hardness with buckram which is a cloth stiffened with gum. There were special "stay-workers" and "stay-stitchers," kept busy upon these materials in each shop. They stitched closely long parallel lanes for the bones which would be inserted, and then trimmed with still further stiffening materials such as braids and cords, edging here and edging there in wondrous designs, and then bound with both fine and coarse yellow galloon. These were the materials which went into stays during the prosperous Georgian days, all sewed together with Ballandine sewing silk. In 1682 one of our ancestors had a pair of "hair-colored stays in Sattin." In the mongrel 1880s, stay

109

bindings were of "twilled cotton, in white, drab and buff color." What a descent!

Stay Laces

Another shop which cousined with that of the staymaker was the "staylace dealer's." Naturally if one's body were to be pulled in until the organs ceased to function, the lacers must be tough and true. The stay-lace or stay-cord was of cotton or linen, and because of its staying powers became a symbol of bringing things up short, or to a finish. To "stay-lace" a person or a movement was to bring them up standing.

The Real Stay

No matter how strongly woven or how much reinforced the staytick may have been, it would have been as nothing against the bulging female form without busks or bones, which were slid into their well stitched lanes to make for ironcladness. Whalebone, sometimes longer than a man was high, was taken from the great mouth of the whale where it sifted the entering food. Whalers at sea were made rich because of women's being trussed up so stiffly, and if the voyage were a long one, the young sailors whiled away their time carving these slender bones into proper length for the stays of their future brides. The last whale-bone cutter, George Messman, died in 1919.

Wooden stay-busks were naturally among early comers, the whalebone coming into greater use after America had developed her great whaling ports and her off-shore whaling. Metal bones came into use and tin is even remembered, although the tin busk is entirely overshadowed by a pair of traditional tin stays.

4. Horn Comb Shops

"D'ye ken John Peel with his coat so gay?
D'ye ken John Peel at the break of day?
D'ye ken John Peel when he's far, far away
With his hounds and his horn in the morning?"

The Horn Smith

If a man lost his comb today and was too far removed from
a shop to buy a new one, he would go disheveled and dis-
traught, while his forebears would have looked about for a
piece of wood and sat down to whittle it into a comb. How
we do rob ourselves of the joy of creation. Not a jot or a
tittle of a dead neat creature was allowed to go to waste. If
death resulted from disease the flesh might not be eaten,
but there was the great and glorious skeleton, tipped with
hoof and horn and tail and sheltered with a skin which could
do wonders under man's hand, to supply the family needs.
The hornsmith had the same feeling for the horns of cattle
as the joiner had for a piece of fine wood, and only he could
have seen the possibilities which lay within these sharp and
dangerous side-arms of the departed beast.

No smith was needed to turn a horn into a carrier of gunpowder, and no craftsman to make the "mower's horn for
hanging at the belt to carry the whetstone in its bath of
water to save spittle at the time of sharpening." Perhaps the
horns which remain to us from the 1700s and are covered
with carved designs of a crude but fascinating art may have
been done by the hand of a hornsmith, and yet we believe

III

them to have been generally the work of the ordinary young settler who filled his odd moments making his powder-horn individual and lifting it out of the plane of a cattle product to a something artistic through his efforts. "Steal not this horn for fear of shame for here you see the owner's name," was probably an old saying when it was carved on a barnyard horn nearly two centuries ago. The base of the powder-horn was blocked up with a piece of heavy wood, and the tip carved and corked, while a braided thong was tied about or through it for hanging at the belt. Some horns were just for calling the workers from the fields, or for winding on a fox-hunt, or summoning to Sunday Meeting, or announcing a fire from clearing to clearing. Some hornsmiths cut horn spoons and little dippers. The term "hornsmith" shows that a smith was after all not only the man who forged or worked in metals, as the letter of the law declared.

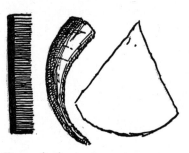

From the horn of a neat creature

"*An Instrument for Adjusting the Hair.*"

The first hornsmiths had no difficulty in getting their material, for the farmers brought in the horns just as they took their hides to the tanner. The first step was to remove the tip and butt of the horn by sawing across. Word of mouth reports on comb-making in simple home or village shops, tell of the horn being then steamed for softening. They were then cut lengthwise, and pressed under some heavy weight. After they had dried they were sawed into the proper width to make a useable comb, and one edge sawed into many inlets for the forming of the teeth. This was the process in a nutshell. Looked into a little more closely the process shows considerable work in getting the "raw" horn softened up so that the "raw horn comb" may evolve. There were several days of soaking before they were pliable enough for working. Sometimes they were boiled in oil in addition to the soaking; again the horns of a bullock were roasted in the flame of a wood fire before their extra toughness was conquered. Slender tongs measuring five or six feet in length were used to hold the horn over a little faggot fire. When this had been accomplished the next step was to get the horn split and clamped in the presses for straightening, the presses being sheets of iron well heated. In addition to straightening the horn this press expanded and thus clarified it. After leaving the press the horn was hardened into its new shape by plunging into cold water, when the roughness was scraped from its surface.

Comb-vise made firm with a wedge

HANDWROUGHT ANCESTORS

By this time the hornsmith had made his material into the fabric of his comb and proceeded with it to his special comb-vise. These vises varied but all seem to have been crude, and effective if they held the horn firmly enough for the sawing of the teeth. One vise was worked by simply slipping a great wedge of wood farther and farther up under one of the wooden clasping arms, until all was firm. Now came the careful and skilled management of the saw in the smith's hands. For this work the smith sat on a low bench with his eyes and hands on the same general level with his work. Thus a passerby might look within his shop door and see him bent forward over the careful placing of each saw-cut that the teeth might be regular. The inner end of each tooth was cut with a plugging awl, while the outer end was rounded with another handmade instrument which took off the sharp jag of the point. So simple a thing as brick dust did what polishing could be done by hand at first. For finer polishing the comb was held against a roller covered with a buffing leather into which more brick dust, or ashes, or rotten-stone had been rubbed. The final rubbing was done by the palm of the hand, helped by a combination of rotten-stone and vinegar, or subnitrate of bismuth. With this hand work a small shop could turn out only a few combs a day.

When more delicate work was called for it was found that by long soaking the horn could be separated into different layers, and that each had its own pith and its own kernel, much as did the hide of the animal from which it had been taken. Fifteen days of soaking in the summer time had to be lengthened to a month when the cold weather came, when the whole horn was taken out and shaken and rubbed until the pith was removed. Boiling water was then necessary for half an hour before the horn could be sawed lengthwise.

Even then there was more boiling to be done before the horn would consent to roll open. When thin edged chisels were applied with delicate care the horn could be divided into two or three layers, according to its thickness and age. The young horn measuring only a quarter of an inch through was split no smaller. When the hornsmith became better equipped with iron instruments he could do with them what the fuller did to the rough cloth, snip off and rub off and smooth down all excrescences and too heavy parts to a uniform thickness. More boiling brought the horn at last to the presses where they were now placed within a cavity dug in a heavy block of wood with a sheet of hot iron between each layer of horn. Here we are reminded of the "cheese" at the old cider mills, which were made of a layer of apples and a layer of straw, and then pressed with a great log dragging a load of stones at one end. There were just so many ways of accomplishing work in the pre-machinery days, and if a man knew the different principles of the six mechanical powers, he could apply them in all of his different kinds of work. Hardening in water brought the horn to the comb-maker's vise for tooth cutting and then for polishing. Wooden combs made by hand-whittling were later turned out by quantity production and at one time could be bought for "a penny a pair."

Enoch Noyes

The man, Enoch Noyes, stands out of the shadows as the early combmaker. In 1759, at his home in old West Newbury, Massachusetts, he started the making of the horn combs in his home tinkerin' shop. The neighbors liked them and gave him the idea of making enough of them to send out for sale through the countryside. Soon he had salesmen walking hither and thither carrying his combs upon their backs in knapsacks. This idea spread and others started the same line of work, giving rise to the largest comb-making business in the country. Leominster was destined to be the world's horn-comb center. A good business was considered a family asset to be handed down and for over a hundred and sixty years the Noyes family made combs, extending their little shop into larger and larger ones until they had factories in Meriden, Connecticut, and in Philadelphia.

To us today the words shop and mill and factory are self-sufficient ones, but investigation shows that even the largest among the early ones depended upon the women in the nearby homes for a part of their manufacture. This "piece work" was eagerly sought. For instance, Enoch Noyes was still having his combs polished by woman handpower long after he had left his humbler shop, for it saved his buying ashes, which mixed with water was the only scouring powder deemed necessary.

Persons who can remember back into the last century will recall the old brass combs found in the humble "comb and brush racks" which used to and still do adorn farm-house kitchens and porches. When the help came in from the fields they stopped in the porch to wash their faces and hands in a dipperful of water poured into a tin basin. This done, they reached for the little community comb, sometimes a fragment of a horn comb, but more likely to be an unbreakable one of brass. These were of Meriden make and cast primarily for the use of negroes.

It was said, shortly after the Revolution, that the women of America had neater heads than those of their English sisters who still clung to their "mobs" to cover their un-

FOR-THE-SAKE-OF-THE-PERSON SHOP

combed and matted tresses, some of which were always slipping down into sight. It is probably to the door of the shop of Enoch Noyes that we must go for the answer to this riddle — a savage country with neater tresses than those of the aristocrats back home in civilization! Enoch deserves much praise for his use of the horns of his homegrown cattle.

5. THE LAUNDER SHOP

"In washing by hand have an eie to thy boll,
For launders and millers be quick of their toll."

Smoothing irons:
A. "Cool" wooden handle
B. Hand forged

Wash Versus Laundry

THE Pilgrims had a regular washday every two months, but time soon shortened this period to more frequent ablutions. The usual "washday" for most Americans has rolled around each Monday, and what has been washed has been the "wash" and not the "laundry," for run of the mill folks. Although popular opinion would probably hold that the term "laundry" is one of elegance which has gradually outmoded the humbler "wash," yet this is not the case, the latter carrying back to the 1600s and earlier. In 1415 England had the word "lawnd" or "lawnde" which was the name for a kind of linen resembling cambric. A "launderer" or "launder" was the person who washed and smoothed, or "laundered" this linen, and "a launderer may be as well a male as a female, by course of nature," they said in 1631.

In 1620 the word "laundresse" was in use and known to our ancestors who came across to Plymouth. It seems safe to assume that the laundresse was the person who laundered for pay, and dealt largely in the daintier garments which needed careful handwork. We shall see that the methods of cleaning the heavier clothing would have worked havoc with dainty "lawndes." The word launder was not only a verb and a noun touching upon washday in a direct manner, but came upon it subtly as well, meaning sometimes "rain," sometimes "gutter," and again a "tub" gouged into shape from a hollow tree.

It is not far-fetched to call a wash-house a shop, for after the days of the more primitive outdoor washing, small shop-like buildings took their place in the cluster of small farm buildings, especially on the Southern plantations. At the end of the 1600s Virginia included a washhouse in her necessary equipment in the "yard" and probably did so much earlier.

Before the Pilgrims were able to come ashore to live because of lack of shelter, special days were set apart for the women, when they were brought to land from the Mayflower for the sole purpose of washing up the soiled linen of the long days at sea. "Washday" should therefore be called our first holiday, for there is no doubt that those days of release from the ship and the opportunity to walk about freely on shore remained in the minds of the women, not as days of hard work, but of happy relaxation from monotony although they had only rocks for rubbing boards, and winter weather to chap their hands at the work.

Brook-washing was common among the settlers and the edge of a quiet bay with plenty of handy rocks for rubbing over, was real luxury. An Old World saying, as expressed in the following warning in 1626, was fortunately not applicable here: "Chalkie Water is too fretting as it appeareth in Laundry of Clothes, which wear out apace, if you use such Water."

One arrangement for "fetching water" when the family washday came around — and it was a real task to carry water from the sea below to the bluff above — was to erect a water-wheel such as was used in 1667: "The water brought to the top of the wheel, in launders or troughs which cast the same into Buckets made in the wheel." This explanation is not as clear as we would wish it, but the thought is clear when we picture a sort of endless chain of little carriers, such as one sees today in a gristmill, but passing over a great wheel and scooping up the water from just beyond the shore down below the cliff and carrying it in small but continuous quantities to the waiting washwomen above.

The Wash House

Because of its climate the South has done much of its domestic work in the open, and although we find many wash-houses in that part of the country, we still find the boiling of clothes being done out under the trees and sky. The Southerner accepts as the usual, the great black iron washpot of many gallons capacity, standing on its three strong but squat legs, pouring up its white breath of steam

*The typical scene in the South, but not the typical
three legged wash-pot. Jacksonville, Florida*

in some cool, shaded grove of pines or palms or magnolias or
"chanee berries," either near a tiny negro cabin or in the
"yard" of a prosperous plantation, with a brisk fire of remnant

wood crisscrossed beneath it. Generally, just enough short wood is cracked up to start the flame and then any available long pieces are pointed into the fire at one end, to serve for their full length by occasional kicks as the minutes pass. It is a carefree, happy way to work out in the open where neither steam nor smoke nor heat can be oppressive and where a mocking-bird may at any moment send his ecstacy out across the flowering oleanders, or a great redbird go darting through the tree boughs in a neighborly sort of way.

Annie, the preacher's wife, was caught at her singing over a steaming tub, doing the washing as it was done three hundred years ago in this same sunny South, and smilingly held her stirring pose while the accompanying sketch was made. At the end of five minutes her voice came tense and beseeching, but still loyal: "Is I got to stan' here 'til King'om Come? I sure is gittin' burn up." For the sake of friendliness and joy at her sudden importance, the old colored woman would have stuck at her post until the water boiled off of her precious clothes and her splay-footed shoes began to smoke — had she been urged — but, released she came over and looked at the effort with a broad grin: "Dat certain'y is Annie. See dat ole stockin' leg cap on her ole head. But, law, Mis', see how crookedy you make my apron look. I don' reckon dose frien's ob you's up No'th will know what I's about nohow. But you done right smart."

Any old black pot would "do" in earlier days for the boiling of clothes, and they still "do" in many cases today, but the usual washpot or "washkittle" is of heavy iron with bulging sides, and holding thirty-five gallons or less. Annie's pot was of galvanized iron, not typical, but dragged out of a modernly equipped inside laundry, because the "white

Thirty-five gallon wash kettle of the South used out of doors. Sometimes the clothes were stirred with an oar

folks kin wash in dey house if dey like, but Annie, she hold by de ole burned place in de sand," and, too, her mistress "didn't make no matter" where she worked. It is quite usual to see the contents of these pots being stirred about with the handle of a broom, the brush part standing up in the air in a dazed and uncomely fashion. It looks a bit awkward but seems to turn the trick, as well as the clothes, and is generally the only available stick long enough to compete with the rising steam.

Washhouse equipment in an old brick or stone building was extremely simple. South Carolina has one with an immense chimneyplace where a fire glows constantly to keep the flatirons hot while the rubbing is being done by an old colored laundress who has known this washhouse ever since she was born. The flatirons have their own built-in brick shelf

123

Homemade clothes drying-rack, Hancock, N. H.
Clothes-bars 125 years old

running part way across the back of the chimney, as a part of its original plan. Here the flatirons are left whether in use or not, while another row may stand across the front of the hearth, where they look like cats on a fence silhouetted against a full moon. Tubs, rubbing boards, a lovely old settee — long since discarded at the Big House but retaining its original beauty of line — holds the clothes which have boiled under the oleanders and a great nut tree, and are now being rub-a-dubbed by long, slender fingers. The windows are small but the door stands open to light and visitors, for the old washhouse is a beckoning sort of shop, with its thick stone walls and hanging vines. Buckets and gourds are in plentiful number, and ironing boards show that more than one laundress has been kept busy here over flounced ruffles and stiffened petticoats. A nest of clothes-horses, neat cross-bars, show by their straight slender standards and broad feet, and their one-paneled structure, that they were made one hundred years ago, if not more; grown smooth with the soft pressure of countless smoothed garments and sheets, they would grace a room for any purpose.

Washing was strenuous if done alone but quite a party if done in company, and especially did the colored laundresses need consolation when they worked alone. Alone or together, "work songs" were needed and colored Florence gives us here the work-songs which have come down through her family for a long time, learned in Georgia. "My mammy she teach me dis yere work-song. It's good to work by — it hit right at you work. You sings each line three times:

> Gib me dat-ole-time-relig-yon,
> It was good — for my-ole mudder,
> And it's-good-enough-for me.
>
> It's good-when-I'm- in trouble,
> It's good-enough-for me
> It's good-when-I'm -a'dying,
> Then it's good-enough-for me.
>
> Chorus
>
> Gib me dat-ole-ti-me relig-yon,
> Gib me dat-ole-ti-me rel-yon,
> It's good enough — for me.

"And the chorus you sing twice more over. Then there's anudder work song my mammy teach me, but dat's a sort of shoutin' song, though.

> I wants to be like Jesus in my heart.
> I don' want to be like Judas in my heart.
> I wants to love ev'ybody in my heart, in my heart.
> I wants to live a Christian in my heart."

125

HANDWROUGHT ANCESTORS

Clothes scrubbed three times over to match up with the song which "hit right at de work" must have been whiter than the proverbial snow.

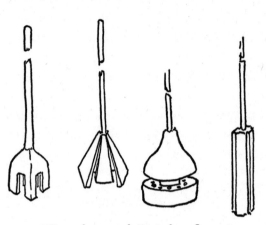

"Pounding sticks" of the 1800s

It comes as a surprise to some of us to find that New England also did some of her washing out in the open in the Southern manner, two hundred years after the Pilgrims did so in their necessity. From a book of ancestor memories done by Mrs. Eva Rich Johnston, of Maitland, Florida, we have the story of Vermont children, about 1810-1820, looking forward to Monday as their great wash and festival day of the week. To quote "The children gathered at the creek to do the family washing. The girls pounded and soaped the clothes on the rocks and dipped them to rinse . . . The boys built the fires and filled the heavy kettles. When the water simmered the boys put the clothes in the kettles and stirred them with long sticks. Then they made a game of carrying them to the creek on their sticks, and they often fell off on the way. The girls then rinsed the clothes and wrung them, one at each end of a garment, by twisting them in the opposite directions. Then the clothes were hung upon the bushes to dry, while the children enjoyed themselves."

Pounding Barrels

If, as has been suggested, to launder was to cleanse and smooth by hand only fine linens, we have a new stumbling block when we find that "lander" and "lender"— words perilously like "launder"— meant to deal a blow. This dealing of blows, or pounding, brings us to the approved method of cleaning clothes during the first two centuries, and also to the "pounding barrel." Here clothes were dropped into warm or hot water and set upon by main force, with a heavy wooden pestle or some sort of heavy-headed stick which beat up the materials as heartily as the pounder could pound. Almost any kind of a heavy plunger with a long handle would do for use in the pounding barrel, and there have been many designs for this implement, some of them continuing to come into existence within the last years, since only a very small proportion of American women are using the improved washing machines so widely acclaimed. From lender to launder the word might range, but the day of the wash was "pounding day."

"Buckin' " and "Battlin' "

One of the first words which meant washing clothes was "buck." One bucked one's clothes on washday, and the clothes-basket was the "buck-basket." A certain tree was called the "buck-tree" because from its ashes a lye for washing clothes was made. One battled with one's soiled clothes, bucked them, treated them roughly, because, alack, one had no notion of the modern way of beseeching dirt from even the heaviest clothes by means gentle enough for fine old lace.

A "battlin' block" in use on an Alabama plantation is described by a young man who saw it in use until he was grown. The name alone seems to tell the story, but his words go still further. "About eighteen years ago I remember seeing our battlin' block set up. Our old negro, Sam Green, set it up in the Yard. A battlin' block could be of cypress or oak, or some hard wood, and it stood about a yard or so high. After the clothes had been boiled in the wash-kettle under the trees the women folded them on the block, and then took a heavy stick, generally an ax-handle, and beat them. Oh, we had it done that way until eight or ten years ago. It was hard on the buttons and the trick was to keep from knocking them off and breaking them. It sure saved rubbing. Later we used the old block to cut the chickens' heads off on. Then the termites and ants got at it and it rotted away and fell down."

Today a lovely "Lily Pond" lies in a green hollow at Maitland, Florida. Forty years ago this pond was surrounded by negro cabins and there were rocks a'plenty on which the women "battled" their clothes with four-foot paddles.

Rub-a-Dub-Dub

The gentler art of rubbing even heavy garments was made possible by the ingenuity of men who took pieces of boards fourteen or sixteen inches across, with the grain running crosswise, and grooved them off regularly down one side, leaving fourteen or more raised semicircular ridges, against which the clothes might be rubbed with no danger of tear or wear. Another scrubbing board had revolving cylinders instead of steady ridges, and the clothes were not rubbed upon it, but laid on and then rubbed by an ingenious little wooden implement which itself had revolving parts and worked against the revolving slats of the larger board. Some rubbing boards had harsh, squared ridges, and after the clothes had been laid upon it, a long "rubber," surfaced with corrugations, was passed swiftly up and down until all soil had been removed.

Bleaching and Drying

"Hattie's wash looks uncommon good, don't it, now?" And,

"I cal'late the new folks over to Hiram's place aint much, jedgin' from the wash I see on the line when I drove out last week." Or,

"Only see those clothes in Sarah's line, now. She always was a dabster at getting her clothes white as snow." Again,

"Shiftless, they be. I know. I see the Monday wash on the line last week."

Final, these opinions, and futile their gainsaying. The die was irrevocably cast. The fame or infamy of a family's daily living hung from its humble clothes line in the front yard or the front porch, for all the world and his brother to see. Almost blessed was the poor laundress who lived on a back road where the neighbors could not see the yellow blowing wash of inadequacy.

One of these blessed ones lives in a cottage by the side of a seldom used wooded road in New England, and from her lot one may understand the difficulties of a washday where a trickling spring is the only water supply and there is hardly enough sun flickering through the trees to sparkle the window panes. A car drove through that old road last summer and its occupants had a taste of the days of the 1600s. A long slack clothes line was fastened at one end high on the corner of the cottage and then looped across the road to be fastened on the high branch of a tulip tree. The car came to a stop — not knowing the way forward against so strange an obstacle. Only a knock at the door brought help in the form of a young woman. She seemed not to think an apology for the appropriation of the public highway to be at all necessary, for all that she had done was to use the only place she could find for drying her Sunday wash. Shyly she smiled and then crossed the road, found a stray branch in the underbrush and then made a statue of liberty of herself, standing with her arm high in the air as she pushed the slack line as high as the branch would go, to let the car pass under. The clothes were sad, colorful, and rather hopeless looking, but still one would hesitate to soil them further by sweeping a dusty car top with them. "Don't make no matter," she said, and the car swept under and through.

Who knows but that this same young washerwoman, placed in a different situation in life might not have rivaled her "whitster" grandmothers, whose bleaching or whiting of clothes brought this delightful term into being?

The extreme cold and drifts of the New England climate are doubtless responsible for the age-old habit of hanging the weekly wash in the front porch. Some New England homes have had front porches strung across their fronts for no other reason than to have thus a convenient drying-house, for many folks preferred indoors to "camping down" on the porch; and even then the women have had to be "uncommon stout" to withstand the blizzards which beat upon them often at the uphanging or the downtaking. One "stranger from off" bought a home in the hills and let it be known that she was going to pull down the ugly and unnecessary front porch, whereupon her neighbors rushed to advise her against so suicidal a step. "Where will you hang your clothes?" they asked. "Why, out in the side dooryard where the sun can reach them." Heads were shaken knowingly, and then, "Wait until the winter snow begins to blow and the drifts climb above your waist, where will you hang them then?" It would be gross injustice to seem to suggest that women washed their clothes snow-white because of the critical glances of their neighbors, for the average woman loves cleanliness for its own sake, but into the front-porch-hanging there has crept a real pride and satisfaction that this hard earned whiteness should hold so conspicuous a position in the public eye. An artist with brush and paints loves praise of his pictures. The artist with soap and scrubbing-board loves it just as well, and surely deserves it quite as much.

We have been told that "praise is comely," and we believe it. The condemnation of the seemingly shiftless housewife may sometimes be utterly unjust, for the water supply may be only a trickling spring, or the rain-barrel water after it has washed the roof clean of many weeks of dust. If a well were handy by, it was comparatively easy to wind up bucket after bucket with the sturdy windlass, or give the well-sweep a bit of exercise going up and down to raise its gallon or so of water from dark depths to the top of the wooden well curb, over and over again, until the wooden keelers stood well filled upon the washbench. This bench was generally a simple puncheon affair, a broad tree split down through the center, one side laid horizontally with the flat side up and with four rough wooden stakes set at a rakish angle back from the four corners. The soft soap for this important event had been leeched and contrived from wood ashes, and grease tried out of remnants of waste fat, and was now spooned out of its great jars or pitchers in dripping yellow-brown gobs which would prove fatal to any unwanted stains. Our earliest ancestors made literally everything used in the great family wash, including the gouged wooden tubs, the later keelers, the homespun hemp clothes lines, and — if they were fortunate — broke the thorns from the thorn tree for pinning the clothes upon them.

Many housewives dispensed entirely with a line for drying their clothes, preferring, or perhaps being forced to the use of the nearby bushes and the branches of the trees. The main point was really not so much the drying as the bleaching, for all clothes would dry in time but not always as white as desired unless the sun had a hand in the doing. The bleaching-green came to America with the first settlers, and while it was not the carefully fenced or protected area of the old countries, it was important, even though the "grassground" of the dooryard took potluck with the other hayfields. Lawnmowers are such recent newcomers and yet it is difficult for most of us to realize that scissors and sickles were the housewives' only weapons when it came to rescuing a spot for the whitening of clothes or the release of posybeds from their encircling waist-high grass and flowering caraway.

The green for bleaching must have levelness to allow for the exposure of all parts of the piece to the sun, and it was counted a privilege to be allowed to lay the dainty linens upon the fresh grass, and even more of a one to sprinkle them occasionally, and best of all to gather them up before the dew began to fall and whiff the sweetness of each piece laden with priceless odors of earth and sun and breeze. America is forgetting this privilege very largely, so that a mistress of a foreign maid said recently: "My new maid does the funniest things with the laundry. She boils the pieces and then takes them all out of doors to lay them piece by piece upon the lawn. After they have bleached for awhile she takes the watering-can out and gives them a sprinkle; then they bleach some more, and are then taken in and rinsed again and then taken out to dry on the line."

Three types of clothes-pins

Clothes-pins were homemade articles for many years. During the early 1800s many families had none of these simple conveniences but sewed the pieces of their wash to the line with thread and needle or pinned them with the inch-long thorns from the thorn-apple tree. When the menfolks began to whittle these little implements for their womenfolks, ease had certainly come in the matter of hanging, and the wet clothes were now free to whip and swing and take full advantage of the air and sun and breezes. It is to laugh nowadays to see the first crude attempts at wooden clothespins in this country, and the poor housewife must have had to cart them to the scene of action in wheel barrows. Pins grew daintier with the years, until a machine-made article was put on the market which fitted the line width

better, though it had no head for easy grasping and stayed
headless for years.

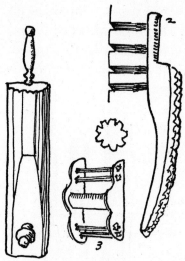

1. Wooden hand mangle. See wooden screw
2. Corrugated rubbing board with rubber,
two feet long
3. Corrugated revolving rubber for board with
revolving cylinders

Smoothing the Clothes

In the hands of the patient, wooden blocks proved to be
successful smoothers of clothes. At Ephrata, Pennsylvania,
in the old Bissell community of Seventh Day Baptists, the
fresh and precious linen used in the love feasts and religious
services throughout the year, were "smoothed" but not
"ironed." One of these old smoothing blocks has been put
into the Pennsylvania Historical Society at Philadelphia
for preservation. They tell one today that this block was
heated before using, but some years ago a "Sister" at the
community claimed that it did its work without assistance of

heat. The family rolling pin was also used for "smoothing" laundered clothes.

At Wiggin Tavern in Northampton, Massachusetts, there is a small collection of laundry equipment of years past, which includes a wooden mangle, smooth on one side and fitted with a handle at one end for pushing back and forth to smooth the clothes.

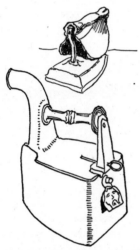

Flat-iron with heat shield
Charcoal flat-iron

What came to be known as "flatt irons" and have continued to be the usual handmaiden of housewives until the arrival of electric irons, were first made on home forges. Some of these delightful old relics remain to us, their handles made with a bar rising from the center of the iron high enough to be well above the heat area, and there bent into a handle of hammered strap iron. Just as a piece of rare old glass will ring out at a stroke against its edge or side, so will the handles of some of these handwrought smoothing irons ring when snapped with the finger, making one wonder whether these two types of manmade articles are not trying to tell us that the earth from which they come is full of music to those who tap it aright.

The "sad iron" was to the flatiron, apparently, what the sledge-hammer was to its smaller brother, a heavy, more ponderous member of the family, and made for the smoothing of thicker fabrics. The "box-iron" of the mid 1800s is still found. Some of these were charcoal burners, like the old footstoves, and others were fitted with an inner piece of metal which could be taken out, heated, and replaced. The fluting-iron had a similar heating method, and fluted the cap-ruffles of women.

A memory of grandmothers and fathers which comes from the present owner of "Two Mile Farm" at Marshfield, Massachusetts, gives us a glimpse behind drawn blinds. "Grandma, who was born in Vermont — she would be a hundred and ten years old now — told me that on the Fourth of July the young girls used to decorate their white gowns with garlands of cinnamon roses. Can't you see how sweet they must have looked? Fairlee, I think, was the town, and they used maple sugar for sweetening their coffee and tea, and the former was some sort of substitute. She was one of ten children and of course the work in such a household was never done, although, as grandma herself did, one generally married and left home when the youngest was born. They say that great grandma had drawn down the window shades toward the road one Sunday, and was doing some necessary ironing, when great-grandpa came into the kitchen. He is said to have remarked: 'Sallie, it won't do any good to pull down the curtains, the Lord can see just as well what you are doing." After all, this busy mother was only following good sage New England advice to strike while the iron was hot. In the old days each piece was ironed, and there was little respect for the "shaking out" method. What a pity that when families were ten or fifteen strong, there were no unironable undies of present day vogue.

There is an old word used in New England which has quite different meanings in different towns, and it is "heater piece." In Thompson, Connecticut, there is a tiny triangle of grassground at the heart of the town, shaped exactly like an old smoothing iron, or flat iron. Thus it is easy to understand the name "heater piece." At Gloucester, Massachusetts, there is not only the "great heater" but the "little heater," shaped also like a flatiron, and these pieces of ground are of real size and dimension, so much so that horses are raced around them and back again, both the great piece and the little piece, and here the name is supposed to have come from the habit of running horses over these lengths of road to get them heated up to running the real race, thus the "Heater Piece."

6. The Taylor Shop

"If it takes nine tailors to make a man,
then the ninth of a man you are."

Cast iron stand

Old Saw

THIS sadly deprecatory remark about the makers of the clothes of yore should have its explanation. There was the old New England custom of ringing the Meeting-house bell when someone in the neighborhood had died. The saxton or sexton was at once notified of the death and set about the ringing of the bell in the Meeting-house belfry. In some places the age of the deceased person decided the number of strokes to be tolled, and because countrysides always knew the details of the habits and health of their members, it was not hard to guess for whom the tolling was going on. One village had a morning made rhythmic by the passing of two women over eighty years old, so that more than a hundred and sixty tolls droned out in a continuous strain. In other places, and this was more usual, the sex of the departed was told by a certain code of tolling understood by all. As it happened, a male was designated by "nine tellers," that is, the bell was tolled nine times in groups of three, and this was repeated over and over. Gradually the ringer himself became known as the "teller" and still later, as the "tailor." Hence, "if it takes nine tellers (or tailors) to make (or signify) a man," one may easily see how the phrase came to be used as one of derision when attached wrongly to the tailorer of garments.

Visiting Taylors

Like the master of the shoeshop, the master of the tailorshop had often to compete with his traveling colleagues,—who went from house to house to cut and fit and sew the suits for the men and boys,— and resented it. These itinerant tailors and tailoresses slept in the third-best feather bed, but acted quite like guests except for this discrimination. Such visitations are still remembered by our older people.

There were tailor shops also in the smaller villages where the tailoring trade was taught. A man wrote of Meriden, New Hampshire: "My maternal grandfather had much to do with this process. It was a prosperous business with them during many years to train the young women, and now and then a young man, in the measuring, cutting, making and pressing of the clothing for the members of the countryside not resident on the farms. When these young women and men had mastered their trade they went from farm to farmhouse turning the homespun into clothes for the men and boys of the household. This process was called 'whipping the cat.' " (This is the phrase which was also applied to itinerant shoemaking.)

The place where this business was carried on was the site of the present village store. The proprietors were in turn, Deacon Samuel Winkley, his son, Mr. Alonzo Winkley, and son-in-law, Deacon Converse Cole. This tailoring com-

139

pany was situated in one of the tiniest little white hill villages, but must have supported and clothed at least two generations of contented Ascutney worshippers.

Many of the tailor shops were in the home of the tailor and not at all on the village Street, but rather on some winding road far from the center of things. Dr. Hubbard, minister and physician of that locality, tells of having his first tailored suit made in such a rural tailor shop when he graduated from the Academy. It meant going many times to stand and wait for measurements, so finally, not to waste valuable time at this crucial age of sixteen, he took along his netting-work, taught him by this same tailoress, and did a goodly stint upon the new tidy for the setting-room rocker. Black broadcloth was the only proper suiting for a young man bent upon the serious task of growing up, and so he was accoutred with that fine raiment.

The Taylor Shop

It is quite impossible to think of the old taylor, or tailour, or tailor, without visualizing a little man sitting crosslegged upon a great table, or shop-board, surrounded by his shears, and spool or quills of thread, his needles and his measuring tape, his bodkin, pressboard and goose. There was, it seems, a tailor's chair with of course no legs, but a back, which must have helped those who had them. It is always an amazing thought to the layman that in this crisscross position a man could sit for hours on a hard board and not grow utterly useless. That this position did have its effect upon one is shown by the old saying, that a man was at once set down as a tailor if, when walking, he carried his elbows close to his sides and his arms below the elbows in a horizontal position.

Following the tape, the shears were of first importance in the making of a suit, and here we run into more double meanings. The great shears with which the cloth was cut were known as "bench shears" and held in high esteem. The smaller shears were likewise held in esteem but of a very low order,— they were nothing but "hand shears" and dubbed "snips." In fact the tailor who puttered about with odd jobs was often designated as the "snip cabbage tailor," or "Snip, the Tailor," or even "Master Snip." So we must not err among our shears.

"Great" or "bench" shears

The thimble of the tailor was, strangely, without a top, quite hygienic for the tip of the finger, but desperately treacherous if wrongly used. The sharp pointed bodkin, a tiny steel rod for puncturing heavy cloth, was a close friend of the small needle. The thread of the early tailors was good homespun stuff made for wear and not for tear.

Tailor's Press Board

141

HANDWROUGHT ANCESTORS

The pressboard was made so that the crosslegged sewer might not have to rise from his green-god position on his bench, when something must be pressed, but simply reach out and seize the narrow board which was equipped not with a high standard, but with a heavy curved block for a base, whittled out to fit between his knees. The sleeve pressboard was small and some of them had a magic about them which dampened the cloth without sprinkling when the heat was applied. We have all wondered, in looking at old daguerreotypes, why our grandparents wore such baggy, untailored clothes, instead of having creases and such, to give greater trimness. This must have been because only the seams were pressed, the rest of the cloth going its own sweet way, and so pressboard and pressers were of a narrow gauge.

The tailor's "Goose" has come down to us in greater numbers than many of the old keepsakes because they were such heavy pieces of iron and therefore hard to destroy. They measured scarcely two inches across although they were longer than the flatiron proper, both of which dimensions fitted nicely to a seam, and they were extremely heavy. The old goose, made on a blacksmith's forge, took varied forms as regards the handle, most of them having two or three twists put into them while the iron was still hot. One rare type had a long handle which turned back, swept across the length of the goose and then turned down, and stayed suspended in air, without fastening again.

The making of a buttonhole was one of the tests of good workmanship, although the button itself seems always to have been held in low repute. "I wouldn't give a button for it," said they of old days. "He has a soul above buttons," was said of a person with aspirations. Still, the button was a most important part of a man's suit, both for use and for adornment. Pewter buttons went the way of window-weights when bullets were needed for wartimes, but after 1812 they came back into style and were freely used by the tailor and tailoress. By this time the pewter button had been somewhat strengthened with a brassy alloy, and was therefore less easily scratched. Today we speak of "button-holing" a person for a quiet word, but the original from which this grew was to "button hold" a person, referring to the button which could be grasped easily, and not to the hole. Live and learn. A bone button made at home from the boneyard of passed animals was not to be despised.

Tailor's goose
"A goose, and then another goose, but never geese"

The New Republic

Besides stealing its pewter buttons, the Revolution had another effect upon the tailoring business in this country. Visitors from England or other foreign lands, began to see a change in the attitude of shop keepers toward their customers, for the new independence — to smaller minds — meant refusing those little attentions and considerations which had previously been usual. This was done that the world at large might know that "I'm as good as you are," no matter what one's position in life. One of these visitors, according to custom, sent to a tailor bidding him come and measure him for a suit. The tailor's answer was: "If a man desire to be measured for a suit he must come to my shop, since for me to go to him is not republican." And that was that.

The "tailor's block" was nothing but a dummy on which to fit clothes for display, and this and the tailor's shopboard came in for some of the sly digs of which the tailor seems to have had more than his share. A youth of too great style or too little brain, or both, might have either of the following said of him: "He's straight off the tailor's shop-board," or "He's naught but a tailor's block."

Coat hangers
That made from a block of wood was for holding
a quilted tricolet wedding coat

7. THE SPECTACLES SHOP

"Poverte a spectacle is, as thynketh me,
Thurgh whiche he may hise verray frendes se."
— CHAUCER

Benjamin Franklin

THERE was one thing which our ancestors did not need to bother with at once upon settlement here, and that was glasses for their eyes. Books were a luxury and many a home was practically without them, while the almanack came along in time to give an insight into world affairs past and to come. While we hear of "early candlelight" as the time when the first dusk fell, it was often the only candlelight of the whole evening, for bed was the order of the day or night after an hour or so of artificial light. There was practically no eye strain and therefore no need for glasses. The Browns of the country seem to stand out as weak-eyed gentlemen, or perhaps among the few who had money to spend lavishly, for the first pair of spectacles to arrive in America came with Peter Brown on the Mayflower, when specs were costing $75.00, while a pair, worn by Noah Brown in the War of 1812, is preserved as a choice heirloom today.

There came a time, of course, when books began to seep into our homes and weeklies edged in too with news of the last fortnight, and early candlelight was lengthened just a little so that grandfather — if he could read — might hang his candle stick upon the back of a slatback chair and study out the letters, or fall asleep and set his paper afire. It was Benjamin Franklin, bless his inventive old brain and amazing outlook, who gave this country her first boost toward the making of really useful optical contraptions. After all, when one thinks of it, it was he who through his printing press began the great inroad upon our innocent eyes by the publishing of his famous "Poor Richards," and so perhaps it was only just that he should provide the antidote. However he himself was sadly in need of eye help and had procured two pairs of spectacles for constant use. He wrote to a friend:

> "I had two pairs of spectacles that I used alternately because when traveling sometimes I passed the time in reading, sometimes, in looking at the country. The change from one pair to the other was troublesome and often was not effected soon enough to allow me to see what I wanted. So I had my glasses cut in two halves, one half of each being put in the same frame. In this way I wear my spectacles constantly."

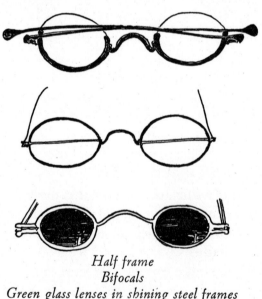

Half frame
Bifocals
Green glass lenses in shining steel frames

FOR-THE-SAKE-OF-THE-PERSON SHOP

The upper half was for "seeing clear," and the lower half for "bringing near," and behold the first bifocals, with a hard line running between the two pieces of the lenses and straight across the pupil.

Glasses cost about a hundred dollars a pair in those days and it is no wonder that the farmers and shop-tinkerers sought to roll their own. Strangely enough the bifocal idea was not taken up universally, for many an old person even until the present day has resorted to a pair of specs on the top of his head and another on the tip of his nose, and found occasion to bring them together when the print grew too fine. From having no eye strain, our forefathers jumped straight into the greatest strain, because of the smallness of much of the earlier print, and because neither candlelight, nor hearthlight nor whaleoil lamp was strong enough to show the way through it without struggle.

William Beecher

As we shall soon see, America was making her own glasses here and there in her home shops and sometimes in stalls along the streets, but she was working with poor glass brought from England, or window glass which by some strange freak of nature achieved here and there a spot of luminosity or magnifying power, in the way that old window glass had. It yet remained for us to become the greatest makers of optical equipment in the world. The following quotation from a short history of American eyeglasses gives the beginnings of this work in a small shop at Southbridge, Massachusetts, in 1833:

147

HANDWROUGHT ANCESTORS

"In a little room over the jewelry store where he worked all day, William Beecher spent his evenings making silver spectacles. Steel ones, they told him, could not be made in this country. But after a little he made those too."

Companies were formed and work begun on the new American eyeglass:

"Those were the days when the newest apprentice trimmed the oil lamps by which the others worked; when the filling of orders might be delayed by the failure of water power in dry weather; when six dozen spectacles was a good day's output; and when the members of the twelve-man working force made each day a few pairs of spectacles from the first shaping of the wire to the final cutting out and fitting of the lenses. There were no dies then; every tiny metal part was filed down by hand; lenses were ground 'at the stone' by foot power."

Importations

While still at the mercy of foreign achievement, our little shops in the cities did their best to supply eyes to the needy. Hannah Breintal kept shop in Philadelphia in 1758, in second Street near Black-Horse Alley," where, according to her advertisement she displayed needed eye-wear.

"Variety of the finest chrystal spectacles set in Temple, Steel, Leather or other Frames. Likewise true Venetian Green Spectacles for weak and Watery Eyes, of various Sorts. Also Concave spectacles for short-sighted Persons, Magnifying and Reading Glasses, Telescopes, Perspectives, with Multiplying Glasses and Glasses for Davis' Quadrants etc etc. Also ox-eye Glasses for taking Landskips."

148

FOR-THE-SAKE-OF-THE-PERSON SHOP

It may be explained that a "perspective" was a "spying glass," and that "landskip" was the word used from 1598 to 1725 for our "landscape." Again, the expression "ox-eye" meant in the 1620s, large, full eyes like the ox, and it was in this capacity that the term was used in this advertisement. One sketching a landskip would naturally want large lenses to take in as vast an expanse as possible, the value increasing thereby.

Tinkered Spectacles

"Whoever make a mistake (*in choice of his spectacles*) buy a master instead of a servant."

Back to the little old shop and we find our forebears undoubtedly buying more masters than servants, for it was not until 1860 that the eye chart developed and mathematical measurements could be made of individual eyes. But, if one's eyes were failing it was natural to try to tinker up some device to help them out. If a man had a forge he would make the frames of slender iron and the bows of iron straps, or turn to lead, which "worked a sight easier," and then find him some pieces of good clear window glass, either white or green, and think he was well set up. It meant careful work though to bend and fit nosepiece and rims and fasten on with metal pins the bows which must be attached by a simple hinge. Once done, though, you had something to "heir" down through coming generations. It was natural that such a splendid pair of crutches should be cherished.

Well enough, said the old tinkerer, to make a contraption to hold two pieces of window glass and fix 'em up with sticks over the ears, but how in heck could you make 'em stick on? Most of the simple bows and temples had slits in the ends or huge rings formed through which twine could be passed for tying behind the head. Some specs could be tied firmly once and just slipped over the head without untying again.

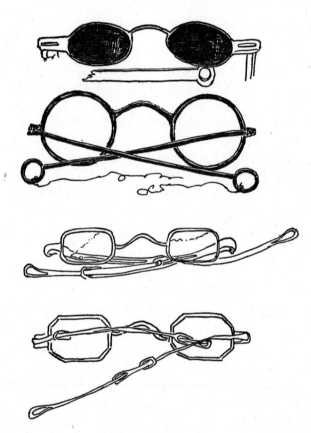

Steel and green glass with sliding bows one fourth inch wide

Homemade pewter frames and window-glass

Rectangular and hexagonal specs with sliding bows

FOR - THE - SAKE - OF - THE - PERSON SHOP

Kinds

The glasses which remain to us from the 1700s and even the 1800s are rather amazing in their variety and their general appearance. They were made of iron, lead, pewter, steel, bone, silver, shell and gold as well as a brassy metal. The rims are circular, oblong with rounded corners, octagonal and elliptical, and vary in size from large enough to cover the whole eye and eyebrow, to less than an inch across the lense at its widest point. This trifling size dates back to the late 1700s when eye glasses were used not so much for seeing with as to attain an appearance of great knowledge and learning, for they are so small and the nose-piece so pinched, that just to look at them makes one's eyes ache with sympathy. In the 1830s they were again popular for actual use. Benjamin Franklin's bifocals were octagonal; the spectacles which George Washington wore in the late 1780s were elliptical; both elliptical, and oblong lenses and rims with curving corners were made in the 1830s, 1840s and until the 1860s, when the angular shapes disappeared for awhile. The heavy bows and rims of the 1780s, had in the 1880s become spidery wire, crisscrossing from either rim across the nose to form the nosepiece, and even with this delicate frame holding the double glass for bifocal purposes. Some clever spectacle-maker did away with the upper half of the rim and let the lense lie in its half-way frame which came up only far enough to hold the bow hinges.

The last mentioned type was made when the bows had become really bowed to fit the curve of the head, but the usual bow was made of two parts three or four inches long which slid back and forth upon each other, extending the bow to fit comfortably upon whatever head was wearing

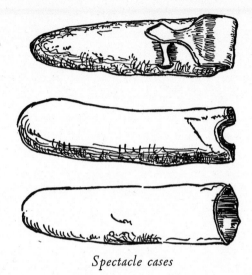

Spectacle cases

it at the time — either grandpa or grandma or Aunt Stephena. Even these extension bows had the hole or slit at the end for holding a tie-string, which had been common on the shorter and straight "temple." As the structure of spectacles progressed, the matter of the hinges underwent a noticeable change. Where earlier temples or bows had used them halfway down their length and even in the center of the nosepiece, they became useful only at the joining of bow and rim, and with the slenderizing of the bows they themselves took on less bulk. It was well for the human face to have this metal gearing grow less and less conspicuous, but it is the old heavy spectacle which is best to look upon as an object of ingenuity and really artistic work, even when it bears no mark of the carving which was applied to the broad spaces of the sliding bows.

The spectacle case used by our forefathers was generally of leather in the shape of a huge peapod with one end left open. Some were equipped with leather flaps at one end where the glasses were inserted and kept safe from falling out by slipping the flap through a tiny leather strap. The inside was made of thin metal against breakage.

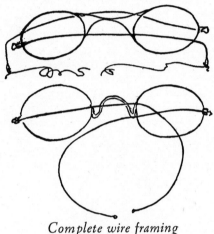

Complete wire framing
Progress in gold

Backgrounds

In a swift backward look it is interesting to see what other parts of the world had done to help the human sight before America began her late ministrations, and in what ways they exerted an influence. Eye glasses seem to have had their beginnings in China in the 1200s, and the earliest type consisted of two round bone rims to hold lenses ground with sand, and fastened together with a two-inch extension joined by a pivot. This type was held in place by the hand. When warriors set forth to battle they could hardly donate one whole hand to the holding of eyeglasses, and so these latter were fastened permanently in their helmets. The war over, the idea was retained by using a strap of leather about the head, and thus the eyeglass became the spectacle. Later, holes were pierced through the rims and strings inserted to be tied about each individual ear; and this led to the strings which went about the head and tied behind. Sometimes a little band went up the middle of the forehead from the nosepiece to the hair or hat, and this in turn led to the two bands which went up across the two temples, giving the name to the short, straight bow. In 1728 the real spectacle bow was initiated, but it still had its rings and string. It then developed its midway hinge or its sliding halves.

Early iron specs with four hinges
Eskimo eye-protector against snow-blindness

Nosepieces, starting with two parts pivoted together, grew into a solid arch, a solid bar, two parts hinged together, and then the gentle arch which laid itself down upon the human nose and did its part in making the lenses remain in position. It was not until 1880 that the pince-nez arrived, depending neither upon hand nor bows for its permanency, and it had taken since the 1200s to accomplish this; perhaps nothing shows more clearly how slowly the world has progressed in its inventions, until it was caught up in the whirlwind of the last half century. It is a long look from China's first spectacles which persisted for hundreds of years, to the great twenty-ton, two hundred inch telescope lense which has been in the making at Corning, New York, and must have years of grinding to bring us the stars.

Finally, "a spectacle is a gazing-stock, or glasses for the sight." A gazing-stock! The store or stock of things upon which the eye looks. How the modern dictionaries, by their delight in filling full the limbo of obsoleteness, rob us of our past glories. So then, our pairs of spectacles took their name from the things upon which they helped the human eye to feast.

To be perfectly fair to the New World we should perhaps remember that long ago the Eskimo had his own type of spectacles, a sun mask against snow-blindness. He had sometimes to wait for years for the special driftwood — Ikshaut — which was swept across by the polar current from north of Siberia. Of this he made a wooden shield pierced with carefully studied-out slits through which he might see his way and yet circumvent the effects of the sun's rays on miles of reflecting snow. Measuring about four by seven inches and tying on with thongs of walrus hide, and having a carefully raised section to fit over the nose, this early product was a real credit to man's ingenuity.

HANDWROUGHT ANCESTORS

8. THE BAKE AND CRACKER SHOPS

"O God! that bread should be so dear,
And flesh and blood so cheap."
— HOOD: *The Song of the Shirt*

Manchmaker and Baker

ALTHOUGH the manchet which he made was a small loaf of fine bread, the manchmaker was yet considered a person of lowly occupation, a sort of stepsister apparently to his well accepted brother, the baker. He is mentioned because he had his place in the feeding of the multitudes, although our immigrating forebears seem to have had their "bakers" established shortly after their arrival. The first year or so of community living which the Pilgrim Fathers tried out, was a natural decision for a group which had so many beginnings to undertake. Why build thirty or forty fires each morning when one large one could cook the breakfasts for all quite as well? Why set each woman to the work of baking bread in individual ovens which must first be constructed with difficulty, when one huge oven, or a few at most, under the care of skilled bakers could supply bread for all? It can hardly be used as an argument against community living that the Pilgrims found it a failure, for it served them well during their cruelly hard beginnings.

The real baker knew when his bread was done to a turn, and how to avoid "doughbaking," or under-doneness. Sugar poured into garden sass does not so much sweeten it as turn insipidity into a flavor, and it was thus that the baker used his salt and his spices upon his various batches. One of the names for old sayings and saws is "sourdough," meaning something which has stood a long time. The baker's yeast might be the dregs of a malt barrel, for the flower of malt liquor when working was a yeast; it might have been set from a tiny green hop, bursting with "raisin' power"; it might have been set fifty or more years before from potato-water, and kept alive and vigorous by continual additions of this effective liquor — if only some seed of some sort of yeast had been dropped in at the beginning.

America's first oven — built in 1565 by the French near the mouth of the River May. (St. John's River) Florida

The Early Bake Shop

The Norseman, the Irish, and other early explorers may of course have erected their bake-shops on this unknown continent for the duration of their stay, but the one built at Fort Caroline on the River May, the present St. Johns, in 1565 by the French Huguenots, may be called our first bakeshop, and its existence is known to us through the remarkable art of Le Moyne. It was a masterpiece, for it combined safety, efficiency, shelter and capacity, and all derived from the material which lay at hand in a strange land. Raised upon blocks or squared timbers, above the ground and crawling things, it resembled an Eskimo's house, in shape, and was plastered with an earthy paste to make it raintight above. It might have been called merely an oven if it had not sported a shelter which brought it into the realm of the work-shop, and this shelter was of saplings slanting back from a timber laid across two crotched poles and slipping down toward the ground at the back, a perfect sun and rain shed.

Famous William St. Bakery, New York City, 1648
Stood for over 200 years

The only thing which remains to us of one of the most pretentious of the early city bakeries is the sketch of that one which was built on William Street, New Amsterdam, in 1648, and remained standing long enough to be modernized in 1828. Over a hundred years later, or in the first half of the 1700s, the term "bakehouse" was still in use in New York City, and one stood at Broadway at the corner of John Street, and its owner, G. Van Bomel, boasted outrageously of its new cistern. One of the nearly five hundred houses still remaining from the 1600s, is the "Old Bakery," also known as the Hathaway House, at Salem, Massachusetts. This was built in 1683 and is a lovely piece of old time architecture. Philadelphia was so late in getting started that it lacks the real antiquity of some other places, but once started it lost no time in setting up a bake-shop, for a Dutch baker named Bom was making and selling bread in 1683, the year after the city was laid out, and doing it from his own humble hut. The second year, Robert Turner built one of the first brick houses out of homemade brick and established therein a bakery and brewery, not an uncommon combination.

Plastered coquina bakery, St. Augustine 1763-1778. Now a garage

Climate, chance and worth have all combined to save for us an old bakery made of coquina, perhaps the only one ever erected in the world. Since this ancient rock was all quarried on Anastasia Island across the bay from St. Augustine, it is not difficult to guess that that city was the home of this venerable shop. Having forgotten its days — or does it remember — of doughs and yeasts, it is now a garage, although one hundred and forty-eight years old.

159

The Baker's Dozen

As long as man has inhabited this turning ball and as long as he shall, there will probably be those who will slice off a layer of butter from the bottom of the weighed pound when the customer is not looking, fasten a false bottom in his "bushel," or hold his hand on the scales during the weighing. Long ago the merchants of London brought upon their heads a heavy fine for such doings. Bread was then sold by weight and the authorities said that after the bread had been weighed, no matter how honestly, an extra piece should be added for safety. So, when a baker sold a dozen rolls or buns he must make the number thirteen instead of twelve. This "vantage" loaf gave us the expression "the baker's dozen" which today means generosity. Only eleven years after the bakers of Philadelphia had displayed their signs, the authorities ordered that "the mayor once in every month gae the rounds to the respective bread makers in this city, and weigh their bread, and seize all such as shall be deficient in weight, and dispose of the same as the law directs."

Daniel Goodman of that city was a baker about 1750, and born the seventh son of a seventh son. This of course was bound to show in some way, either in his bread baking or in some more occult way. His home was on Second Street between Market and Chestnut and it was not long after he gained his majority before he was advertising along with his baking the power to cure "King's Evil," which was a disorder of the glands. To show that his name was no misnomer he would do this curing for nothing. This was even better than the thirteenth loaf. His seventh-son power extended also to the infallible curing of mad-dog bites, and to the curing of the dog itself. If a "manor woman" ran amuck of the mad dog she could be saved for five shillings, while the dog could be saved for only two and sixpence.

Signs and Implements

The sheaf of wheat was a popular bakeshop sign, but a long wooden peel was a better. The real peel, when of iron, measured perhaps seven by five inches in the head, with a yard long handle, but when it was of wood it might have a handle which would go five and six feet high, and have a head a foot square. This was for placing far back in the great brick oven the dozen or two loaves and for getting them out again when baked. Another quaint sign was the picture of a mule turning the long wooden sweep of a grist mill where the grain was ground between revolving stones. Brick ovens well plastered with local cement might protrude from one wall of the shop or stand by themselves under some sort of rough shelter. Often erroneously called the Dutch oven, they were really entirely unlike this small iron kettle into which the dough was placed for baking, covered with an iron cover which held hot coals, and then placed in the hot ashes of the hearth.

An oven which had been slowly heated for an hour or two with quick burning twigs, raked clean, and then had balls of dough laid within its redhot bricks, baked a very different tasting bread from that baked in any other oven. It mattered not at all that there might be a soft blow of ash still left upon the surface of the oven when the dough was turned directly upon it, just as the corn pone of the South has always been baked upon the uncovered hearthstones.

Six-foot wooden peel

Cook Shops

We must not think of the bake shop as being a place where only bread was made and sold, for it had a much broader base of usefulness. As the weaver carried his cloth to the fuller for shrinking and pressing, so did the housewife carry her bread, her beans and even her meats to the baker for baking or boyling or roasting. In some New England towns it was a familiar sight to see great batches of bread or beans nicely covered, being carried to the bake-shop to be left for twenty-four hours or until they were done to a turn. For the carrying home there was a certain blue and white checked handkerchief known as the "bundle handkerchief" into which the bread was put and hung upon a shoulder stick. We have always laughed to see pictures of men tramping along the country roads with their few belongings hanging thus in a bundle, and thought that it was always a sign of poverty. On the contrary these bundle handkerchiefs were manufactured for just this service, and must have been handy and easy to carry. Surely we can trust our ancestors who did much of their traveling on Shanks' Mare, to have the best way to transport their meagre luggage.

Tin cookie cutter

To the much criticized New Englander who wants his pie for breakfast may come, as a handy weapon, the note from Bucks County, Pennsylvania, that "for common living in the early 1700s, bread and milk and pie made the breakfast."

The Cracker Shop

One of these hung on the edge of a dusty country road over a deep ravine, and started the fortune of one of our millionaire families. But that was long ago. A cracker, in the 1700s, was "a noisy boastful sort of fellow or a kind of firework which had gunpowder at its heart." Babies were never fed this kind. What became a cracker in the late 1700s and is one today, simply was not. There was, though, the biscuit, a kind of hard, dry bread, which was invented and produced because it kept longer than did bread, and it had its own shops. About 1700 Jacob Yates erected a granary in Chester, Pennsylvania, and used the first floor for an "extensive biscuit bakery." Theodore Pearson of Newburyport had a "cracker bakery" in the last of the 1790s, and here and there in many of the smaller villages such cracker shops sprang up under the newer name. It was not until about 1900, when we found ourselves being advised on every roadside signboard that we needed a biscuit, that we took back the old word, at least for ordering purposes. But, while we may pay for a "biscuit" we still eat "crackers."

The measure of a man in one New York village, was the obscure cracker. Throughout his life and through the many years which have passed since his death, he has been known as the grocer who broke a cracker in two to make the exact pound.

The cracker stamp made of wood, with iron spikes inserted in it in a row, and sometimes the family initial whittled in relief in the center, is the outstanding antique of this kind of shop. It was applied after the dough had been dropped upon the board, so that it might be flattened and properly pricked to let the air slip out.

Some notes on early bake-shops:

A swizzle- stick, or natural growth egg-beater

164

One of the early egg-beaters was called a "swizzle stick." It was a thin branch of the pine tree — which throws its little new shoots out in a circle about its stalk. One of these with about seven shoots made a perfect swizzle-stick, if they were cut back to within two or three inches of the stalk, and, held above by the stalk, would beat at a furious speed.

Some egg-beaters were the human hand with the fingers widely outspread. Used in a bowl they were said to out-beat any made instrument.

Some eggs were beaten upon a flat platter, with a turkey wing which had been picked and stripped and boiled into a fine white skeleton framework. The slant of the feathers and the nubbin where they met together at the body, made a perfect beater with a perfect handle.

The best ice-boxes were either a bucket suspended in a cool, deep well, or a stoned recess in the well wall, where the thing to be kept cool might be swung in upon the shelf at the end of a rope. Another was a locker in the cellar wall.

Johnny-cake, a form of bread made of cornmeal, was best baked upon a clean board leaning toward the open fire. This Johnny-cake board was a little over a foot long and about four inches wide.

Bread dough was made in Florida by softening the roots of the bamboo in a hollow tree mortar, then putting it in a sack through which water was poured. When the water was drained off, a pone was made from the result-ing flour.

✧ VI ✧

1. THE BLACKSMITH SHOP

"Under a spreading chestnut-tree
The village smithy stands;
The smith, a mighty man is he,
With large and sinewy hands . . ."

*Old "King's Forge" where iron work was made for
Fort San Marco, 1638, and Fort Marion (the same
fort) 1754, St. Augustine, Florida
Site still called "The Old Forge Lot"*

Smithy and Smith
LONGFELLOW did his best to differentiate between these
two words, but it is fair to say that most of us believe that
both smithy and smith mean the blacksmith himself. Do
we not see him "standing" beneath the spreading boughs,
and yet for aught the poet says, he may have been leaning
over to shoe a horse at the moment of writing, while it was

THOSE WHO WORKED WITH IRON

the little shop which was doing the standing. Since in a recent issue of a wellknown newspaper the error of calling a smith a smithy, was made, perhaps we should draw a sharp line between the smith who does the forging and working in metal, and his shop, smithy or even smithery.

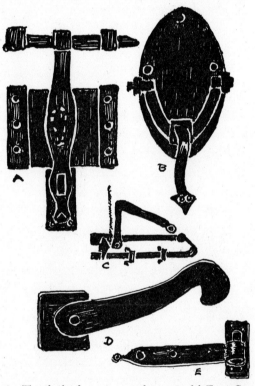

A. Triple lock on court door of old Fort San Marco, St. Augustine, Florida, showing sliding bar, hidden keyhole under flap, and eye for padlock
B. Combination knocker and door latch handle. "Snake Eye." New England
C. Latch and bolt on a New Jersey door
D. Seven inch handwrought hook. Pennsylvania
E. Spanish-American hinge

HANDWROUGHT ANCESTORS

Having thus pried apart the smith and his shop, we may as well call attention to the "blacksmith" and the "farrier." The latter word is seldom heard today but was familiar in earlier years. Both were smiths, and both, working with black iron and charcoal soot and smudge, were "black" smiths, but the definite work of the farrier was shoeing horses and neat critters, while the blacksmith proper worked in iron for the making of many articles. Of the farrier we can speak later in his own shop.

For most of us the word blacksmith means the old man down the road who shod horses and oxen in the summer with smooth shoes, and sharpshod them when the ice and winter came, but long before there were horses or oxen to be shod in this country the blacksmith was one of the busiest and most vitally necessary persons of a pioneer settlement, and those near the coast — and our settlements were mostly there — were apt to have three or four forges running at one time, so often did shipbuilding call upon them for careful work, work which would keep a ship afloat at sea or anchor it when in port. One who can claim a blacksmith ancestor is sure of having had at least one thoroughly handwrought one, and if he can claim one he can generally claim more, since this important and artful trade generally ran from father to son, sometimes for several generations. Coming down to our own times we have seen such men as "Jim Pratt" of Essex, Connecticut, continuing at this trade, his business reputed to be the oldest in the country which has been continuously conducted by one family. There may easily be other cases in other parts. Then there is Edwin F. Hambly, of Tiverton, Rhode Island, who was still working at his forge on his eighty-fifth birthday, and whose shop, where he himself has kept busy for sixty-seven years, has been owned by his family for one hundred and thirty-five years or longer. Fine blacksmithing has not been limited to white men, for down in Tenille, Georgia, one of the ablest of his day was old John Haskins, a colored man, who is remembered for his fine work and the "ting, ting, ting" of his hammer on the anvil. He also worked a large plantation. Most of the lovely handwrought ironwork of balcony and window for which New Orleans is famous was hammered out by colored coachmen who were forge and anvil artists.

Smithery Equipment

The blacksmith who worked in iron for other purposes than shoeing animals, loomed large in the old scheme of things. The story of how early American iron was found in the sledges in meadow or swamp, broken with a "sledge hammer," and the ore turned into a workable substance, is a story in itself. The few remaining old-time blacksmiths tell us that in their day the American smith used the Norway iron, because it was the best in the world at that time. Already in *Candle Days* the author has gone into the subject of the old blacksmith shop, its equipment and visitors, but it may be repeated that unlike most of his fellow craftsmen, the blacksmith had to make nearly everything with which he worked — and many of the tools with which others carried on other trades — except of course the iron itself. He built his forge of homemade brick wherever he was located near brickmaking materials, and his chimney as well.

The forge once set up, there must be a bellows, and this was one of the giants of the small shop, a great man-long

Old Spanish type of lock used in the South

affair of light wood, and leather, and brass nails and thongs, suspended from a heavy wooden rack. The work of the bellows was of course to pump air into the forge to make the necessary under draught for the hot charcoal fire which alone was hot enough to heat iron properly. These old "leather lungs," as they were called, were made the same shape as a hand bellows, but measured four and six feet long, the rear part swelling out to a great width and made of pleated leather so that when the pumping was going on the lower and upper parts were pushed far apart, extending the leather in between to the height of a couple of feet or more. The end of the bellows which connected with the lower part of the forge chimney, was run down in size to almost a point so that the air could be lead directly through the metal tube and into a small opening in the bricks. The handle was as long as the bellows itself, and in some cases longer, for at the far and lower end of the bellows a great iron hook was fastened connected by a chain with the end of the handle which was suspended above the lung from the crosspiece of a rack. That the blacksmith might stand at the forge and still work his pump, the handle reached to the forge.

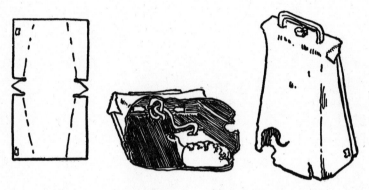

Forge-made cow-bell with pattern and showing chunk-of-iron clapper in interior view

In the end-pages sketch we have the old Beckwith black-smith shop, at Drewsville, New Hampshire. Here we see that an old shaft was made to serve as bellows handle, and it is not hard to visualize the old smith who used to stand by that forge talking with his neighbors and leaning back upon the handle of his leather lung, working it all un-consciously with his left hand held behind him while with the right he used his tongs in the flame of the forge. One can almost see the great bellows rise and sink with each deep breath and see also the flame dart up and die down. Today the old shop is used for the redoing and sale of "antiques," but the old bellows and forge are undisturbed, for the owner,

HANDWROUGHT ANCESTORS

Mr. Charles Russell, loves each old thing which he finds in place and leaves it there. In the upper part of the building there was formerly another bellows, rather unusual in so small a shop, and this was uniquely circular in shape. The shop stands close by the highroad, convenient now as in the old days, and its rear peeks down over the brink of a hundred foot drop to Cold River racing among its high falls and swift currents, and beyond this the Green Mountains of Vermont paint the horizon for many a perfect sunset.

Of course the anvil stood within arm-reach of the forge so that the smith could turn from one to the other with his redhot irons without taking unnecessary steps. At one end of the forge was either a barrel or watertight box full of black water into which the hot iron could be plunged. It is the anvil, because it has a tongue of its own, which has always caught the attention of the passerby and become almost symbolic of the blacksmith shop and work, given rise to anvil choruses, and to any number of old sayings, such as "Strike while the iron is hot," which are calculated to lead us on to victory. The making of an anvil was a very nice job and no botcher could turn out a worthy one. The first blacksmith at Newbury, Vermont, so late as the 1760s had a rock set upon a stump for an anvil. The stump was however the usual pedestal for the finest steel anvils, being fastened to them with great iron clutches and bolts.

Even the "coals," which were really charcoal, had to be made by the smith himself, this annual task taking three or four consecutive days and nights when he stayed alone in the woods, charring a great mound of cut logs. There was nothing which gave so hot a heat as charcoal.

THOSE WHO WORKED WITH IRON

Blacksmith's "head" or "set hammer" or "flatter,"
for smoothing wrought iron

A smithery on the plantation of Ralph Wormley, of Virginia, from 1698 to 1713 had this equipment:

1000 lbs. trash iron
1 pr. bellows
1 anvil
1 back iron
4 great vises

4 hand vises
screw plates
taps and files
hammers
tongs

New England handcuffs with key

Some of the Virginia blacksmiths of this early century were landed proprietors and their work savored of the jeweler rather than the worker in heavy iron, for they did the work

173

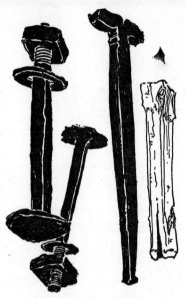

Irons from old Tucker X Covered Bridge built
across Connecticut River in first decade of 1800s
Bellows Falls, Vermont and North Walpole, New
Hampshire. Recently torn down
Handwrought iron spike clinched at end
Oaken "framing pin" squared at one end, split at
other to hold a wedge

of the silversmith, mended guns, and restored the temper
of damaged swords. Their acres might easily run into the
many hundreds in number and their tobacco fields stand
lush on a vast share of them, but handwork was handwork,
something to be kept for personal happiness and the doing
of the more artistic things in life. It would be impossible to
say just who was the first blacksmith to come to this land,
for there is no question that every ship that touched our
shores as far back as those first mythical ones, had aboard

their decks at least one man who worked at the forge and could keep the ship in order and condition, with chain links forged and braces firm. One of the first recorded blacksmiths here was Thomas Walford, who came to Weymouth in 1623. Here again was a man of importance in his neighbor-hood. Walford settled later at Charlestown, but still later went to Portsmouth, New Hampshire, "being expelled for his Anglican tenets." He died in 1666 "with broad acres."

Works of Art

Not in spite of this hard work before he was able to claim any output, but probably because of it, the blacksmith was able in his home-wrought shop to turn out just about any-thing in the way of ironwork which his neighbors might need. Here are a few of things found necessary to nice liv-ing which his "large and sinewy hands" and "the muscles of his brawny arms" made possible to his community. Not all of our ancestors were angels and it sometimes became necessary to slip handcuffs over their wrists to keep them in place. It was the blacksmith who made the needed cuffs or the ankle irons. A bridge was about to be swung across a river and it is the blacksmith who must make the bolts, the nuts and washers to hold it in place against tides or spring freshets or ice jams. When the Tucker Bridge, joining New Hampshire and Vermont, was built in the early 1800s to replace the first bridge across the Connecticut — which was at Bellows Falls — it was the usual covered "X" bridge, the sides crisscrossed with heavy timbers in a huge lattice-work of X's, which gave the bridge its name, and necessitated many iron pins and bolts. The Tucker Mansion, home of the builder of the bridge, stood at the foot of Fall Mountain where railroad tracks now bedizen the land, and every pin and bolt which went into the monstrous structure was under the personal inspection of Mr. Tucker. All of the ironwork was undoubtedly made in the local blacksmith shop, and when this second bridge was recently replaced with modern concrete, the old iron pins and bolts came tumbling out as perfect as when put in, to show the handwork of their master.

*Sheep-markers of wood and iron, and a branding
iron for a larger animal*

Sheep grazed in our pastures and meadows in earlier days in surprising numbers, and it has always been necessary that these tireless little wanderers wear upon their flanks some designating mark of ownership. The iron sheepmarker was therefore quite a usual article of manufacture for the blacksmith, who beat or cut out the initials of the owner, sometimes leaving the iron letter ready for the attachment of an iron handle, sometimes affixing a slender iron handle for holding the letter when redhot for the marking. One clever smith formed the letter "D" by forging a bar across the opening of a ready-to-hand horseshoe. Iron skates, iron pot-hooks for lifting pots from the crane and others for holding the pots thereon, iron cowbells made to a nice pattern and folded and riveted, with a huge chunk of rough iron for a clapper, iron shutter holders, all sorts of iron hinges and latches, locks and handles were called for and produced in varying degrees of loveliness, and the spit for roasting meat and the spit-rack, all were made in the smithy by the smith. It would be impossible to remember half of his output, some of which in all probability we have never even heard of, for the old days were the days of ingenuity, and variety.

Handwrought ring, hook and staple for well stone,
raised with rope over wooden drum. Quodic, Conn.

HANDWROUGHT ANCESTORS

Condemned to continued hard labor in a wayside well in Quodic, Connecticut, is a nice piece of old blacksmithing in the shape of an iron ring, hook and staple, which hold a monstrous well stone to a rope which passes over a feeble looking drum overhead, for the drawing up of water.

Mr. N. R. Ewan of Moorestown, New Jersey, tells of iron latche plates found upon some of the houses built in that vicinity in the 1700s. These plates were perforated with the initials of the owners and sometimes those of two generations, showing that the custom continued with the years.

Works of Torture

One gruesome task which befell our handwrought ancestral blacksmiths, was the occasional "ironing" of the Southern negroes for the chain-gangs. In the middle states there was the "brank," or "scold' bridle," or gag. This brank was a hoop of iron which enclosed the head. It opened and closed with hinges and fastened at the back with a padlock and staple. This terrible hoop extended inward so as to fit into the mouth and press upon the tongue for a gag. Later the hoop changed in shape to look like a cage or lantern or mask which covered the whole face, with holes for the eyes. So villainous were some of our handwrought ancestors that the victim was paraded through the streets in this headpiece by the town bellman, the beadle, or the constable. As an added incentive to virtue some of these cages included a little knife which cut the tongue if it dared to waggle in protest. Just what headpiece was strapped on to the ugly husband in his high moments has not been recorded.

There was the iron strait jacket and the more terrible body cage in which a victim could be hung up to die. The

THOSE WHO WORKED WITH IRON

New York Times of December 28, 1924, gives us a hint of this gruesome process, or of some equally cruel torture, as it describes the finding at Hempstead, Long Island — founded in 1620 or thereabouts — of a human skeleton encased in a "crude metal cage — an iron spike six inches long protruding from a hole just below the right eye." This was found by some small boys who were digging in a vacant lot. The cage is described as being made of four vertical metal stripes, an inch and a half thick, with four similar bands running crosswise, and other bands compressed at the neck to form a circular mask to hold the head. At the top is a ring by which the mask was hung. The early dwellers on the Island are saved condemnation by the supposition that pirates or men of the seas may have come ashore and buried this horrid affair some dark night, in the days when the high-seas ran with blood as well as with water.

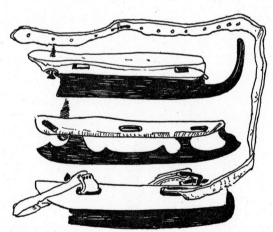

*Handwrought iron skates with wooden foot-hold,
and leather straps*

179

HANDWROUGHT ANCESTORS

Perhaps the busiest of our blacksmiths were those whose shops stood close to the seashore where shipbuilding was going on. Here three or four forges could be kept busy while the blacksmith and his helpers took care of the "ironing of the ships" under construction, making the needed plates, bars, chains and anchors necessary to safe passage. One of the earliest blacksmiths who kept busy at this kind of iron work was Robert Bond, who arrived in Southampton, Long Island in 1643, and then established himself as a settled smith at Easthampton in 1649. Lances, and harpoons, "harping irons," had not only to be made, but their sharp and barbed points made like a swordpoint for cutting. Much of this blacksmithing for the sea was done in the little shops of the seafaring men who could look after their own iron work when ashore, and had their own shops in their back dooryards, or as they were called on Long Island, pightels. Perhaps, the inland blacksmith at the country crossroads was kept busiest, with his shoeing of horses, ironing of wheels whose "tyres" would get loose and beyond the help afforded by driving through a brook to swell the felloe, and doing those countless things in iron needed for the running of farms and their equipment.

Handwrought shutter hook, "Central House"
Stoddard, N. H. 1800

180

THOSE WHO WORKED WITH IRON

One bit of iron work which may have been done in a blacksmith shop, and was surely done somewhere in Volusia County, Florida, a hundred years ago, was to trim one's hair with a red hot rod.

2. THE FARRIER SHOP

"Heat a horseshoe and drop it in the churn — t'well burn the witches out of the cream, when buttermaking."

Farrier's kit

Relics of the Past

THERE is no more striking example of the devastation — along with the good — which the coming of machinery wreaked upon simple handwork, than the sight of deserted and tumbling blacksmith shops which linger along our roadsides and at village crossroads, where indeed the ubiquitous gas station has not already pre-empted not only their old sites but their very memory.

THOSE WHO WORKED WITH IRON

One young blacksmith who had been learning his trade ever since he could toddle out to his father's shop as an infant, and was inheriting the business of the entire countryside in shoeing and wrought-iron needs, found the motor cars eating up his chances of a livelihood among horses, and closed the old shop and turned the key in it forever. Even if there had been no car rivalry, he had decided that shoeing horses and oxen was too much work, and standing before a hot forge another hardship. To be sure, as far as shoeing horses was concerned, he would have had to make neither the shoes nor the nails, as his father had done for many years before him, but bending over a horse's hoof, trimming it and acting the nursemaid to any animals, was more than his two hundred pounds of brawn was able to visualize as a life work. It was much easier and pleasanter, he thought, to drive a truck. Perhaps if he had had to make the shoes and not been left the monotonous job of just nailing them on, he might have seen more to pull at his muscles. It has been the slipping away of the need of creative handwork which has worked the havoc, and left us the little deserted, open-door, vinewound shops with their now breathless bellows waiting for ultimate destruction by small boys, countless iron tires and used horseshoes, moldering coals on a dead but unburied forge, and windows across whose tiny panes the magic work of spiders has been weaving glorious tapestries. The old center of "neighboring" has passed and left a vast, unsatisfied need, while the chipmunks scamper from sunup until sunset across its roof and on its walls, and its timbers slowly give up their supporting bases to the ravenous gnawings of creosote-hungry porcupines.

No one may rightly blame modern youth for taking advantage of the easier ways of living, but while the old blacksmith was a leader in his village or town, the son who now drives the truck all day and spends his evenings at the movies, is just one of the many. Is it fortunate or unfortunate that he does not realize, for all his gains, what he has lost? Ease has taken its toll in the privilege of creation through handwork and its resulting uplift of mind and heart.

One of the sparks of hope that some day men may go back to the forge for their outward and inward needs, is the fact that blacksmithing has been so deeply ingrained in the heart-oak of some family trees that the latest branches are working at the forge and anvil in spite of themselves and their other interests. Robert Burroughs of Alstead, New Hampshire, is a keen young carpenter and because he is modest few know that the trademark of his blacksmithing ancestors is plainly branded upon him. He is as much at home before his forge as before his carpenter's bench. His best friends speak of his work as though he were a blacksmith of a hundred years ago: "Rob can take an old nicked ax-head and draw it out on the forge and make it so that it is tempered as beautifully as a steel head." And "beautifully" is exactly the word to express how work of high art was done before the old smithy forges.

Shoe for work — worn hoof

The Farrier

A farrier, technically, might be both a shoer of horses and a horse-doctor, the word veterinarian being of rather recent date. The motif of interior decoration of the blacksmith shop of the past half hundred years has been the horseshoe, repeated over and over, the new ones in circular rows upon their wheel-tire racks suspended from ceiling or side wall; the old ones in piles upon the floor where they have been flung after being wrenched from tired old feet, or swept into corners, or rescued in part and hung upon outstarting hooks in jamb or window frame, or clinging for dear life to the end hook of a chain dangling helplessly from its own nail, or lying overlooked upon the open floor. Horseshoes were just about everywhere that one looked, for by this time they were being bought in quantity and hoarded in quantity after their first usefulness was over. Not that many of them would be used as shoes again, but a blacksmith shop must have just so much "co'lat'al" around, and old scrap iron may always come in handy.

It was different in the old days before the easy commercial shoe came upon the market and each shoe must be forged by hand, and when the ox-shoe was more used than the horse-shoe and did its share in interior decorating. It took years of practice before a man was able to make a perfect horseshoe, three, four or five, and they must be made for great plugging plough-horses, and the lightest of dainty feet of the "speed-horses" which were raced to the village pump at the center of town or along some even length of road or around a field after the mowing was finished in July. Old blacksmiths talked of the shoes they made for these speed-horses in terms of ounces rather than pounds, and they knew to a nicety just which horses toed in and which ran heavily on their left hoof edges, and made each pair, or each set of four, as though they were fitting a glove to a lady's hand. Yet with all of this pains taken in individual work, a farmer might drive his horse up to the blacksmith shop and have it completely reshod with ordinary shoes for the sum of sixty cents.

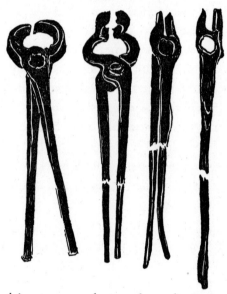

A tool for every need — made at the forge where they did their work

It would be interesting to know how much it cost the owner of a draught horse in Gloucester, to have him shod. One shoe, remaining from his old equipment, measures nine inches from crumpled, turned-over toe to the artistically turned-back ends of the heel, and eight inches from side to side, and "hefts" five pounds or more. A raised bar of iron which runs across the toe for digging in to the road, must have done its share in accumulating this weight and four of these great iron pedestals must have made mere walking difficult with no cart-load at all — a round twenty pounds of shoes.

Swedish iron rod for horse-shoe nails.
Over 50 years old. Bellows Falls, Vermont

The process sounds simple but the skill which saw it through was learned only in a long and exacting school of experience. The fire must be just at the right peak of heat, the coals red and keen, and the shoe which has been lying in this bed of redhot coals is lifted with long tongs, sprinkling sparks, but of a dead white heat. Quick as lightning the smith has it on his anvil and is hammering it with short, sharp strokes, the anvil chorus, first with the "sledge" and then with a smaller hammer with which he can more easily fashion and shape the shoe to the foot of the waiting horse. A dip into the water barrel and it is not long before the smith has the horse's hoof between his cloven leather apron and his sturdy, viselike knees.

Not only did the farrier make his own shoes but he made his nails as well. An old blacksmith still living spent the best part of his youth making and pointing horseshoe nails be-

187

cause they were just not to be found for sale. He says that old Norway iron was called the best for general work, seventy or eighty years ago, but that the iron which went into horseshoe nails was the Swedish iron. This came in slender strips or "nail rods" which were scarcely more than a quarter of an inch in width and many yards long, bendable enough to be folded up like wire to be sold in any quantity desired by the farmers who did their own horseshoeing and made their own nails. "Blacksmith and Nailer" was the sign over some blacksmith shop doors, which shows us how much time was spent in making this small but important part of the shop's equipment.

"Jiminy Crimps! I call it a fellar didn't know what to do with his time after store nails come in. Why, I was pointin' nails every odd minute between jobs, when I was younger." Thus, almost regretfully, an old smith spoke.

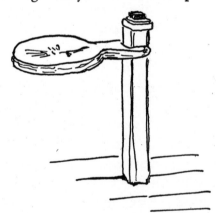

Seat or "horse" for hammering out horseshoe nails on rectangular piece of steel

For hammering out nails there was a special device used by some smiths, a sort of chair convenience. A square post cut high enough to come to handheight when a man was seated, was cut and nailed with spikes to the floor of the shop. On the top of this was a cap of wood into which was fitted a small piece of very hard steel. A few inches below this a seat was hollowed out of a circle of wood and fastened to the post at right angles. This made a nice comfortable seat for the blacksmith, or nail maker, which he could straddle in a jiffy and work at his nail pointing with ease. Even with plenty of soft iron nail rods on hand, a blacksmith could rarely make more than ten or twelve pounds of nails a day for each one took some twenty blows to form it. A cross section of the nail rod showed an oblong and so the holes punched in the horseshoe with a piece of steel, were likewise oblong, but the bringing of the whole to a slender and perfect point which would not turn until it was through the hoof and ready for locking down flat, was the trick of no novice.

Shoes for one ox foot

The Cleft Hoof

Of course the horse was not the only animal to be shod, the oxen taking far more of the blacksmith's time, both because he arrived earlier and in greater quantity, and because he wore eight shoes at one time instead of four, not to mention the effort and minutes taken to manage him before he was ready for his shiny new shoes. It is a question whether a farrier proper would have made a livelihood during the days of the first settlements and on through the next hundred years, when horses were a luxury, if it had not been for the cumbersome old oxen's need of iron footpads. Of course many a farmer did his own blacksmithing and shoeing, and in some sections the ground was so free of rocks and so swampy that an animal needed no shoes to protect his feet. Certain parts of the South did not shoe their horses, oxen or mules, the biggest work for these animals being to snake great trees out of the swamps. To keep the hoofs clean and well trimmed was all that was necessary. It is said that during the first two centuries in Bucks County, Pennsylvania, many of the farmers had no blacksmith shop within seventeen miles of their farms and so horses and ploughshares went unattended by the blacksmith, the one going shoeless and the other bent and jagged, except for the efforts of the owner.

There is probably nothing more tottery in appearance than a great pair of oxen teetering along a country road on their small cloven feet. But if they seem likely to crumble up it is all in the seeming, for these tiny feet really have an extra grasp of the earth, which allows them to swing their bodies in the mighty heaving jobs which fall to their lot, as no well-footed horse or mule can do. Feeble and tottering as to underpinning when they have all four feet on the ground, it is not to be wondered at that when the time for shoeing comes round and one of these feet must be raised, the animal would really crumble to the ground if he were not supported. Long, long ago the blacksmith or farrier met this situation by means of a great wooden wheel, a massive wooden frame or stall, ropes and chains and a belly-band of stout cowhide. Literally the ox had to be hung up in the air, or at least enough to take the weight from three of his feet while the fourth was being attended, safely lashed to a low slanting upright.

New Jersey called these contraptions "ox cramps," and New Hampshire called them "ox-slings." There may have been other names as well. Old New Hampshire went about shoeing her oxen this way: the owner of the ox, led — with difficulty — the animal through the broad open door of the shop and directly into the sling frame which stood almost on the threshold. The frame or stall was long enough to hold the ox with its protruding head through the heavy stanchion at the far end, and with room left at the rear where the smith himself might stand to shoe the hind feet. Suspended at one side was a great strip of cowhide with straps fastening it above and others below for fastening under the animal's belly. In the loft above and over the ox's head was a huge wooden wheel, made almost solid of shaped planks, and from this, extended over the animal's body, a huge timber to which the sling was attached. All of this was visible from below in a dim, cobwebby murk. Close to the ox's head a rough ladder led up to the loft, and its sides were heavy enough to have fastened between them, half way up and between two of the rungs, a wooden windlass. When the leather sling had been adjusted and closely buckled under the animal, this windlass went into action from the hand-crank at one of its ends. Then the great wooden wheel above began to revolve, turning the huge timber and with its straps raising the animal from the ground.

The floor of the sling frame was a low, heavy platform, with two low slant-top posts at each side well toward the front to which the front feet were chained or roped or tied with leather thongs, in an easy position. At the rear there were two more uprights for use when the rear feet must be worked upon. The last move for readiness was the tieing of the animal's horns so that he could not move or weave or "get his head" in his first struggles after the unnatural raising.

Ironing Wheels

One of the distinctive bits of equipment in an old blacksmith shop was the arrangement, differing in different shops, for the holding of wheels when they were brought for their first application of iron tires or for new wine in old bottles. One contrivance was a huge bottomed cask which had been hollowed from a tree, filled with rocks half way up, and the upper part growing smaller in the way of some casks, until it came to a finish where it was well hooped with iron for strength to hold the wheel when its hub was inserted. The need was for something which would support the spokes, be hollow in the center to allow the hub to slip in, and make a steady support for the felloe while the tire was being applied. A very ancient way and the best of all for this need, was the great granite table, measuring a good six feet across, six inches thick and with a center opening about sixteen inches across. This table was set upon granite posts to make it table height, or if very thick, upon the ground, and with this beneath his hammer the blacksmith had no thought of how hard or how lightly he should strike.

Two of the sturdiest and yet most symbolic signs ever set before a blacksmith's door, and not at all as signs, but rather for convenience, were a pair of granite posts. The one at the left was more slender and had only a smallish iron ring in its head for a hitching post for horses awaiting their turn within the shop; the other, which stood at the right

THOSE WHO WORKED WITH IRON

and directly in front of the door which opened to the ox-sling, had an immense iron ring and a bar or rim of iron surrounding the top of the post, lest frost follow the staple down the stone and freeze and burst the granite. It was like the big and little bear, each serving its own size.

Above the door of this Meriden, New Hampshire, blacksmith shop is perhaps the loveliest bit of ironwork which ever served as a sign. There are two horseshoes, one too large for any horse, and slightly back but embraced by the larger shoe, one so small that no horse could ever wear it either. Two generations of blacksmiths have used this old shop. Perhaps this is what the sign is trying to tell us now although the doors have been padlocked for many years, "one man worked alone here until his son came to do his share along by his side, and then the son did it all — alone."

To join the chinning throng at a blacksmith shop, came each day a pompous resident whose very bearing showed his vast superiority to other men. His entrance was magnificent. He would then stroll up to the forge, take up a poker, lay it in the red-hot coals and when it had heated red-hot itself, take it up by the cool handle and light his pipe. One day as he was seen approaching, one of the neighbors took up the poker and laid it, handle-first, in the coals. Just before the magnificent entrance he took it out and laid it handy on the forge. That day magnificence gave way to something else.

~~~~~~

3 BLACKSMITH AND NAILER SHOP

"That's the time he hit the nail on the head."

~~~~~~

The Farmer a Nailer

THE simplest definition of a nail is that it is an iron pin.
Another is that it is a stud, and the old fashioned stud was
a heavy nail with a large head, and long enough to go
through two or three thicknesses of wood, such as went into
the making of entrance doors in the 1600s when a man's
home was his fortress against prowling and battering-ram
Indians. When used in this capacity the nails were generally
driven in staggered rows, so that they formed — as does a
cornfield — straight lines running vertically, horizontally
and obliquely, making a simple all-over design across the
surface of the door. Once driven through the wood, the
nail's point was "clinked," or clinched, or smashed back
flat against the wood so that it was locked and could not be
drawn out from the outside. This was the usual "studded
door."

Still another definition of the word "nail"— back in those
days when names were earned because of value received —
was a measure of length, or one sixteenth of a yard. This
would make us believe that the original nail was about two
and a quarter inches long, and that the stud was a large
brother which deserved another name but still belonged to
the same family.

It is safe to say that in early America the nail was practically always a homemade article, fashioned in the indispen-

THOSE WHO WORKED WITH IRON

*Blacksmith shop with "wart" at rear over brook to
accommodate the great bellows. Mill Hollow,
East Alstead, New Hampshire*

sable home shop, or within the house itself. Just as the farmer
went to the gristmill to have his grains ground, so he had
also to make occasional trips to the "rolling mill," for nail-
rods from which to cut himself some new nails. The rolling
mill rolled the iron out into a thin rod from the larger bars
of iron, and then "flatted" it. These rods the farmers took
home in rolls, ready for cutting and heading into a real nail.
After a while this iron could be procured at the village store

by a trade of eggs, or yards of homespun or knitted feeting — the long warm socks for men. Carried over the shoulder a'horseback, or in the ox-cart, it was like bearing home a new golf stick for filling in one's occasional hour of leisure. The rod was cut to the desired length with a short, stocky cold-chisel, sharp at the lower end and heavy at the top for the blow of the hammer. The nail once free of the rod, one end was then slit and the hammer descended at this point to form the head. Some of the old nail heads are strange looking affairs, with no rhyme or reason in their formation and style, except the mighty chance. From Vermont we have the tale that nails were made in its kitchens, and, strangest of all, "at a corner forge." This was of course used only in winter or rainy weather.

Cold chisel to cut nails

The Cut-Nail Maker

Although nail slitting machines came among the first inventions, it was not until 1800 that machines for cutting nails came into use, and then not generally, but before that time all sorts of devices were tried out to hasten this slow manufacture of a much needed article. New Hampshire paid bounties to whoever would make 100,000 nails in a certain stated time. Some men rigged up small water-power for the cutting, and planned a simple foot-power for the heading. Jeremiah Wilkinson of Cumberland, Rhode Island, was a famous early nailer and pin-maker, who "cut cold" his nails before the beginning of the Revolution. "They were first cut by a pair of shears from an old chest lock, and afterward headed in a smith's vise. Sheet iron was afterward used and the process extended to small nails."

Up to within ten years the old folks of New Hampshire were apt to use the first name for our common carpet tack, which was "tack nail."

Their Weight in Gold

So recently as ninety-eight years ago nails were considered among the really valuable assets, even to a man who had a shop for their making. There is a story of two boys who were so innocent as to gather up two nails found in the smoking ruins of a burned-down shop, to be saved as keepsakes of this exciting occasion. When they reached home and showed them to their mother she was aghast at such thievery. She rescued the nails and wrapped them carefully in paper and then made the boys carry them back to the robbed shopman and confess their misdeed. One would suppose that the price must therefore have been prohibitive, but although each nail had been pounded out by hand, their cost was only fifteen cents a pound.

This "pounding out by hand" leads us to the fact that rolling mills were not always handy and many a nail was actually pounded out from a piece of scrap iron on the home forge, from tip to finish. When a lightning rod was affixed to a meeting-house in New England in 1788, the necessary nails for this job were bought and paid for by the number purchased and not by their weight. Thus do we come to the reason behind the naming of different sizes of nails as "eight-penny," or "ten-penny." However many one received for a penny, so was their name. Today we buy nails by the pound, but they are still so-many-penny nails.

There was one development of this scarcity of nails which became serious in the early colonies. In a time when some roofs sheltered three or four generations at the same time with a scattering of boarders or strangers, every shelter, no matter how small, was riches to the colony. It became a common practice, if nails were needed for a new building, to burn down an old one to procure them. The authorities wanted more houses as well as better ones, and by this practice one got nowhere in the better housing program of the time. The Governor of Virginia hit upon the clever plan of discouraging this razing of needed buildings by offering to give to the owner as many nails as the old house contained. Think of knowing how many nails there were in any one house, and yet, so valuable were they, that this was the case.

THOSE WHO WORKED WITH IRON

4. THE PIN MAKER'S SHOP

"Needles and pins, needles and pins,
When a man marries his trouble begins."

Small but Oh, My!

WE have already found that a nail is an iron pin, and now we discover that a pin is a peg, or a pointed, short wire, and that wire is a metal drawn out, or spun into threads. There seems to have been some sort of a grudge held against early pinmakers in this country, or more probably England was nipping in the bud any industry along this line which would spoil her home trade. Nathaniel Robinson of Plymouth Colony, tried very hard in 1666 to set himself up in the business of pin-making but "was not let." In 1677, the most famous of our pioneer iron workers, Joseph Jenks, petitioned the court at Lynn for the use of a room and funds to make wire, but thumbs were turned down likewise upon him. Somewhat later the making of wool cards and pins was actually allowed because "there were tools in the town" for their manufacture. Someone had been clever and cunning, apparently.

The pin-maker at first made his pinheads by twisting one end of the wire back upon itself for an eighth of an inch or so, not aspiring to any more noticeable capital for his slender column. Although made differently, the spiral-headed pin, was in use until after the Civil War. By this time the pin-making process had advanced so far that a boy could make 1600 in an hour, and he must have been an amazingly capable boy to have achieved so much in such a crude way. The wire was cut the length of six pins and he took a handful of these at one time and began sharpening them at each end on a grindstone. Then from each end the length of the pin was cut off with heavy shears, leaving two new ends on each wire to be sharpened and in their turn, severed. Then the third set was sharpened and cut in two, making a complete harvest of six pins from each wire. For heads these pins would wear each two spirals of wire which had been coiled on a spinning wheel, and then upon the smith's anvil, hammered fast to the body of the pin with a hammer worked by footpower.

These pins, in style a hundred years ago, had a brass base which had to be tinned over in a vessel made of copper in which a solution of tin and lees, or dregs, of wine, had been mixed. To polish the now tinned-over brass pins, they were dropped in quantity into a revolving vessel or drum with a mass of coarse bran, and kept turning until they were elegant enough for the thread and needle shop down "the Street." There are many alive today who can remember, from childhood, being repeatedly cautioned not to put pins and keys in their mouths, because they were "brass"; and when they forgot, quickly ejecting these mouth-watering delicacies because the brassy taste was not at all satisfying after all — when the outer trimming or tinning had worn off.

One of the great famines of even the early 1800s, was that of the common pin. At this time even shawls were sewed on with a few stitches when farm women went neighboring for a tell and had not one pin in the house, nor one procurable for miles around. The thorn tree was still being resorted to for its donation of sharp prongs and prickers, for want of the thing which we broadcast today with no consciousness of guilt or waste.

> See a pin and pick it up,
> All the day you'll have good luck.
> See a pin and let it lay,
> Ba-ad luck you'll have all day.

Thus went the little lesson in pin thrift, when a pin was worth much more than its weight in gold to the woman who needed it and had it not.

Unusual hand-bellows of the far South

❧ VII ❧

1. THE COOPERAGE

"Every tub must stand on its own bottom."
— BUNYAN: *Pilgrim's Progress*

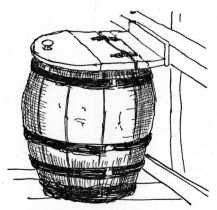

*Barrel for running spring water in a
New Hampshire kitchen*

Men of Parts

ONE of the oldest names in America is that of Alden, and under it ranges a wide progeny. One of the most interesting and beloved old houses and homes in the country is the old Alden house at Duxbury, Massachusetts, built by a son of, and shared with the original John Alden, cooper, who was picked up at Southampton just before the Mayflower started on her long voyage to this country. A cooper would be a very necessary artisan in a land of no shops but with millions of miles of forests from which to carve out cask and barrel, tierce and pipe. It was thus that John Alden became a member of the Plymouth band, and since he was a personable young man he had soon won Priscilla Mullen for his wife and started the family whose numbers are today legion — and a cooper shop.

Young John Alden would have been amused if, when he signed up to ship as a cooper with this highminded and serious band of religionists, he had dreamed that one day he would be counted a Pilgrim Father of high reknown, he, a simple cooper whose job was to stave and hoop a cask and make it tight. Since the date of the landing of the Pilgrims is the one date which no American ever forgets, we may be sure also of the date of the arrival of our first cooper. There was probably no lace at John's wrists, but there was strength and muscle and skill which was not to be sneezed at by lord or lady. So it was with many of our shopmen, who knew one thing well and could live comfortably and often handsomely upon that knowledge.

Early Wooden Containers

To coop a thing up was to shut it in, imprison it, or cage it. The cage was called a "coop," and the person who made it, the "cooper." The word cooperage has three different meanings, first, the making of barrels, casks, or other rounded vessels; second, the cooper's workshop; and third, the price paid for the cooper's work. Technically, the barrel or cask which the cooper made had sides composed of separate staves held together by surrounding hoops, but the work of the cooper was much broader than that, taking in the gouging of tree trunks for the forming of casks without staves, and turning out all sorts of wooden vessels upon demand.

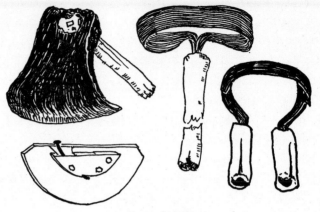

Cooper's adz
Cooper's shaves
Cooper's curve plane

New Jersey antiquarians claim that their colony's barrel business began because of the fine apple orchards which they had planted early in the vicinity of Newark, which in time led to the pressing out of cider and the immediate need of barrels in which to keep it. They did not however wait to have their cooper make barrels from staves, but hunted about in the surrounding forests for gum trees which had rotted at the heart. These they cut into sections barrel height. The centers were then burned and gouged out, probably by laymen as well as coopers, and one end was floored across with a bottom of inch or two-inch board which was pinned in around the edges with small wooden pins scarcely larger than a match, driven in from the side. These pins were tree nails, or "trunnels."

Whatever might be contrived, of wood or iron or stone or fire, to gouge or hollow or shave the inside of a log or tree into the semblance and usefulness of a vessel — and "vessel" first meant anything which held liquids — was seized upon by our handwrought forefathers, for not all could be coopers. There were little iron shaves or gouges with wooden handles which cut a near circle out of the heart of a small log by repeatedly shoving it in and pulling it strongly out again. There were gouges to shave a flattened arch, and some which were barely curved and made to follow the form of a great log with huge circumference. Like the woodturner and the cabinet-maker who had numberless cornice or molding planes with which to catch all angles and curves in their ornamentation, the man who hollowed wood into all sorts of vessels must have all sorts of curving shaves.

The gumtree was gouged for use in many parts of the country, wherever the gum tree grew, and the light basswood came in also for hollowing into vats and casks, in the New England States. Sometimes the sides were left scarcely thicker than cardboard, and sometimes they measured two inches through. They were used for "grain-boxes," for smoking hams after a little door had been made at the base for tending the smudge, for mortars for grinding corn, for storing smoked meats, for leaching ashes for soap-lye, and many other things. The South turned them into beehives. This "beegum" has been a familiar feature of old plantations. A young man gives this description of some in use until recently: "A board was nailed across one end, the joinings stuffed with rags as one would cork a boat. Then the log was upturned to test for water, not that water was put in it, but because the bees insist on air-tightness," then, as an afterthought, "June was bee robbing time."

Bona Fide Coopering

Following these crude but splendid dugouts came the real barrel or cask made of white oak staves and built especially for holding liquids, and the red oak barrels with hickory withes for holding dry goods. Along the Jersey coast the stave was cut from cedar. Thus "cedar coopers" were spoken of, and "oak coopers," for men used the best wood in their own vicinity. Then there were hogsheads for molasses, bound with red oak hoops, and barrels for fish. In time these subdivisions under barrel-making came into existence: the tight, the wet, the dry, the slack. This might easily have been but two divisions for the tight and the wet were the same, and the dry and slack. The former needed greater skill in the making for the vessel must be water and airtight, while that which was to hold solids or dry goods could be made with less care and greater slackness, and of such softer wood as the fir tree.

One of the bright ideas which visited that group of Englishmen, who sent others to do the hard work in the vast Virginia of the wild New World, was that here was an exhaustless supply of trees for making both pipe staves and clapboards. Many grants of land received by the settlers contained the little catch laid down by the Orders and Constitution of 1619-20, that the owner should produce a certain amount of these valuable articles each year — to be sent home — and the allotment was 15,000 annually. The "pipe" referred to was one of the vastest of the barrels, holding two hogsheads of cargo. At this time the clapboard was shorter than we use today, measuring probably not much longer than the pipe stave. Thus although Virginia had a large barrel stave output she must turn most of it into the maw of the colony directors. In South Berwick, Maine, pipestave shipping gave the well known name of "Pipe Stave Landing" to the point of departure.

Finally sawmills cut the staves and bundled them, and hoop-mills were running along country streams. One of the early hoop-mills was at Carlisle, Massachusetts. Here and there an old barrel, hooped years ago with a twisted wooden withe, comes to light in loft or shed, and is well worth saving from the welter of modern barrels with their machine made hoops of iron.

Log horse for splitting withes

The Making of a Tub

This was set down that we might know the ways of the early cooper, and so is here set down again. "For a tub: Timber cut to right length with firewood saw. Split into pieces with a frow — curves correspond to curves of vessel. Shaved on edges with straight drawing knife — those used inside with a concave form — convex on outer. Jointed on long plane. Shaves thus prepared are set in a truss hoop, and after this has been drawn down, one or two others which are to remain are put on. The outside then smoothed with a convex'd knife and inside with smoothing plane, the edge of which is circular. Inside of smaller wooden vessels are generally made smooth with crooked drawing knife. Staves sawn down to same length at bottom. Groove cut for insertion of the bottom, with a cutting instrument fixed in a gauge. Bottom boards smooth with straight'd knife, then being slightly fastened together with wooden pins. The whole is inserted in its proper place by drawing it down from the top on the inside. Finished by driving on the hoops and making holes in the handles." Thus ends this lesson.

A New York farmer who remembers barrel-makers at work in their shops when he was a boy, tells us a little less and yet a little more.

"Well, a man sat down with a pile of staves nearby. The staves up in this section were rived out of quarters of white oak. When withes were used they were of hickory. A fellar could set up a hundred barrels a day. There was a bench with the staves in a bay at his side. He used two truss hoops. Why, they were two hoops set steady to start the barrel with, not to be a part of it when it was done. He'd set enough staves and then slide over two permanent hoops. Then he'd draw in the top and set and then draw in the bottom." Simple enough.

A nearby neighbor gave it this way: "They done steaming of the barrels in the rear room out there in the shop. They took the staves and fixed them into the truss hoops, to get them in final shape. Then they steamed them and when they were shaped right, they put the final hoops around." So it is always, with many witnesses, one sees and remembers one thing, and another remembers something else, each to his special interest or liking. So do we get the whole story, although each thinks that his part is the whole.

The usual barrel — not made for some special cargo such as resin which requires a thick and almost straight stave — had each stave curved to make one segment of the whole barrel, cut broader at the center to form the necessary bulge. The edges were beveled to fit exactly the next stave. Since no man could hold all of the staves upright without help, a circular wire frame was used in some shops fitted with truss hoops, which held the loose staves until the permanent hoops could be slipped over them. To the rope which was used to draw the staves together at the top, a windlass was sometimes fastened to facilitate the work. We have seen the steaming suggested and the final encircling of the hoop; and the joining or locking of these winding hoops was a careful job which only the expert could manage.

To get the "head" a perfect circle, wooden compasses were used, often homemade affairs which had been pinned together or bent and steamed into shape. The ends of the barrels were finished for the holding of the head by the forming of the "chime" or bevel at the ends of the staves, and the cutting of the "croze" or groove into which the head was slipped. The finished barrels had their heads fastened in by the slipping on of the lowest and the highest hoops, which held them safely within the croze. A cooper with a single helper could make two casks of white oak for liquids in one day, and four or five of red oak for dry goods.

While it was the work of the miller rather than the cooper, a later arriving barrel was made without staves. Great trees were cut into sections and set in a vat containing a biting liquid which helped to soften and remove the bark. The following day the logs were fastened on their sides between two revolving spikes. As they turned, a knife cut from their length a thin sheet of wood, a mere veneer. This was twisted around into a circle to form the barrel and the bulge was obtained by cutting little V gores from the upper and lower edges. The two ends were then joined and hooped as necessary. Such barrels were slacks and used for dry goods.

A withe-bound barrel and a "locked" bucket
An oil can

Barrels which needed bung-holes in their sides for drawing off the liquor, were perforated with a tool called a "bung-hole borer," which was really a huge pod auger, fifteen inches long. A pod auger was the original bit and brace, but of solid iron and shaped like a carrot, and ending with a few spirals or threads cut into the lower part. The handle was a crosspiece of roughly shaped wood for grasping.

There is a story of a stranger who came to one of our old taverns and after getting his drinks and running up a good score, asked the bartender if he knew how to make wine out of cider. The gullible and innocent countryman denied such knowledge and was all for acquiring it. To the dark cellar they went. A hole was bored in one side of a huge cask and the tavern keeper told to place his finger therein to keep the cider from flowing out. Into a hole on the other side he put a finger of the other hand and thus hugging the cask waited while the stranger went to his gig to get some special charm. The wait was a long one, but the owner held on lest he lose a drop until it dawned upon him that he had lost a long hour of the day, a good tight cask and the pay for several good drinks. There is a tale of a strong countryman who lifted a barrel and took his drink from the bung-hole.

The Measure of His Work

It would surprise some of us today if we knew how many things used to be packed in barrels which now have much more elegant containers, such as shoes and money and bolts of cloth. Tobacco was of course "rolled" to the coast for shipping in huge casks with an airhole in one end, and turning on an iron axle which ran through them from end to end and to which the traces of the mules' or oxens' rigging were attached. Cavalcades of these great "tumbling barrels" made roads where there were none, crushing down the underbrush and by yearly returning constructing their own highway.

It would be surprising too if we knew all of those things which the cooper was asked to make, and how many he succeeded in delivering. A cooper of Virginia, in 1655, sent out the following bill, which gives us an inside glimpse of his resourcefulness:

"for settinge up of six tunne of caske"
  (Tunne or tun was the size of four hogsheads)
"for the making of a cradle to shale corn"
  (shale was to husk)
"mending of 5 hogsheads new headed and hooped
"making of 2 newe milking pailes
"Ye hooping of 4 Duty anchors and making new coverlids"
  (Anchor, equalled sixteen gallons)
"new coverlid for a powdering tub"
  (powdering tub, a tub to salt meat in)
"cutting of an English tearce in two and new hooping
  of them and putting new ears to them"
  (tearce, or tierce, is a measure of forty-eight gallons)

HANDWROUGHT ANCESTORS

Sap bucket and wooden tankard

An intimate description of an old powdering tub is given by an old gentleman who remembers them in use: "A powdering barrel was about three feet high and two and a half across the bottom. The top was drawn in smaller. It was made of pine and on the bias. When the pork spoiled in it, you better throw the while thing right out, it's no use any more."

Dash churn

BUILDERS AND VEHICLE-MAKERS

Bird-house from a bucket

An early New England milking pail was a wooden piggin with one high stave with a hole in it, to serve as handle; a washtub of the 1800s was a keeler, made by the cooper, with ears at opposite sides for handles; sapbuckets for catching the flowing sap from maple trees were similar to the milking piggin but drawn in at the top while the former had straight sides; sap troughs were small gouged logs; the dash churn was a cooper-made article sometimes slanting at the top and sometimes at the bottom; a coomb was a corn measure of four bushels; a wooden tankard was a huge drinking mug of wooden stave sides; and the cooper was even a maker of wooden pegs and pins. Perhaps the most universally useful product of the cooper's tools was the old gum tub with a movable board fitting well toward the bottom and bored full of holes. Those who own them today claim each a different usefulness for them, some insisting that they were for pounding grain and letting the husks pass through the holes to the ground beneath; some are sure that such a cask was used only for crushing grapes and letting the juice run through the three-quarter-inch holes into a receptacle below; some know that their's was used for pressing cider from apples; others call it a leech tub for the making of soap, and so it goes. Undoubtedly it served its many masters in many ways, and always well.

Wine Measure

2 pints — 1 quart
4 quarts — 1 gallon
16 gallons — 1 Anchor of Brandy or Rum
18 gallons — 1 runlet
31½ gallons — 1 barrel
42 gallons — 1 tierce
63 gallons — 1 hogshead
84 gallons — 1 puncheon
2 hogsheads — 1 pipe or butt
2 pipes, or
4 hogsheads — 1 tun

He could make them all.

There has always been just one thing against a barrel and that is its bulk when one wants to shove it out of the way. An old couple in a New York crossroads store found this difficulty. There must of course be a few around for flour and sugar and salted fish and sitting purposes, but enough is as good as a feast and so all extras were carried out to the farm for storing. One day a neighbor came in to get a barrel and the old storekeeper said: "No, there aint no barrels here to store. We'm take'em up to the farm. If we'm want 'em we know them there. And if we'm don't, then there yet." Surely a wise way to dispose of such unbendable commodity. Queer as Dick's hatband but always desirous of pleasing, this old man was often the butt of neighborhood teasing. A young man went into the store one day and asked for some Scotch plaid sewing silk and cross-eyed needles. "Yep, we'm got 'em," the old man answered quickly, and then embarrassed that he should be found out of stock added: "No, my stars, we'm out."

Ancient sap trough 27x11 inches. For New Hampshire "sugaring"

2. The Carpenter Shop

"Let thy converse be sincere,
Thy conscience as the noonday clear."

The Woodworker's Shrine

"The afternoon sun was warm on the five workmen
there, busy upon doors and window frames and wainscot-
ing. A scent of pine-wood from a tent-like pile of planks
outside the open door mingled itself with the scent of the
elder-bushes which were spreading their summer snow
close to the open window opposite; the slanting sun-
beams shone through the transparent shavings that flew
before the steady plane, and lit up the fine grain of the
oak paneling which stood propped against the wall. On a
heap of soft shavings a rough grey shepherd-dog had
made himself a pleasant bed . . . and was lying with his
nose between his forepaws, occasionally wrinkling his
brow to cast a glance at the tallest of the five workmen. . .
It was to this workman that the strong baritone belonged
which was heard above the sound of plane and hammer
singing, ' . . . thy conscience as the noonday clear.' "

A mallet with a handle or "shaft"
A maul with a "shail"

216

BUILDERS AND VEHICLE-MAKERS

THIS picture of an old carpenter shop which George Eliot painted in *Adam Bede,* has never been surpassed by pen or brush. There is the wood to be wrought into many things, its odor, the movement of the tools, the offcast shavings curling away, the content of the faithful dog, the beauty of the world outside the door and above all the serenity and happiness of the true carpenter at his beloved work. One never forgets the slant of the evening sun shining through those age-old shavings lying all about the floor of that little English shop, at Hayslope, in 1799. While many of our own shops did not keep five men busy, this shop may yet be called typical of those worked in by our carpenter ancestors. Such a shop might belong to a carpenter, a cabinetmaker, a chair-maker, or other woodworkers, for all must have their bench and vise and all those other things used in Hayslope.

To the lover of tools the following equipment found in the carpenter shop of John Cumber, of Henrico, Virginia, in 1679, may suggest the kind of work done in that faraway time

jack-plane	gimlet
smoothing plane	pair compasses
small plough planes	1 piercers
files	hand irons for a turning lathe
bramble bits	chalk line
keyhole saw	wooden gauges $\frac{1}{2}$ foot square
$\frac{1}{4}$ inch guage	tool chest
$\frac{1}{2}$ inch guage	handsaw
$\frac{1}{4}$ inch short auger	pocket-roll
$\frac{1}{2}$ inch short auger	jack and line
$\frac{1}{4}$ inch heading chisel	a holdfast bench hook
$\frac{1}{2}$ inch heading chisel	pincer bits
mortising chisel	file for handsaw

broad turning chisel	whipsaw
paring chisel	foreplane
small squares	crosscut saw
bow saw	bramble saw
broad axes	leather doublets
adzes	

For all the crudity of the small shops to be found throughout the country, we here have evidence that among those who had money for ordering their tools from the Old World, the very best was available and used. It must be remembered too that the lack of fortunes in the Down East sections led to the many tinkerin' shops where New Englanders developed a skill in workmanship which was not general in the South, where until the middle of the 1700s much of the household and farm supply was imported from England. 'Tis necessity that is the mother of invention, with small exception.

If the claim of Virginia be true, however, that she built a vessel to set to sea before 1611, the old claim of Manhattan that Adrian Block built his *Unrest* there in 1614 as the first ship to be built in America, must be waved, and credit given to the wealthy South for immediate handiwork.

Home Shops

One of the smallest, by foot and inch measurement, of these old home shops, was probably the shoeshop where the farmer made shoes during the winter for cash or barter. These were so small that today we sometimes mistake them for old chicken houses or playhouses, and yet their output was large in comparison. Like the tinkerin' shop, the usual carpenter shop stood for the one word, INGENUITY. Did the

218

housewife need anything, did the farm-help want for supplies, did leather or iron or wood give out . . . get ye to the shop then and make it new or make it whole. Sugaring time was almost due, for the days had begun to thaw and the nights were still freezing, and new troughs must be hewed out of a log for setting beneath the flowing trees, and boards must be hollowed with numberless little sink-holes to hold the maple-sugar candy after the sugaring-off; new shingles must be rived out before the long spring line-storm; a chair rung must be turned to replace the one which granny's feet had worn through in her low-backed chimney-place seat; a scoot, a heavy stone-boat with wooden runners, called for a different treatment, but the treatment was there on call; whatever, and whenever, and however, with no questions asked. This was the old "shop" of our forebears.

Bed jack and holding-pins for carding a bed

One old shop still active by the roadside was once a tiny district school. How more than the teacher and his desk were accommodated in it is a puzzle, but it cared for the young in numbers, in its day. One old shop recently removed, stood handy in the farm dooryard, but flush with the weeds of the dusty roadside. In it good sturdy chairs were made for many years — of course only in the winter — and while they were not called suitable for the best parlor, they served well in the humbler stations of life. For years the old chair-maker plied his trade, making the furniture for the newly married in the countryside and for many an old couple, but never did he win the title of chair-maker, remaining always just "old Jim Stamford who tinkered with chairs in cold weather." Today his old slatbacks are eagerly sought for living room and front hall, for they were made " 'pon honor."

Pounded ash for splint bottom chairs

Another shop is pointed out as the old cradle shop, where four sides and a bottom were dovetailed together to make a nest for rest. Oddities developed in different cradles, some being made without a bottom board, some — as in Florida — having the bottom board well perforated with holes in a neat pattern, some with high hoods, and some with high posts for holding a net. Not only for the baby was the cradle made, but for two or three babies and almost any number of children within the same four sides. A family which lived in Brattleboro, Vermont, in 1754, had a dirt floor, one-room cabin, and the parents slept in a corner with boughs and blankets beneath them. Their children — number unknown yet a'plenty, according to tradition — slept in "the cradle," which measured bed-length and twenty-seven inches across. It is still standing in the loft of the old homestead barn. Old

BUILDERS AND VEHICLE-MAKERS

Wallace Supernon, whom the neighbors called "sprung" in his mind, slept in a cradle all of his life, with his knees drawn up. Many women had their cradles, if stories are true, and one of the candle-light tasks for the tired hired-man was to keep the cradle of some sleeper moving with his cowhide on the rocker. So, although cradles did not wear out for several generations, we can see that there was demand enough for them to make them attractive work.

A New Hampshire district school bench and slate

There was the man who turned his shop over to the making of "corner cubbards," or "cobards," to the making of crickbeds or fourposters, or "pairs of low drawers" of the 1700s, commonly called "lowboys" in modern vernacular, and of "high chests" called "highboys" today. "Seatin' chears" was another shop work, and sawing out and pinning together the wooden "suttles" for the chimneyplace. A man might make the loveliest "blackboard" looking-glass frames, or "teasters" for fourpost beds, or gate-leg tables, and yet not always be termed a "cabinet-maker" by his neighbors. Nicholas Disbrow who started making the famous "Hadley Chests," around 1675, and John Townsend of Rhode Island, who drew out from nature's trees the loveliest of block-fronted desks and chests of drawers, worked in little shops and had no thought that some day they would be immortal because of their simple but honest output. When maple was "curled in its grain," or a newly felled cherry-tree showed possibilities for polish, they were set aside for some day making into something that ma would like in the best parlor, or needed in her bedchambers.

Bullfinch with his curves and McIntyre with his straighter lines and pin-point designs, and Phyfe with his reeded finishings, were skilled "beyond common," but their shops started like the shops of the less blessed, and the skilled and the less skilled grew in greatness of soul worth as their work grew. One of the most careful of the old carpenters or cabinet-makers was the mortise-man who made those intricate little joinings even in the foot of a table leg, tying crosspiece and leg together in an unslackening embrace, which only occasionally come to light under the hand of some curious cabinet-maker of today. The skill needed in inserting the tiny "trunnels," or wooden pins, is not often remembered. Until less than a score of years ago a sign hung on a tree in Essex, Massachusetts, pointing the way to the maker of treenails.

The paint which was applied to some of the old hardwood chairs and tables seems to us today in the nature of sacrilege, but paint was a long time coming, and when it came it was seized upon as the great preservative. Perhaps if we had handmade some fine old piece, we too would have helped ourselves to its safety and long life by reaching for the paint-pot. Rush seats lasted a couple of hundred years longer if they were well painted; and slat-back chairs, which the men would always tip back against a wall to make a little bit comfortable after a hard day's work, lost some of their squeak and looseness when given a coat of bright green or blue. Vermillion paint was only for the well-to-do, but there was that nice Venetian red which could be bought dry for two cents a pound and mixed with linseed oil or skimmed milk —and there was brick dust for the scraping, to be mixed the same way — and one had a "strong paint" for almost nothing.

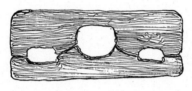

A Rhode Island pillory made in a local shop
Grasped from above in thumb and finger holds, this
shingle made a fine flour ladle

What's on the Floor

"What's this?" one enquires as his foot strikes something projecting from beneath an old shop bench. "That? Oh, that's an old sled runner. Goin' to get at that some wet day. We'll be needin' that when we get to haulin' up ice from the pond." Another obstacle: "Well, what's this nice old thing?" as one stoops to investigate. "That? Oh, that's a frame I cut to steam into shape for a bushel. The old one's lost it's binder. I'll get at that some day. Just leave it up there. I'll remember me then to fix it for ma." Standing all by itself behind a pile of boards is a block of wood with the top well rounded and polished. "That's granny's old hat block. She used to braid palm leaf hats and fit 'em over that block. Some cold morning that'll make me a good fire in the stove. Ought to be dry enough, hey, to give an uncommon good blaze. 'Bout a hundred years old, seem's if it ought to be about dried through."

An old sign of 1839 read:

"Hats !
    Which were made on block-heads, but will fit
    The man of learning, sense and wit."

There are treasures not only under but over the bench, hanging to the wall. Imagine the joy of finding an old brass-bowled tasteing-spoon, with a slender rat-trail handle of wrought iron, made fast with copper rivets. It had hung there for years and nobody wanted it, until . . . Cobwebs may try but cannot hide the little things of real value and worth which lie waiting for recovery in some of the old shops, things which show us the wealth of skill which lies behind us and may for that reason still lie in our own hands, for the trying. One thing in a shop which never strays, is never lost and seldom stolen, is the old wooden vise, fastened to the front of the bench and tightened and loosened for years of holding-fast, recalling its old name, the "hold-fast."

Riven and Cleft

Shingles and clapboards might easily have been the first to demand shops for their making, for one of the first demands of the titled backers of our provinces was for their export to England, but both of these commodities could be made quite as easily without a shop as within one. The early shingles were a good yard long and the clapboards perhaps twice that length, so that there was a good deal of riving and cleaving to be done before the great first-growth trees had been whittled down to these small proportions, but the work was, after all, outdoor work.

BUILDERS AND VEHICLE-MAKERS

In a nutshell, we have the manufacture of clapboards given us in these words: "Clapboard Cleaving. Pine and cedar being sawn in short butts and cloven, shaved and finished for clapboards." Shingles might be described in the same way, but the former had an extra bit of work put upon their narrow ends, for one must be shaved under and one over, to make the proper overlapping with the adjoining clapboards. The shingle, long up and down rather than from side to side, was nailed into place with a wooden pin, or trunnel, and later an iron nail, and the next shingle laid upon it one above the other, with the sides simply fitting up snugly against its next neighbor.

Natural growth shingle-horse, six feet long, for holding shingle during shaving

A tree trunk was cut across into several butts or sections the length of the desired shingle, and then the butt was laid upon one face so that its other might be marked off for cutting or riving. A description of this careful marking and cutting has been given in *Candle Days* by an old man who remembered the plan. The tools needed for the work were the froe and the beetle, the former a long iron blade with one sharp and one broadly blunt edge, and with an upright handle of wood affixed at one end. The beetle was a heavy wooden mallet bound with small or broad bands of iron, against cracking. In cutting a pie all pieces head in at the center in wedge formation. In cutting a cross section of a tree trunk the same thing is true, so that a couple of cuts would

225

make a shingle, small on one end and broader on the other. The cutting was done by laying the sharp blade of the froe on the mark and striking upon the broad upper edge with the beetle.

The shingles once cut, the shave-horse was then straddled or fronted, and its iron clip, for holding the shingle held fast by pressing a treadle with the foot, while a cord tied to a spring of wood on top helped the release. Sometimes a forked log on its side held the shingle, under one side, over the other. The shaving was done on one side only, with a straight drawer-shave, the shave being pulled toward the worker. The under part of the shingle which was not exposed to weather was left rough to assist in clinging fast to its mates. No matter how carefully these shingles might be shaved and fitted against each other, the weather might still slip in and surely the wind would, and so, since there were no roofing or siding papers in those days, the bark of the white birch was often peeled off and laid in between lining boards and outer shingles. An old house in New Hampshire has a lining of mica behind its clapboards, but the fact had not been known by many generations, until the mica sheets began to slip out of place and come sidling down into the light of day again. When the moon shines upon them they glisten like stars across the back of the old house.

Many an ancestor would laugh if he could see us cherishing some of the outputs of his old shop, which to him was nothing but "knittin' work" to fill up the wet and blizzardy days. What he would point to would be the fine old houses which he built 'pon honor and which we dare not start upon here, for fear of never ending.

BUILDERS AND VEHICLE-MAKERS

3. THE COFFIN SHOP

"We have loved the stars too dearly, to be afraid of the night."

Boss Wright's coffin shop early 1800s. Work room on left, "lay-out room" on right

Boss Wright

SURELY no one in hunting a site for his own dwelling could have found a sightlier place in the heart of a pretty village, than the one which was chosen in the early 1800s for a certain coffin shop. It stands close beside a brook, which was a convenience as well as a boundary of beauty, and there are trees arching above it, and the dusty road passes close before the grassy dooryard. Since even houses as a rule did not hold their heads high in the air in those days, except when money thrust them there, the workshops naturally

227

remained low and comfortable looking, as though they felt a kinship with the earth upon which they stood and with the folks who trod the beaten paths to their doors. Especially should a coffin-shop have felt a certain affinity with the good earth for which its work was destined. So it was with this story-and-a-half coffin shop of old "Boss Wright," near Schenectady, New York.

In following the course charted by this able man, we see also the course of coffin-making when it was still a village industry. Boss Wright was an expert ship-builder when he left the coast and came inland to the village of white houses clustered on a ridge. There is no second-best to the work done on a ship, for here life is at stake, and so a ship-builder must be an exact and able carpenter and cabinet-maker. Since ships could not be launched and floated across sunny fields, Wright took his tool chest and went hither and yon building new barns and houses and little home shops. Having vision, he finally decided to make a sideline to his work and so built himself a shop and became the village coffinmaker, and so of course the undertaker as well — for undertaking was rightly simple in those days. He must have succeeded in his new line, for although others succeeded him in his sideline, his name still looms large in tradition.

Some of Boss Wright's ship-cabinet-work over his coffin-shop door

As an instance of his natural bent toward careful work, one has the front doors of his coffin shop. They were no mere whacked together makeshifts, but built with the most careful workmanship, just such work as would have been fitting for a great ship bound for distant parts and representing a country proud of its handwork. In design they are perhaps unique, the long side pieces deviating from the usual straight line and slanting in suddenly where they meet the center cross stile, to give an elaborate effect and a pleasing one. Even the overhang above the door attracts the eye with its unusual carved darts which finish its lower edge. It would have been so much easier to make it straight or, if ornamented at all, with a single line of points sawed out in the usual way. This however was not Boss Wright's way. From this care in his outside work one may judge of the work which went into his coffins. A far cry from ships to coffins, but the same standards held in both.

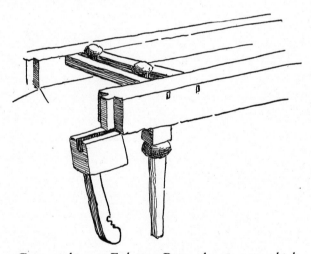

German bier at Ephrata, Pennsylvania, on which the dead body was first laid on the "cooling board," then on the ice-box and then with handles at ends raised, carried to the grave by four men. Movable wooden knobs to hold box in position. 1700s

HANDWROUGHT ANCESTORS

The double front doors led to Boss Wright's work shop, while the single door by the brookside opened into the "layout room." When one were laid out at home, a door was the usual couch, but here was a permanent place for the body which was fitted out with a tub of ice on all four sides and a tented sheet over the whole. Speaking of doors, one woman seemingly in her last moments, suddenly caught sight of her man removing the chamber door, and became so angry at his evident speeding of her on her way, that she recovered.

An elderly man who knew Boss Wright when he himself was a mere stripling, says: "I remember seeing him filing up his saws to make his coffins — he did it out front. It took a lot of filing too to get them to suit him. It was my father who sold him the elm for the coffins." To the man who knows the hardness of elm wood, and how these great trees are seldom drawn to mill for their lumber but left to make broken skeletons through the countryside because it is so difficult to "work 'em up," there would be no question that a saw applied to them would have to be well filed. One of the freaks of fate was that a man who was willing to work with hard elm should have settled in a community of Friends, whose religion demanded plainness in all things and thus adjudged the common pine the wood best suited to their coffins, and pine was the easiest to work up. Nor was this all, for there must be no stain applied to make a false coloring, no paint, no varnish, no ornament of any kind, no handles — all of which would have been mere vanity. Boss Wright was a man of understanding as well as of undertaking, and did as the "plain people" asked.

"Those old coffins, though they were nothing but pine, were quite a fair heft, and had to be handled kind of careful.

It was the way then to walk to the burying ground and it was right handy there behind the Meeting-house, and so it didn't matter much that there weren't any handles on the Quakers' boxes. The men just heaved 'em up on their shoulders and marched along with the village folks, to the grave. And there weren't any stones put up after, for many of 'em." Carrying coffins to the grave was a usual custom in the country.

For those few others in the village who were not "plain," Boss Wright could spread himself with boxes of native cherry which took a polish and waxing to cheer his heart and artist eye. Of course in his day there was more to the making of a coffin than a simple oblong box with square corners. The coffin was made to fit the man, closely, almost like the clothes he had so recently worn, and so was narrow at the top, either slightly pointed or straight across, but only the width of the head. From here the lines led outward to the width of the shoulders, and from there they drew in again until they formed the bottom of the box, just broad enough to enclose the feet. This of course meant many angles and fine joinings and must have been as balm to the soul of the shipbuilder who loved his work. Here was a heaven for a natural-born "joiner."

The lining of these boxes must come later, but lined they were in this little old coffin shop. Then the styles in coffins changed and large factories opened for modern work, so old Boss gave up the nice making of the boxes and laid bodies out in fitting settings.

A Successor

Following old Boss Wright in this same shop, came Abraham Wemple, lovingly known to his neighbors as "Old Abe

Wemp." During his regime the work of lining the coffins was turned over to his daughters, and a fine pride they had in this important work for their neighbors. As a sign of handwroughtness to the worker, in even so gentle a task as this, we have this remark of a descendent: "Mother was a very fine sewer, as was her sister also, and it was at the casket shop" (note the change of name) "that she learned it. It was such very particular work. . ." The "Wemp" caskets were made of pine, and stained, or painted a shiny black. Later they were covered with a sort of black broadcloth. These of course called for an outer "rough box."

One sweet old lady tells of lining coffins when she was a girl: "We lined them with what was called "book muslin," and pleated it carefully all around and then tacked it with little silver tacks. We could do one in three days. They had to be painted and varnished and they were made with fancy screws, and had a silver plate."

Forehanded Ancestors

Having a coffin shop in the neighborhood was a very convenient arrangement. Sometimes Boss Wright had a dozen coffins made up ahead of time, when there wasn't much sickness around; and some of the citizens in his section thought they would be forehanded too and get ready on their own account. A woman in this neighborhood remembers an afternoon which she spent playing at the home of a school friend:

"We were playing hide and seek all over the house, hiding in closets and spare rooms, under the tables and under the beds. Once Nellie took me into her father's and mother's bedroom and I started to crawl under the bed, but there were two coffins there ahead of me. Her father had had them made and had carried them about to his different places of abode. One for him and one for his wife. By having them kept under the bed, being put into them would be no work at all. Just pull one out and pop him in. I heard later that he finally sawed them up for firewood and was buried in a modern one after all. She — oh, she is still living."

Another man had his coffin stored in the freight-house of the railroad station. This plan failed too for when he died and they went for the coffin the worms had eaten it up too much for his use. One man made his own coffin and slept in it one night to be sure that it would fit. Some used their coffins for benches, some kept the winter beans in them; one was made for a little girl who was thought to be dying, and when she recovered they used it for the cradle for the baby.

The Sexton's Shop

Being a sexton in New England where drifts and frozen ground make burial impossible for three or four months in the winter, meant being also a maker of coffins. Graveyards — "the yard"— or burying grounds, received little attention esthetically from the digger of graves, until the hay was high enough to swell his crop for the winter. Thus relieved from the daintier work he could find time for digging and nailing coffins together. This work of making coffins was done on his own workbench. During the summer it did not take long to whack together the box within the fatal three days and have it in the ground by sunset of the last one. In the winter it was different. More people died, trying to make March-hill and failing. Bodies went into the vault and it was only necessary that by the first of May — sure and no fooling — there were enough boxes ready for all the bodies which had been waiting in the vault, to be slipped away into decent seclusion.

An old Vermonter tells of his father's work as a sexton when he himself was a boy: "It was nearly midnight of the last day of April and father must have seventeen coffins ready by morning for the buryings. They were all done but one and for that he had lost the measurements. To help him out I offered to go up into the yard and take it for him. Before the words were out I wished I hadn't, for it meant going at the ghost hour with a lantern into a pitch black place, for the vault was in the hollowed damp part. But I wouldn't back out. I unlocked the vault and went in, walking to the bodies over a narrow plank which bridged the accumulated water. I made the measurement and then didn't dare turn around to walk out. Those bodies — I just had to keep my eye on them — so I crept along that narrow plank backwards, holding the lantern so I could see the bodies all the time, and that made the ground dark all around me. I got out though and father had the seventeen boxes finished for the burying the next day." One body left in this damp vault for a long time before burial was, when finally taken out, turned to stone.

Coffins

As far as is known the first coffins were hollowed rocks. Then came a stone-lined grave. In our own South the gum-tree, so useful for many purposes when hollowed out, was used for burial, a length being hollowed out like a water-trough, with the ends left solid. The cover for the coffin was the piece which had been sawed out on one side, replaced. The made wooden coffin could be had to measurement, but many a body was made to fit its coffin, when the coffin-maker had been forehanded and wanted to get rid of his stock. Those old body-shaped coffins were generally painted black if they were full sized, and a dull red if the size were small, although some of the larger ones becoming exposed in burying grounds which have later become hog-pastures — and there are plenty of them to be found — have borne the more cheerful color. They say in Salem, Massachusetts, that the man who built coffins often used his left-over red paint on tables he might be making, and the left-over black on his chairs.

That part of the many-sided Paul Revere which was a silversmith, made a specialty of the engraving of the silver plates which were attached to coffins for possible later identification. In his notebook is a sketch of a coffin pinned to the last page. Strangely enough old silver plates turn up today in desk or garret and sometimes at auctions, having been removed from the coffin just before its burial as being too valuable to bury underground — serving better as a badge of family prosperity.

The words coffin and casket were used interchangably when the latter came into use in this capacity. In the 1600s the definition of a coffin was "a pastry cup of milk and butter." In the next century it was described as a "chest for dead bodies," and the word corpse had not yet won its final E. In the 1800s, Webster has the single meaning for the word casket, which was, "a small chest or box for jewels."

One of the requirements of a coffin until about 1750 was the pall, a black cloth which was thrown over it. Salem and Marblehead were sadly lacking in this respect and a clever captain found a profit in the circumstance, advertising thus:

HANDWROUGHT ANCESTORS

"The Towns of Salem and Marblehead . . . have no
Pall to accomodate a decent Funeral . . . . Captain Joseph
Majory, at his house in Marblehead, has provided two
handsome black Velvet Palls to Lett, suitable for such
service." Strange land trail for a captain to follow. Boston
papers carried an ad for "palls for grown persons at 7—6,
for children at 4—1 "

The signs hung out by undertakers varied, but generally
carried either a death's head, or a picture of the so-called
"octagonal" coffin, which was generally content with only
six or seven sides. Above the lists of deaths on a family-tree
record, a lonesome looking little black painted coffin rubs
elbows with the red blossoms above the "births" and the
bleeding hearts of the "marriages."

4. THE CARRIAGE SHOP

"He's got the cart before the horse."

Springing Comfort

The Pleasure Waggon

"OUR folks used to have the pleasure-wagon for going to Meetin' in. It was about five feet long with one seat up front. It had good wooden springs sawed out of lumber, and a heavy hub, and even with a plough-horse hitched in, it could travel a mile in three minutes. Lucky it could go, too, for when midweek Meetin' came round, there wasn't much time to waste. Father'd hurry in from the field, slip his false bosom over his workshirt and put on his Meetin' hat and hurry off. He didn't mind touchin' the horse up some either, even on Sundays he'd pass a team — which of course he shouldn't.

"I remember once I didn't go to Meetin' but went after Mother to bring her home. She always liked to take the reins — yes — she was a good horsewoman — and father and me didn't generally mind. But while we were goin' along that morning, I see, out of the corner of my eye, that Joel Pitcher was overtaking us, and I reached over for the whip

237

and give the horse a touchin' up. Blamed if that horse — he was awful lifey — didn't up and put his foot right through the buggy floor. It come right up between mother's foot and mine. If she didn't splutter! She knew every team for miles around, far as she could see 'em comin'. She lived and died up on the Street."

In quite another part of New York and a good fifty years earlier, or in 1823, this sign appeared in a local news sheet. "A two-horse pleasure-Waggon for sale."

The "pleasure-wagon" was therefore a rig of many years standing, at least in the country sections where one was apt to cover a good many miles on an ordinary trip. The wagons and carriages used for pleasure during the last days of the horse-carriage, were much more graceful and comfortable. They included the phaeton, the landau, the surry, the ubiquitous buggy, both covered and uncovered. The coach stood in a class by itself and was of the ages, coming early to the post-roads and ending on the Fifth Avenues of the land, one of our grand "e-quip-ages." The little old chaise and gig were vehicles used by the doctor and the parson and those who must travel alone up and down dale, where no pleasure was anticipated.

The Shop

The carriage-maker naturally made the vehicle of the period, but whatever it might be, he must have certain equipment for making the routine parts, such as body, thills or shafts, dash, step, seat—with or without back,— fifth wheel and the four other wheels, for the carriage-maker generally knew how to make the wheels, just as some of the wheelwrights knew how to make the whole wagon. Small communities could hardly be expected to support each of these craftsmen since the vehicular needs were not great, once they were supplied. Whether he had an order for a buckboard, a two-horse wagon, or "a leathern conveniency," such as Robert Murray ordered in New York City in the middle 1700s — thus achieving one of the first private carriages — or whether as a plain waggon-maker one must turn out the cumbersome ox-cart with wooden axles, or a lumber wagon, his shop varied little in appearance. For the carriage there must be tools for finer finishing, but these finishings were done on the same littered bench, with the help of the same wooden vises and hooks and clips and clamps that had worked on the coarser work, and the same cobwebbed windows let in the same sunshine upon the cart and the coach, and the same black-smith ironed the solid wooden wheel and the finely spoked one.

The best woods for the body were ash and cherry and pop-lar, while the wheels and running gear were of hickory or maple or some others. These woods were normally seasoned by exposure to air and light, and for two good years of time. The wheels were made and left for shrinkage inside the shop before being finished and ironed. A carriage-maker with plenty of work did most of it within his own shop, having one room for a smithy, one for the making of the wheels, a "body room," another for painting, and still another for the final trimming.

The era of the carriage for common use was really very brief. Vermont had her first carriage shop in 1817. There Thaddeus Fairbanks, at the age of twenty-one, made pleasure-waggons. In 1815 he had come from Brimfield, bringing one pleasure-waggon with him, and had thereupon set up shop and made another. The horseless carriage came at the end of that century.

HANDWROUGHT ANCESTORS

Original Springs

Perhaps the most interesting work done in the old wagon and carriage-shops was the making of the springs, for here each man had a chance to use his own ideas of what might produce comfort in travel. The spring did not have a place on the cart or heavy wagon until the early part of the 1800s. One old drover, who generally walked beside his team, would occasionally climb onto his seat, and there tuck beneath him the pillow which he carried as a shock absorber, knowing no better way. The idea that even a work vehicle might be made easier for the human spine gradually seeped into man's consciousness and then all sorts of wooden contrivances were made. Of course the stage coach had swung for ages upon its squeaking straps slung from front to back, but a coach was a coach.

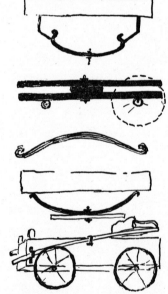

"Jus' sawed out o' lumber"
Home-grown wooden wagon springs

BUILDERS AND VEHICLE-MAKERS

The first place to which the spring was applied was not to the body but to the seat, and this seems quite natural since it was the seat upon which one sat. A great half loop of iron was fastened to a heavy plank which fitted across the bottom of the wagon, the upper ends grasping the ends of the seat. This was advanced thinking in comparison with the type of spring shown in the sketch. This was used only in lumber wagons, and was simply two stout poles which passed under two iron hooks placed on the outside of the wagon sides, and caught at the rear through two more iron hasps. Upon the raised ends at the front the seat was placed, and had the benefit of the spring for the entire front half of the poles.

One type of spring had the women in the back seat in mind, (as well as the men who sat in front and got the best view, but whose self-respect demanded this honor, for survival). It should be mentioned that most of the spring devices of wood did not depend upon the springiness of the wood, but upon the spaces left between the boards which would allow of a nice bouncing up and down, for lack of support. This special type of spring had two spring boards passing from axle to axle, upon which were placed short pieces of wood, upon which the body was in turn placed, but fastened and touching only in the center, which left the front and rear parts free to spring and bounce. Thus men and women at last sprang in unison. The acme of ease was procured when, in addition to a springing body, the seats were placed upon their own springs as well. Now body and seat sprang separately or together as the rocks might decree. When it was decided to trust man's life to a single thin board hung between the axles, which would spring at the approach of a pebble, the real joy riding had been achieved, and the "buckboard"— a significant name — had come to stay as it happened, for a very few years, due to the coming of cars.

The years brought more and more style and adornment, a touch here and a touch there, but the proud couple who drew up to a toll-gate and had to pay extra toll because of the new-fangled aprons adorning the under part of the buggy-body, soon removed their aprons.

The Paint Shop

Of course each well made wagon, cart or carriage, must receive its coat of paint, when paints became available, and this was not until the first half of the 1800s, for general use. This painting could not be done with a careless hand or a heart devoid of artistic leanings. There was far more than slapping on a black or a red or a blue color. The body, as did the wheels, received one coat of paint before going to the blacksmith to be ironed, and after ironing many a wagon or carriage in the late 1800s received eighteen coats of paint, each one slowly dried and rubbed down before the next was applied. After these coats had been administered there were the most careful edging lines to be applied to the body, and painted in almost hairlike slenderness along smooth spokes. There was the great chance for a telling brush stroke upon the backs of sleighs — done during the hot months — and by fall there would stand out among foils and foliage little village spires among leafy trees, which would have a fine chance for exhibition as the sleigh made its rounds of the snowy countryside through the winter. The sleigh-painter of the late 1700s, of course made use of the newly crowned eagle in his designs, the splendid creatures fairly screaming in glory and paint from many a high-backed, wooden runnered sleigh.

*Wagon-maker's shop and paint-shop in ell—
Ramp at rear*

One typical carriage shop in a tiny New York village, had a two story building to itself, using the main floor for the manufacture of the carriages, and having an outside ramp up which the finished vehicles went for painting. This ramp was a usual device too for the country blacksmith shop. During the summer, sleighs and sleds were painted for the winter, and during the winter wheeled vehicles were painted for the summer. In between, there was time too for painting houses and farm buildings, and since one of these carriage-painter brothers could never let his brush rest, he painted landscapes. Today these old oil landscapes are valued in the old village where the carriage and paintshop still stands, now the Post Office. Each painting was presented to the parents and grandparents of the present owners, by the carriage-painter, Lewis Hunt, when a job was finished and the bill paid. They hang in many homes made snowwhite by his skillful brush. In the Hunt Carriage Shop, ten men were employed and they turned out each year seventy-five wagons and carriages.

Now the only sign on the old wagon-shop

The man who trimmed the carriage seats and made elaborate linings and trimmings for the carriage, was never the man who made it. This man must, like the painter, have an artist's soul, to produce grandeur and elegance to please the eye. With tiny brads he fastened yard upon yard of silk and silken fringes, binding silks and silken buttons to each body and the making of these trimmings became a business of large proportions in itself. The art work of the carriage painter and the coach trimmer was something which no machine could ever steal away.

Horse and Buggy Days

Within the last year the last surviving wagon factory in the country was sold at auction in St. Louis, and by wagon factory we mean the overgrown wagon or carriage shop of country beginnings. The expression "horse and buggy days" is coming to mean as definite a period of American history as "the Civil War Days." It generally means the latter half of the 1800s, passing only when the motor car outdistanced its champion in speed and popularity. It stands not only for the quiet years before the storm of electricity and gasoline broke upon the land, but for a time when folks were happy in making something out of nothing, having a good time even though staying home occasionally, walking

244

the face of the earth and loving it, seeing a buggy-ride as an event each Sunday afternoon, and feeling the warmth of summer sun and the boon of moonlight as something to be taken slowly and with quietness.

When folks rode in buggies they heard the brooks sing and the birds; the meadow-lark's challenge — "You can't see me," was not drowned out; violets showed for what they are, single blooms of loveliness and not just a sheet of vanishing purple among the roadside weeds. The best that could befall a country woman when her Monday's wash was done and her Tuesday's ironing, was to "ride out,"— there was business then for the buggy-maker. It might be necessary to think up some obscure errand, for to ride out without purpose was almost like sinning time away, but it was good to peep about the close black curtains and see the far flung fields and the neighbors' gardens, and how high the brook was down at the forks. "All the women folks is out today. I cal'late it'll rain tomorrow." The truth was that it had probably rained for several days before and this was a lifesaver from monotony.

There was some style to a spinning buggy when it first came from the shop. There was elegance in the hold of a long whip. There was magnificence in the loud "Whoa!" with which the young spark announced that he had come to drive his lady love out along dusty roads. Once, a girl was too shy to walk out alone to the buggy and waited for her swain to come in for her. He continued to cry "whoa!" and when she did not come, he drove away. Alack for the course of true love in buggy-riding days.

Perhaps the strangest vehicle which ever traveled along our roads was drawn along a dusty one in New York one

Sabbath morning a century and a half ago. The family cart had broken down and yet Meeting must be attended. The farmer went to his woodlot, felled a fine big hemlock and dragged it to his shop. Here he inserted an iron ring in the bottom of the trunk and hooked on a pair of oxen. When the family drove into the Meeting-house yard there were gay welcomes. Spread upon the branches were blankets and upon these the women and children were perched, protected from the dust of the road, while the father played drover and guided the oxen straight to the horse-block. When a thing was to be done, t'were well to do it.

Buggy step

5. THE WHEELWRIGHT'S SHOP

"It's the fifth wheel that makes the loudest noise."

The Spinning Wheel

THERE are stories of wheelwright's who when spring came knocking, saddled their longhaired beasts of burden, looked well to their rope "riggin," lest halter, rein or bellyband play false on muddy roads, strapped to their own backs a great bundle of wheels and sallied forth to turn the winter's handwork into hard money. The nature of these wheels will be exactly known by those who have delved into the days of spinning, and learned to discriminate between the great wool-wheel, the smaller quill-wheel with its extra broad rim, the still smaller flax wheel, and smallest of all, the two wheels which went into the chair-shaped frame of the spinners of flax in New York. It is possible that some wheelwrights were giants and so may have peddled cartwheels on horseback, but surely not many could have been carried at one time, in spite of old tales.

One of the very first wheels ever conceived and put into use was for the purpose of spinning, so history tells us, and many a settlement made by our forefathers had the spinning wheels running a long time before a single wheel was even glimpsed as an aid to transportation. In many places the wheels of the ox-cart which had drawn a family into the wilderness were the only ones for miles around. There was the distaff for spinning before there was the wheel, and women spun and twisted their flax as they walked about

247

their villages and visited with their neighbors, but there was a limit to even the trained hand and arm. The wheel is one of the six mechanical powers and has always stood for both power and speed. No hand or arm could move as fast as a revolving spindle propelled by a banded wheel, and it was this spindle speed which was necessary if cloth were to be turned out in required amounts. So man, or perhaps the spinner, or spinster herself, conceived the idea of a light wheel which could be turned by the merest touch of the fingertips or the easy foot treadle, and connected it with a twine band to the spindle head. Wheels were of great importance, but without the most humble twine band to connect them with the scene of action they would have been powerless, and this twine band was the work of the spinster who made it upon the very wheel which it was to turn. The very first one was probably twisted by hand or braided of fine silk or hair. This wheel band was called the "driving band" and had been spun and twisted and double-twisted and its ends joined so smoothly one to the other, that there was no perceptable lump or the tiniest hitch as it made its way around the wheel head.

Hard wood was used for the wheel itself, and the head, turned out in perhaps another shop, must be of the finest workmanship and smoothed to silk texture. When a wheel was sold at a farmhouse door the wheelwright no doubt assisted in the adjustment of frame and wheel and head, for unless all worked together perfectly no good spinning could be accomplished. Women cared for their wheel-heads as faithfully as they did for their babies, and one which had its perfect band which would not bind nor stretch was guarded jealously.

The large wool wheel, with over a yard's diameter, had

simple turned spokes, sometimes larger at the circumference, sometimes larger at the hub, and quite far apart, and its rim was of wood split to almost paper thinness, generally a little over two inches in width and overlapped and fastened, where it met to form the circle, with tiny wooden pins or brass tacks to a perfect evenness to carry the band without roughness. Occasionally a slender groove was cut in its center to help the band keep its position as the wheel turned round. Into the making of the smaller wheel for flax spinning went a great deal of beautiful handwork, the spokes being elaborately turned on a lathe and the broad vertical rim decorated with delicate moldings. No matter how long ago they were thrown away as useless, or how madly they were rushed back and forth across garret floors as improvised hobby-horses, they seem never to break or even bend away from their first fine building.

The wheel which the wright could make with less time was that for quilling, or winding the quills for the shuttles of looms. This was in size about half way between wool and flax wheel, with a broader wooden edge and fewer spokes, and for rough quaintness perhaps the most appealing of all. The little wheels for the chair spinning wheels were made of the same careful workmanship as that of the flax wheels.

The Wheelwright

The man who wrought in wood was a wright, in the old meaning of the word, and he was one who was skillful and able in the matter of construction and contriving. Although the carpenter also worked in wood, he seems always to have been the "carpenter" and never the "wright" unless he were building a house, when he became the "housewright." There is something very substantial about the word "wright," and naturally the work of the wheelwright had to be substantial, needing a keen eye, a trained hand at the lathe and sure fingers with the shave. Sometimes the wheelwright was also the carriage-maker and waggon-maker.

"Shoe" to slip under one wheel to act as a brake

Like the light that flashes in the dark and catches the eye, so the whirling wheel was an outstanding part of any equipage, and we had "the wheelers" or the horses closest to the wheels, in contradistinction to "the leaders"; instead of talking about the toll collectible at a toll-gate, they claimed "wheelage."

Those Turning Wheels

During the approach of Burgoyne's army toward those fields near Schuylerville, New York, which were later to be known as the battlefield of Saratoga, the settlers across the Hudson packed such of their household goods as they could crowd onto homemade vehicles and started upon their flight to safety. "Some traveled on sledges on the bare ground, others on trucks or carriages that ran on a sort of wheels made with the end of a large log sawed off and holes made through the middle and put on axle trees." This axle tree was a tree indeed, six feet long, squared to eight or nine inches and hewn down at the ends to fit and be made fast in the center of the solid cross sections of tree which would revolve upon its bark and make the simplest and yet the heaviest of all wheels. For such wheels the wright was not at all necessary, for any farmer with an ax and an adz could hew them out and fasten them together. Anything for a roller! And then if there were time before the army reached the opposite shore, an iron tire or two would be forged and spiked along the outer edges of these wheels which would measure perhaps fifteen inches at the nave and eight or more at the edge.

"His manageable steed with horns" and four uncertain wheels

Only the finest wood went into a well and regularly made wheel, for this whirligig must travel many miles and over roads of all kinds, and no part of it must be weak, for, "the chain is no stronger than its weakest link." Strongest and toughest of all must be the nave, or hub, and for this the almost iron-like elm or "el-em" was often used, as was also hickory, and the tough wood of the gum tree. The word hub seems to have been an arrival after the Revolution. One hardly knows how anything in this country could have been dated, if there had been no Revolution, for it stands out like a sore thumb, making a background for the many things developed during that busy period of the Western World. The hubs of the heavy work wheel were shaped much like a cider barrel and often nearly as large. With iron bindings on each end they looked even more like a barrel, with its top and bottom hoops fastened in place. Slenderer wheels had slendered naves, and their shaping could be done upon the wheelwright's turning lathe. Whatever the size of the nave it must have a hole bored through its center lengthwise. This was done with a great pod-auger, or "reamer" or a piece of iron shaped like a carrot with one open side, with a few threads cut in the point, and a crosspiece handle of simplest construction. It was yet a mighty tool, but hard on the muscles when compared with the brace and bit which came to lighten labor. It really did the work of two tools, for it not only broke the way through the wood, but enlarged the hole by its greater width at the top.

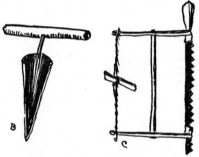

B. Pod-auger or reamer for rimming or boring holes
in wheel hubs
C. Whipsaw for making spinning wheels
Tightened with twine

Axles or "Xs" were also made of wood, and since this meant the turning of wood upon wood within the great hub, some plan had to be found to save wear and tear and cracking, and the squeak which is sure to follow when wood disagrees with wood. A New Jersey blacksmith who still uses old methods and finds them good, tells of the simple preventive used in that State. "With the wood-on-wood axle you fill the hole in the hub with tallow and then keep putting hot stones in for a full day. This will make the wood get to be just like so much iron, so you couldn't saw it to save your life. That'll make your wooden axle turn forever."

A. Spoke shave

The Spaka or the Spoke

For those slender bars which keep the hub and the tires of our wheels from falling into each other, the Anglo Saxons had the word "spaka," and from it we have our "spoke." Sometimes the wheelwright turned his spokes upon his "spoke lathe" and they would show circular in a crosscut, but many spokes were hand formed, being drawn into shape — sometimes elliptical — by means of the drawer-shave. Once shaped, they must be polished or smoothed so that they would less easily collect mud in their travels. One way to polish a spoke was to place it in a sanding barrel, which was turned by means of a shaft connecting with a millwheel. This was really a great tumbling barrel, containing sand which, rubbing swiftly against the spokes as they fell over and against each other, took off the rough places and in time smoothed them. Some of these sanding barrels contained no sand and depended upon the quick revolutions to achieve the same result.

For many years one of these old sanding barrels was left

to rot away not far from the old woodworking mill which had once had it connected with the tumbling brook in the rear. It was at least eight feet long and perhaps four high, with holes in the ends for the axle or shaft to pass through, and an oblong opening in one section of its circular flanks where the spokes of baby-coaches had once been pushed in and set turning for their ultimate beauty. It was finally knocked to pieces because one of the local ne'er-do-weels had made it his home for three winters, with a bundle of hay as his only furnishings. Once in and the door drawn close above his head, the old fellow had a roof over his head and no rent to pay, while the nearest neighbors paid his board bill at their kitchen doors — and table. Shut up like the spokes which had preceded him in the old tumbling barrel, the freeze might yet have caught him, and there would have been no merry turning to keep him safe.

Hollowed stump, filled with stone and with a steady-ing timber run through its base, upon which to repair or iron wheels

In the meantime their destined hub had been prepared for the spokes by having a double row of holes cut about its

middle which would fit their ends when they had been
morticed with a hand chisel and wooden mallet into a shape
to make certain their continued firm position through the
years. The "dished wheel" was used during the 1800s for
the nice wagons in which the family rode to Meeting or
the Street, and must be kept as neat and unsplashed with
mud as possible. This dished wheel had its spokes thrown
outward, which brought the rim of the wheel out over the
outer end of the hub, and was supposed to aim the mud beyond the wagon area. Speaking of mud and the water which
caused it, it was bees' wax which gave all of the nicer wheels
their final waterproofing.

Although wheels were put together and then left to
shrink before finishing, it was yet one thing to get a new
wheel and another to keep it fit and fine with no loosening of
its spokes, since mud and sand and wet and dry are hard
on wood. There were several ways of treating spokes to keep
them firm and without a rattle. One was to take them from
the axle and stand them for half a day in the water trough,
turning them occasionally to give each spoke its chance at a
soak. There was always the brook where one might drive and
remain for a quarter of an hour, with the happy assurance
that the drink so badly needed was being taken greedily by
each spoke. "Gid up, Dobbin, take another step and let the
next spokes soak awhile." It was the usual thing for a bridge
on a country road to have a bypass trail down to and through
the brook which it spanned, so that drinking and soaking
and swelling might all be attended to under the happiest con-
ditions.

Felly and Tyre

It is not a long step from "felloe" which means the circumference of a wheel, to the shorter, terser, more intimate

"felly" or even "fella" which were so popular when wagons were more in vogue. While this outer rim contacted the earth as did neither the hub nor the spoke, it was yet but the slender periphery at the tips of the more closely built center. Some wheelwrights used ash or hickory exclusively for their felloes, while some living in New Hampshire, clung to maple as the perfect felloe wood.

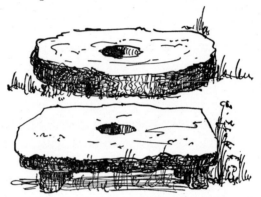

Granite slabs for ironing wheels. New Hampshire

Some one gave the making of a wheel thus curtly: "Use the saw, the ax, the drawing knife, the spoke shave, the chisel and sand paper, and then iron 'em." The ultimate of a felloe was generally the ironing of it, but to support this ironing there must be form and strength. The wheelwright had his forms and patterns of varying arcs which helped in the cutting out of the outer rim. Some of these curved forms would themselves have made heavy rims, but others were solid wooden segments with the desired curved edge, but both gave the pattern of the curve to be copied. The felloe in time was pierced with a row of openings which would hold the end of each spoke. These once in, the iron tire could be added, or the "ironing' of the wheel" accomplished. Sometimes the wheelwright depended upon the blacksmith for the iron work, and sometimes he did it himself. Whoever fitted the tire upon the wheel was sure that holes had been cut out of it so that the fastening nails could be driven through.

We have already seen, in the blacksmith shop, the various schemes for holding the wheel flat while the iron was being applied. The best of all was the great granite slab raised upon four low granite posts which formed a table of the proper height for easy work. The new hub was set within the central hole chiseled out of the rock, while its spokes and felloe might lie with no strain upon the broad flat surface. Some of the rocks measured six feet across, were square or oblong or round, and some so thick that they needed no raising to bring them within easy swing of the hammer.

D. *"Run it round the fella, then round the inside of tire and take out what's too large"*

In some old shops today one will occasionally see hanging from a nail a little iron wheel which at first glance seems to be an old revolving gridiron for broiling meat. Investigation will prove it to be a little wheel with a handle which the blacksmith used for measuring the length around a felloe, that the tire might be of the exact length. This little implement is not more than six or eight inches across, of flat, thin iron, and with two crosspieces to form its four spokes. The slender arm is fastened on with a thin pin which allows the wheel to turn easily and do its measuring around the wooden rim. So many times around the wood means so many times around the iron with a little extra thrown in. Then, that the tire may fit perfectly, it is heated red hot before applying, so that it can be drawn close at each point of the circumference.

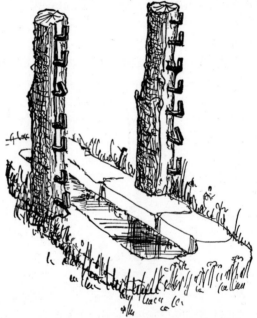

Warren Blacksmith and Wheelwright Shops,
Malvern, Pa. 1770. Pit about 5 feet long for
"freezing" red-hot tires to wheels. A pole was run
through the hub and placed across the iron hooks,
allowing felloe and tire to turn in the cold water
"Old Forge Inn"

BUILDERS AND VEHICLE-MAKERS

Back in the days of Benjamin Franklin when roads were being measured and stones set up to give the miles to Anywhere, men drove over the road sections and counted the revolutions of their front off wheel. This was a job for a patient man who could keep his eyes tirelessly on that wheel and never lose count. At the end of the route by multiplying the revolutions by the length of the wheel circumference, the desired distance was ascertained; unless one had detoured around too many rocks or stumps, or turned far out several times to meet another team, or made those little brook trips which ate up a few more feet of distance. But, by and large, one knew in a general way how far it was from Perryville to Thunder Town.

If there is one thing which takes second place in the cluttering of a blacksmith shop where wheels are often ironed — the first place having already been claimed by the horseshoe — it is the old iron tire which has presumably had its day but is still allowed to linger handy by because old iron should never be wasted. Suppose an old tire has parted company; this is no reason for thinking there are not years of usefulness ahead of it. Everywhere in the shop one sees it in use, for door gudgeons, for strap hinges, for braces, for holding horseshoes old and new, for fencing off space around the "lumber," for binding poles and hitching posts, for strengthening wooden sled runners, and for an untold number of things. "There's no iron today. It's got to be steel to be worth burning up your charcoal for. The old iron was good stuff and as good any time as the day it was first drawed out for use," says an old blacksmith today. "Iron was iron in them days, I call it."

The old saying that a man has put his shoulder to the wheel, is still being proven today, and showing its effective-

ness. A picture rises before our eyes of days or nights when we
have been stuck in the mud and some able-bodied and willing farmer has believed it his job and his joy to lend a hand.
Out of his house or barn he comes swinging his lantern and
bringing with him that shoulder which will soon be applied
so gladly to our muddy, slough-bound wheel. Planks and
burlap bags may be called into play first, and shovels and
"crows," but in time the farmer will put his shoulder to the
wheel as naturally as he puts his head against the cows'
flanks at milking time.

6. The Saddler's and Harness-Maker's Shops

"If two ride on one horse, one must ride behind."

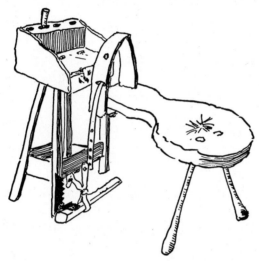

Saddlers' horse and vise, Northampton, Mass.

The Saddler's Leathern Versatility

IT mattered not whether he made saddles, harnesses, shoes, breeches, or whatever, the man who worked in leather had an amazing skill and breadth of capability. One might settle down to the thought of a saddler's shop and find himself considering, quite as much as saddles, a sturdy faggot-carrier of cowhide bound and run with rope for carrying in wood for the chimney-place, a nifty leather hatbox of rawhide well stitched and rubbed and brass name-plated for elegant service, or a great ox- whip with an eight foot lash of rawhide and an eight foot handle of hickory, such as Alabama produced, or even the implement in the hands of the public-whipper, for wielding which — back in 1753 — Dan'l Pettiloe of Philadelphia received ten shillings the year. One might go on for a long time enumerating the different articles which the saddler included with his saddle-making, and among these would be "Military Furniture for the Army."

While the saddler knew his saddles from start to finish, he had workers in other materials than leather to turn out those parts which could not be produced from leather. For instance, the frame or "tree" of the saddle was made by a special wood-worker who knew wood as the saddler knew leather. When there was need of iron, a blacksmith — either in the saddler's shop or nearby, did the work. This applies in general, but there were undoubtedly saddlers in the first shops who could themselves manage it all.

The first covering of the wood was done with canvas. Over this was put the "straining web," then came the wool padding, or the wool and hair padding, and over this was stretched the linen cloth. Over this went "Hog's skin." The seat was now pretty well attended to. After this came all of those necessary straps and the girth for making all secure. Following this the stirrups were attached. Some of the quaintest of our keepsakes are the early stirrups made of wood. Twisted roots or branches were discovered circled about upon themselves, and these were peeled and rubbed into perfect circular stirrups which had cost not a penny and would hold a boot as firmly as the best make of blacksmith stirrups. An old Spanish pair still remains in St. Augustine to delight us. The first of our handwrought iron stirrups were slender affairs, quite lovely in their line and satin finish.

The saddle of the ox—which was often pressed into service

as a beast of burden — and that of the cow, were of wood, great cumbersome affairs curving up to a shallow peak over the animal's spine, and extending well down over its flanks. With a heavy raised border of wood curving down on either side they were burdens in themselves, but must have made a fine foundation upon which to pack the family goods. Whether the saddler made these saddles is a question, and the probability is that he did not, for they lay more up the lane of the crude woodworker.

Harness-maker's bench and vise

Harnesses

Although we include the saddler and the harness-maker under the same general heading, since both had a hand in outfitting the horses and the animals of the bovine genus, or "neat critters," when they took to the road, the saddler preceded the harness-maker by several years. Men rode beasts for many decades before they had roads suitable for vehicles, and the demand for saddles was felt among the first needs when four-footed animals had become available to the colonists. Of course fine harnesses were probably brought from across the waters — a lovely phrase that, "across the waters" — but the usual harness was little more than a collection of thongs and ropes knotted together more or less crudely. The very name was "gears" or "riggin'," rather than harness, this latter word meaning the traces for horses. And if the truth were told, it was the shoemaker who was saddle and harness-sewer in many a town which was without an established saddlery or harness-shop.

In 1750 the simple "gears" included a hold-back, the word "breeching" being unknown. There was the head-stall, and a collar of braided cornhusks which could be made at home before the open fire at one's leisure. There were the hames of curved wood fitting over the collar to which the traces were attached, if any load were to be drawn, and these were cut and drawn into shape by the carpenter. If the farmer could not himself manage to turn out the reins from rope or sewed together strips of cowhide, the shoemaker could, while heavy twine did more than its share of service for reins as well as tying the different parts of the riggin' together. Old men still alive can remember seeing just such equipment in New England districts when they were boys, and the Southern mules and occasional neat animals which one sees on the roads today coming slowly out of some sandy trail in a hammock, are similarly equipped.

When a man achieved some kind of a gig or cart or even a stoneboat or wooden scoot, the matter of connecting it with the animal arose. Our present day shaft was a "thill," and the horse which became the proud walker between a pair of thills, was a "thill horse," or a "thiller." Quite different gear was needed now, if utter simplicity can have differences, and the gear used for this new advance in travel was called a "set of Thiller's gears."

His work once established, the harness-maker's work was as varied as that of the shoemaker. The equipment of these

BUILDERS AND VEHICLE-MAKERS

different leather workers, was however somewhat different.
In the saddlery there was the saddler's sewing horse of wood,
a broad curved seat with a wooden vise on the forward part
which was controlled by a stirrup attached with a leather
band, or by pressure of the knees. Some of these horses had
an iron ratchet which was held by a treadle beneath the saddler's foot; sometimes these little horses were connected with
the tool bench.

Harness-makers' vises, New Hampshire

For both the saddler and the harness-maker there was a
vast amount of stitching to be done, and a vise was most
necessary for holding whatever was being worked upon.
Many of these old vises, or "jacks" had a rough, unfinished
block of wood for their base from which rose up whatever
device the ingenuity of the leather-worker might produce.
Some had screws to draw in the two sides; some had simply
two boards which looked like barrel staves and so fastened

265

at the outer edges of their block that they were naturally thrown against each other at the top. Knee-straps were sometimes the vise, or the knees themselves, grown like iron in muscle and in flesh.

While a "jack" was really a small vessel made of leather, such as a mug or a can, the word "jack" was applied to every little device which held on like grim death, helped to lift weights, or made itself generally a helper in a hard job. There is the bootjack which hauls off boots which hands cannot budge: there is the bedjack used on the old corded beds to give a twist that human muscles could not supply; and the cobbler's jack and harness-maker's jack, until one feels that the word should be started with a capital and mean an omnipresent individual by the name of "Jack."

Harness-makers' punch

In both shops there was the endless sharpening of knives, and iron punchers for making holes in straps both for buckles and sewing, and hempen thread and the hog's bristle for making the "waxed end."

266

BUILDERS AND VEHICLE-MAKERS

One of the popular games which used to be a part of the entertainment at country picnics and fairs was called the "Peg Race." Just why is not clear, but the game depended entirely upon a man's familiarity with his harness. Two buggies were placed side by side. Two horses were then placed close by, with their harnesses on the ground. When the gun was fired two men sprang at the harnesses flinging them onto the horses to see who could be quickest at the job. The harnesses on, there was a rush to "hook in" to the buggy. Then as a test that the harness was properly in place, the next step was to jump aboard, drive twice around a prescribed track and try to come in first. Some one won the prize. Quick harnessing sometimes meant a difference between life and death, and such contests were as valuable as learning to save from drowning or fighting a fire.

THE SHOPS OF MANY AN ANTIQUE

❧ VIII ❧

1. THE YOKE AND BOW SHOPS

"As crooked as a yoke-stick."

〰〰〰〰〰〰〰〰〰〰〰〰〰〰〰〰

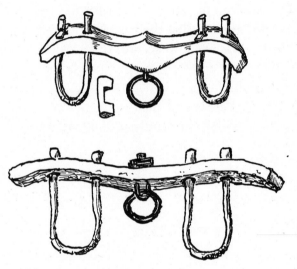

New Hampshire ox yoke, bows and key
Southern ox yoke and bows

The Ox Yoak

"MY uncle made a crop of cotton," said a Southerner, "with one Jersey ox, last year," and this is good to know, for "last year" was 1935 and both the South and the North were using the old methods of labor in many places. Sometimes four yokes of oxen are chained together — the chains running from yoke to yoke, to haul or snake one great tree out of a Southern swamp or a Northern lumber camp. With this in mind one might expect to hear that some new way of yoking oxen together had been substituted for the old, but the ways used in the early "yoak shops" still obtain.

The ox-yoke was and is a contrivance by which two of these animals can be coupled together to draw great weights and over the roughest of ground. The yoke is simplicity itself, consisting of a great curved piece of timber in which four holes are burned or bored and into which the ends of two bows — slipped over the animals' necks — may be inserted to be locked fast with a wooden key. Underneath, at the exact center of the yoke, an immense handwrought iron ring or hook is fixed, its shank running up through the yoke for bolting on top. Into this the hauling chain is fastened.

"To lerne to make his yokes and his ox-bowes," a man needed strength and patience and but small shop equipment. A good log of ash or hickory would make a good yoke for strength and lightness, and this was "sawn out" by hand or hewn and cut out with one of those vicious tools called a "foot adz," with which a man endangered his feet every time that he raised it and brought it down in some great log. The cutting was rough work but the final shaping was done with the draw-shave, so that the yoke was nicely "drawn" into curved edges and rounded surfaces, the shave being really a modeling tool when in the hands of an adept. The yoke was broad enough to lie across the necks of two great oxen standing a short distance apart and side by side, and to leave a short curved-down hangover at the outer ends. Four holes were then bored from above for the forthcoming bows. Although these old yokes were soon well greased and polished by animal sweat and constant rubbing, it was yet necessary to grease them with tallow when finished, since the sweat alone would roughen the wood. Thus did the "yoke-stick" grow.

The Ox Bow

Then came the making of the bows and often in a shop of their own. These two curved pieces of wood which were to fit under the necks of the oxen, measured from one inch to two and a half in thickness and were also made of hickory, preferably the "second growth," since that in growing quickly grew very straight. In Maine sweet walnut was used in the bow and was called harder than the bitter walnut, with red elm as a good second. The heart of the timber turned out the toughest wood. If only a few bows were needed for home service they were easily made in the home shop, being shaved with the straight draw-shave at first and then the curved shave to take off every bit of roughness and leave only curved surfaces. Then because the wood was green the bow could be twisted and dropped for a half hour or less into boiling water where it became pliable enough to bend the full sweep necessary to fit loosely the great neck for which it was destined. It was then passed through the holes in the yoke and left to dry and harden into permanent form. Not far from one end a small hole was pierced to admit the key.

Various pokes and yokes

Where the making of the ox-bow was the sole industry, choppers were sent early in the fall into the woods to fell and split the trees for finishing in a sawmill or a woodworking mill. There the wood was subjected to a roughing-saw which debarked it, when it was cut into the required lengths, the heart wood opened out, the shaves applied, and the seasoning accomplished. Instead of boiling the bow, a steambox in time was fitted up over a great iron kettle on a fire in the open where the wood gradually gave up its stiffness and became bendable in the bow-maker's hands. He then worked it into its final form.

An early way of shaping the bow was to build a mold into which it could be placed after boiling or steaming and remain until it had become solid in its new shape. Such a mold was roughly whacked together, being nothing more than a heavy plank for a backing to which was spiked another piece of plank which had been cut out to the shape of the desired bow. Nicely pinned in with "trunnels" or wooden treenails, the bow could remain until it had not only shaped itself but done some seasoning as well.

The making of the yoke-key was a simple matter of whittling for a man with a sharp jackknife. The key was of hard wood and measured about three inches long, so that when it rested upon the yoke it would not protrude on either side. It was scarcely an inch in height, about a half inch through at the curved top and running down to a narrow wedge edge at the bottom. Two upward cuts were then made in the lower edge and a third of the lower part removed — or the width of the bow — so that it could turn within the bow and lock it fast. Once thrust in and turned, its ends lay comfortably upon the top of the yoke until the work was done and the yoke ready for removal. It was generally necessary to lock and unlock only one end of the bow.

It is remarkable that in our own Maine woods timber was

cut and bows made for the elephants of India. They were of course much larger than those of the ox-bow and of great weight. The horn-yoke was a much more elegantly finished article than the usual neck-yoke. It rested upon the horns of the animals, thus necessitating no bows, and was of hard polished wood, intricately cut and fashioned, and not typical enough of our old shop work to need more than a mention here.

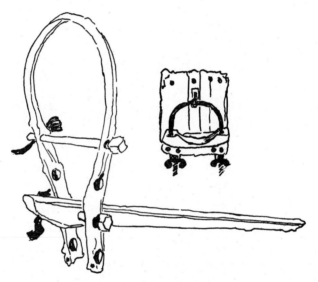

A. Horse-poke, against fence-jumping
Of oak and rawhide
B. Bog shoe 8x9 inches, for horse

Tethers, Pokes, Ties and Bog Shoes

To enable a horse to travel through a bog without sinking in too deeply, a heavy wooden bog-shoe was made on the principle of the snowshoe. Its base measured about eight by nine inches, and was of two layers bolted together to ward off warping. A short distance back from the front edge of the shoe was an iron hook from which swung loosely a sort of stirrup through which the horse's hoof was placed and bolted fast. The front of this stirrup or tie was an iron half-hoop and the back a block of heavy wood, gouged and curved to fit behind the hoof without rubbing; although smaller by far than the ox-yoke stick it resembled it in its curved depressions and curves.

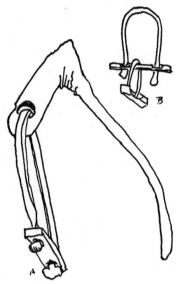

A. Cattle poke
B. Cattle tie, 1754, for tethering to a stake

The man who made bows for yokes also made bows for all sorts of wooden "ties" and "tethers" for barnyard animals, the horse, cattle, sheep, even turkeys and geese. There was little friction to a nicely smoothed and greased bow, whether applied to the foot or the neck of an animal or about the tree from which it was being tethered. Sometimes one tie worked within another for greater freedom for the bound animal and also to avoid the tangling of rope or chain. When it came to animals who loved better to roam than stay at home, and found a wall or fence no barrier, the poke was made, and always it must have its smooth bow from which the long stick or pole depended.

As Florida Spaniards made their riding stirrups of tough twisted wood, curling it into a near circle whose ends overlapped for fastening to the strap, the work of the bow-shop might be considerably broadened by local needs.

*Old Florida stirrup of bent wood locking
ends together*

2. THE MAKING OF KNIVES

"By corpus Domini, I will have thy knife,
And thou shalt have my distaff, and go spin."
— CHAUCER

❧❧❧❧❧❧❧❧❧❧❧❧❧❧❧❧❧

IN spite of all that today has to offer in the way of machine-shop equipment and conveniences, there is nothing which has ever taken the place of the jackknife. It is our greatest tool. No man or boy of a few years back considered himself fully clothed without some kind of a knife in his pocket, and the red-blooded ones of today seem to feel the same way. Back in Chaucer's time, to judge from the above lines, the knife was the symbol of masculinity, and the female scorn which could suggest swapping it for a distaff, must have been immense. In Chaucer's time too there was a little custom still prevalent in our own South among certain groups, for we read: "A sheffield thwittle baar he in his hose." To "thwite" meant to cut down, to whittle, to pare or shave, and in the 1500s men were still busy "thwittling with their thwittle-knives" or "whittles." Here we see another obsolete use of a modern word.

The jackknife's oldest granddaddy was a sharp stone, and we see its succeeding ones giving the names to the succeeding ages from the "stone age" to the present. Knife-shops were not among our initial industrial centers for we leaned heavily upon Sheffield for a couple of centuries for our run of knives, finding the famous old "Barlow jackknife," especially, something not to be improved upon. It is safe to say that no matter how far we may go in our labor-saving devices, man will never — and may he never — lose the love of the feel of a knife in his hands, "for to do a little whittlin'," if no more than enough to gain him time in which to think things through or do a bit of quiet visitin'. We are already going back to our old fashioned whittling.

The tinkerer was, not always, but often, a whittler, and the carpenter of the more isolated New England hills still stops to reach in his pocket for his more personal tool — the knife — when a nice curve must be made around a corner beam or a shelf made to cousin with its support. Benjamin Banneker, a negro, back in 1754 whittled a clock to strike the hours, with only a sundial and a watch for suggestion and a jackknife for a tool. If we must be businesslike in speaking of the simple jackknife, it may be said that it works by pressure and never through a blow, and that when its time came for going higher in service, it became part of a plane, and so began its climb into great intricacies.

Famous Cutlers

English Sheffield cutlery needs no introduction for it sprang into being many generations ago, but it was not until after the middle of the last century that America procured some of the well-watered roots and planted them so that today they bear, each year, knives by the million. It is claimed that out of Sheffield came the well-known "Barlow jackknife" so dear to our handworking ancestors, so dear in fact that it was lovingly remembered in written records. In time America began to make the "Barlow" knife, the name "Barlow" seeming to have become synonymous with the usual jackknife, for both were pocket knives, meaning that they had a single blade which could be turned back into the protection of the handle. The English originals were popular for over sixty years and "sought after for over a century." As to the American copies there seem to be various claims. One is that the first "Barlow" made here was the "Russell Barlow" made in Southbridge, Massachusetts, but then here comes another opinion from a popular source, as well as from a man who has sold "Barlows," for forty years:

The famous old "Barlow" would never recognize its offspring

"It's a clasp knife stamped with the name BARLOW, a maker famous in the United States in the early 1800s. It's the "Billy Barlow Knife," why everybody knows that. Has a bolster or jaws — the metal piece at the end of the handle into which the tang of the blade fits. The handle is about three and a quarter inches. Cow's shin bones for handle, stained brown, and left unpolished, roughish looking, you know."

Another man tells of a Barlow thus: "The handle's of bone, left with the grain rough, not smoothed off, sort of flat and light brown. It has one blade, like a blunt spear, pointed, and the bolster is of iron, and there's always three Roman numerals on it, "I X L." I don't know what they stand for, always wished I did."

Another famous name is that of "Bowie." Colonel James Bowie was of Texas and he, like many another man in need

Homemade bowie or hunting knife — of a file,
wood and iron
Scabbard, handsewn of lead and sole-leather

of the best material for a knife blade, turned to an old file
to find it. Every old man who ever made his own knife always nods his head vigorously when an old file is mentioned.
"T'was the best stuff you could get." Colonel Bowie was
not out for whittling clothes-pins peacefully in the barn door
and philosophizing with a chance neighbor who had dropped in for a spell, he was looking for a knife which would
stand the gaff in time of attack by man or beast. The broken
sword he had found more effective than a long unbroken one,
and so he made a knife the length of his file which happened
to be shorter than a sword and measured between fifteen
and twenty inches beyond the hilt, or bolster, now that he
was talking in terms of the knife. It had one keen edge and
a curved point. This point has been described thus: "The
knife had a blade with the back straight throughout most

278

of its length and then curved concavely to the point, to which the edge curved convexly." The bowie-knife was invented about 1835-6, and the type became known as the bowie-knife or hunting knife of the country, although the blade was considerably shortened. One Reese Fitzpatrick has been called the first maker of the bowie-knife by some claimants, but his name seems to be against him.

Homemade knives, razor blades, and wooden handles, with designs cut at the top into which hot lead was run to hold blade and handle together New Hampshire

Not Famous At All

Very few of us know of W. W. Baxley, a blacksmith who lived in Orange County, Florida, about Civil War time, but he did the same clever primitive "making something out of nothing" in his pioneer district, that made settlers of two hundred years before famous as "tinkerers" in New England. Baxley supplied himself with iron from the guns thrown

279

away by soldiers who had been busy in that section on some unproductive mission, and whatever other iron he could pick up. With this material, at his forge and anvil he became well known for the fine pocket knives which he turned out, good butcher knives too, and bowie or hunting knives made from broken files found in his rubbish piles. For linings of the handles of these knives he used the brass hoops from old muskets, while the horns of bucks were turned into the handles of the knives. These bowie-knives were popular with the Indians. Today there are slender little "killers" which are worn in the stocking by many of the Southern negroes who feel safe in this world only when thus equipped with trusty arms.

Knife-makers tell us today that a piece of steel that is of the proper texture to make into a razor is not suitable for a pocket-knife, and that what would be suitable as a temper for a pocket-knife blade would be entirely wrong for a carving knife. Such unimportant niceties had no place in our forefathers' lives. Some of the best old knives left to us were made of broken razor blades fastened into a piece of wood and held there by niching the wood and pouring in lead, while long bladed carving knives still show the crisscross cutting of the original file. Some of these knives are found driven into a beam in the shed as hooks for catch-alls, sometimes point-first with the handle sticking out and sometimes with the handle gone and the blade tang driven into the wood.

To be perfectly honest, the author does not know of any old shop which was set up for the exclusive making of knives, until about eighty years ago when some of our great hardware and cutlery concerns had their beginnings. In the 1700s Jonathan Crookes was dealing in knives in Boston, but it is not known that he made any. He may have been a "cutler" of the first and original order, who made knives; or he may have come under the second and later regime when to be a "cutler" meant to deal in knives. Knives however were made in many a shop and called for some of the best tinkerin' which was brought into play anywhere. Knives too began to be slipped into wooden contrivances to assist in some big job. Take the apple-parer. One New England man tells us: "There was an old soldier lived on the farm at home when I was a boy. He'd some falls pare five or six bushels of apples. He'd sit on the old parer and hold the knife just as good, and, say, he'd pare those apples so the skin wasn't thicker'n a hair! Then the folks would quarter 'em and take out the seeds and core, and then we children would string 'em up and they'd hang over the stove to dry, or else lay 'em out on the frame and dry in the dooryard." The apple-parer was a good example of the knife caught in simple mechanics. It had a crank or treadle which turned a little wooden wheel from which a head of four prongs extended and upon which the apple was thrust, and the knife — a narrow blade inserted across the end of a wooden handle — was steadied against an upright of wood a short distance from the turning apple. It meant very careful work to hold the knife "just so" and pare the skin thin enough to meet with housewifely ideas of thrift.

Blades and Handles

As with other manufactured articles so has it been with knives, the first were made from start to finish by one man while the later ones pass through many hands in our modern division-of-labor plan. Just what is being done to man through this taking away of the joy of watching a thing grow beneath his own hands, and substituting the monotony of a single repeated act on a single part of a whole, is not pleasant to contemplate. Less than a man is an automaton, and less than vital must we be growing who know only the one repeated stroke of the hammer upon those thousands of unfinished parts which slide hourly past our bench. In the early days of Sheffield one man made the entire knife; now each knife needs the skilled touch — and often little more than a touch — of nearly a hundred skilled workmen.

Case knife belonging to the Edward Stablers of Greenwich, Connecticut. 14½ inches long and ¾ of an inch thick. Of yellow bone and iron. Blade 1¾ inches across

One man in the early days knew how to stand at his forge and then at his anvil and draw out the edge of his fine old-day iron, temper it and hone it to a perfect edge. If he were making a caseknife, which was the large knife with a solid handle at one end, he drew out the "tang" or little rattail on the blade and cut a corresponding hollow in the handle, and bound them together. If the knife were destined to fold and become a "clasp knife" there must be a socket or hole made in one end of the blade through which a rivet might pass to hold it firmly between the two sides of the handle. These old claspknives were generally large affairs, hardly pocket knives, for they measured well over a foot in length, with a great curved handle and a great curved blade which, coming together at the two ends looked like a doubled-up lobster claw, and yet were a great improvement upon the "caseknife" which in its nakedness had needed a case or sheath to make it safe or portable.

The lining of the knife was oftenest of brass, and although called a "lining" was the frame into which the blades shut and to which the outer handle was formed. At the end of this brass work the blade was hinged, and to this hinge in time came the spring which turned the old regime knife into a modern one, and gave it its new straight line as opposed to the old curving sweep. Wood and shell were used for the handles of the old knives and sometimes horn was treated as it was for the making of a comb and then shaped into knife-handle form; again the shin bone of a dead cow could be cured and polished into a creditable handle.

We may sum up the knife then as passing through forging, hardening and tempering, grinding, handle cutting, jointing and assembling, finishing of handle and final polishing of the blade.

Keeping Them Sharp

A hone was a free grinding oil stone or whetstone, or a true block of fine compact stone for sharpening edged tools. One hones a razor but grinds an ax upon a grindstone. It would be interesting to know why a "grinder" might "grind" something on a "grindstone," and the long "i" be used in the first two words, and the short "i" when the word "stone" was added. But so it was until the Revolution in all of the word-books and still continues to be in parts of New York where they use the heavy old monsters. The good cutler knew that a sensitive blade could be burned in careless grinding, and that a blade edge of uneven thickness would never make a clean, smooth cut, while a well ground and sharpened edge would cut a long even taper in whittling with almost no guiding from the hand. He knew that the sides of a knife blade should be slightly rounding, the under part more than the upper, and that if the blade were hollow ground there would be but little support for the thin cutting edge. He knew that the flat or hollow ground blade would cut into wood, but would not clearly cut out and free itself.

The old fashioned games and tests of knife-throwing at trees and bulls-eyes, which took place at country fairs or before the crossroads store or at the mill or wherever young men gathered, were but other examples of how many of the old so-called "games" which seem rough to us, had behind them a grim meaning. A knife had its possibilities of swift protection.

Old stone shop, Wallingford, Vermont

3. THE TOOL SHOP

"It's a poor carpenter who complains of his tools."

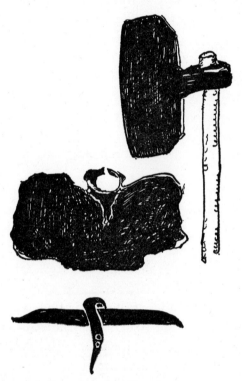

Homemade broad-ax handle, thrown to one side,
for hewing to a line. Two dug-up New Hampshire hoes

Scythes and Reaping Hooks

BESIDE the highroad at Wallingford, Vermont, there stands
one of our most lovely old tool shops, called today the "Old

285

Stone Shop." No longer used in its original capacity it still retains its step-right-in proximity to the sidewalk, carries the same old entwining vines upon its native stone wall, rests in quietness beneath the overhanging shade trees and is proud of its old sluice-way which still shows slipping along underground through holes in the surrounding lawn. This is but one of New England's numerous old birthplaces of those tools and implements which a tinkerin' and inventive part of the country would naturally need. The Old Stone Shop, is not really old, a mere eighty-nine years, and yet its lifework has been finished for some time because its beginnings were too close to that time of arriving machines and those larger shops which swallowed up the little ones like so many tidbits. Here in the coolness of summer days and when the winter winds howled, one Bachelar made pitchforks, and later rakes and rakehandles came into being.

Back in 1646 the famous Joseph Jenks had his eye on scythes and procured a patent from the authorities to "improve sawmills and scythes." They seem to have needed considerable improving, for the first to come over from England were more like our present bush-scythe than a grass or grain scythe, having a short blade and a handle which was practically straight, and long as a staff. The straight tool handle throughout the first two of our centuries, was the "stale," often misspelled "stail," and it was not until the third century here in America that we find the word "snath," our present name for the handle of a scythe. It is believed that the first snath was invented by a man named Lamson who lived at Windsor, Vermont, when for the first time the curve, which is now usual, was first installed. This man Lamson was a hard thinking and most independent character, and a man of high standing in Windsor. Once when he had voiced some radi-

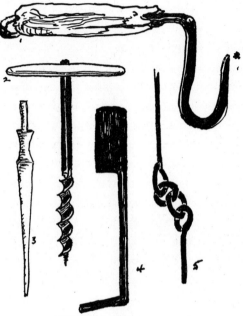

1: *To lift pot from crane*
2: *Wimble.* 3: *Flax Swingle*
4: *Peat cutter* 5: *Surveyor's chain.*

cal opinion, the town decided that even so prominent a man must be suppressed if the national government were not to fall. He was therefore taken to the village jail and locked up. When his few days had been served he was unlocked and told that he might go free. He refused to budge and they began to wonder how they could get him out, having once put him in. He remarked: "I didn't put myself here. Let them that put me here take me out." At last two of the guards made a seat of their crossed hands and offered him a ride through the doors to the street. To the crowd of fellow villagers who had assembled to see him delivered, he said in a loud voice as he rode comfortably forth: "I am more honored than Jesus Christ. He rode on one ass. I ride on two." His snath was so great a success that it has never been improved upon in all the years.

The scythe was a farm tool for mowing grass. To mow meant to cut the grass or hay and then it was mowed away in the haymow, that dark, high, warm part of the barn which all of the farmhands liked to avoid if possible on a hot day in July. The greatest praise which a farmer could give a man was to say that "he takes his mow without being told," when each was taking his turn at the different jobs.

The scythe was composed of the blade, the snath or snead, its two nebs or jutting handholds on the snath, the wedge, the wrench and the iron ring. When the scythe had been augmented with great wooden sweeps to hold the grain and drop it after each stroke in a proper spot and in order, we had the "cradle." One of the failures of modern industry is the sickle which is turned out supposedly to follow in the footsteps of the graceful old hand "reaping hooks" of our past — not only of Biblical days. The reaping hook of today lacks the grace and beauty of line of the old tool, and seems never to hold an edge, and certainly is limited in its reach compared with the fine old ones.

In 1774 John Adams wrote in a letter of a scythe mill at Durham, New Hampshire. Says another: "On Lebanon Brook there stood a snath and rake factory, I've heerd tell."

Tools with Stales

The old name stale or stail, while dropped for the scythe in favor of the snath, continued as the usual term for a handle which projected in a straight line from the tool, and was not attached at a right angle, like a crank, or shaft, or "handle" with which one would pound. The stale stood

more for the thrust. The mallet had a handle, and the maul
a stail.

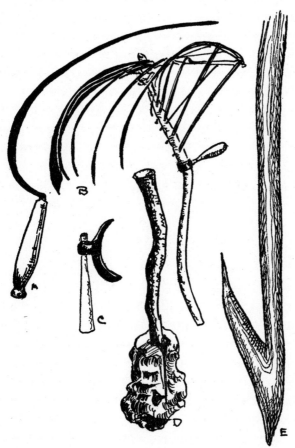

A: Hand sickle. B: Early cradle for grain
C: Bill hook. D: Natural maul. E: Natural hayhook

Many woodworking shops turned out hundreds of stales
just for local use, never thinking of sending them away in

quantity. Around some of these old rake shops the long white wooden teeth of the wooden rake keep turning up as the frost heaves them up in the spring where they have lain buried for years, and one hears: "If there aint some more of old Cy's teeth turning up again!" Sometimes the longer teeth of that implement for raking-up-after, or the bull rake, are found, fine and strong and squared off and of stanch ash, making wonderful window sticks where the little sashs are innocent of fasteners or weights and have grown lighter as the weather has been gathering their strength year after year.

Tools of Wood

They were legion. They were as the hairs of man's head, and as difficult to count, but each man made his own — of a sort — and thus added to the country's supply of variety. Some of the little shops specialized in one tool, and some made whatever was called for. When we say tool we give the word a broad meaning, covering all of those single devices which man needed on the farm, along the shore and in the mountains, for tools were agents or instruments, doing the work which man might guide them to do. To mention just a few of these devices, there was the "tool" for winnowing grain. This might be of steamed wood and look like a great shell upon which the grain bounced and danced when shaken about for the clearing out of dust and husks, or it might be a basket or a sieve of leather punched with holes or having a braided leather bottom; there were snow shovels of light basswood; the flax swingle, or wooden knife for beating the flax; the one-piece hay-fork made from a piece of ash or hickory and split at the bottom to make three tines, and a fourth in the rear added for strength; the common grain shovel with a short stale and a small piece of wood pegged across at the top to form a handhold; and many, many more, calling for many, many shops.

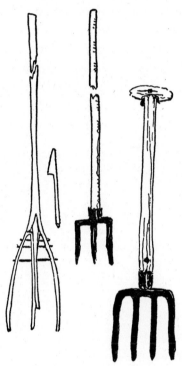

Split tine hay fork — Garden fork — Spading fork

Florida still has in her possession an old handmade plough, a natural elbow of heavy wood and a maul which suggests the muscles of Goliath, and it is from these simplest of tools — made from chance and natural formation of growing trees — that we are able to realize how our forebears managed in their days of stinting.

Notes worth noting: The prongs of a farrier's pincers overlapped, while those of the carpenter just met.

HANDWROUGHT ANCESTORS

The pod-auger was without a screw on its point until about 1800, just as the screws of only two generations ago were innocent of points. The "carpenter's square" was made in Vermont soon after the War of 1812, by Silas Hawes, a blacksmith of South Shaftsbury, and marked in inches only. They were first sent out by peddlers and sold rapidly. Some men paid several dollars a piece for them so necessary did they believe them to good work.

Among his Poor Richardisms, Franklin said:

"Handle your tools without mittens. Remember the cat in gloves catches no mice."

THE SHOPS OF MANY AN ANTIQUE

4. THE BROOM SHOP

"I enclose you some whisk seed; it is a kind of corn good
for creatures; it must be planted in hills like Indian corn.
The tops make the best thatch in the world; and of the
same are made the whisks for use for velvet. Pray try if it
will grow with you."
— BENJAMIN FRANKLIN *in a letter to Boston.*

New York "broom"

Primitives

THE simplest American broom has doubtless been the top
fluff of a hemlock branch or pine, the latter still used throughout the sandy sections of the South to keep the dooryard

neat. When several of these tops were tied together the broom had progressed. The Indian birch broom was a work of art in comparison with these natural makeshifts. A two or three inch sapling was splintered in long strokes to within a foot or so of the bottom and until about half of the thickness had been splintered. The splinters were then turned backward and down and tied with thongs of leather or wooden withes, or some of the splinters themselves, and the lower part of the now rough bush trimmed straight across for an even sweeping surface. When the white man made this broom he used hempen twine to do the fastening. Birch Indian brooms were made by white men for two hundred years and sometimes so small that they could be used for scrubbing the dry-sink of the farmhouse. Such brooms, or brushes were said to have "wooden brustles." In North Carolina these Indian brooms were made of hickory and called scouring brooms. Then there was the shuck broom made of corn-shucks or husks, fastened to the end of a long stick, or drawn through holes in a block of wood which was fastened to a stick or pole. Especially in the South where heavy and tall grasses grow luxuriantly, has the grass broom been common, and the small palmetto pines offered ready made brooms for the taking and tying.

Whatever was broomlike or had broom possibilities was used as a broom. That was the way life was lived by our ancestors, and a wise way it was. What need for a feather duster from the store or across the water, when one could wing the dust with a chicken wing or larger turkey wing. Women have wung the dust for centuries in this land. Whittier in his "Snowbound" says: "We sat the cleanwinged hearth about."

THE SHOPS OF MANY AN ANTIQUE

Flat vise for holding the "brush" of broom-corn
Pressed by pushing under a wedge

Broom Shop Ways

One old Massachusetts man who knew broom-corn in his youth and the making of brooms, said: "Huh! I swan, if there aint some old broom-corn! Gosh, I scraped a ton of broom-corn, we had seventeen acres sowed to it. The seed was good for the pigs and we fed 'em it —'twas as good as oats — if the frost didn't come. There was a good broom industry to Montague, one of the old broom-makers used to tie the brooms on his knees. He run the ferry to Turner's Falls then." While this is not very enlightening as to processes, it at least gives a hint as to how one man held his broom-corn as he bound it to its handle, as well as the necessity for scraping or hatcheling the corn to remove the seeds before it was ready for broom construction. A simple iron flax hatchel was used for this part of the work before the broom machine included it in its responsibility.

While many a broom never saw the inside of a shop, but was born out of doors or before the chimneyplace, there were yet small shops in which brooms were made from the broom-corn introduced by Franklin in one of his inquisitive moods in the 1780s. The little shop produced some crude beginnings but initiated a vast American industry. The result of

295

this primitive shopwork was good, therefore the method must have been so. Some of the quaint and rough looking broom machines are still to be found, but not often, and to the novice they often have little resemblance to each other. One is described by a man who knew the work:

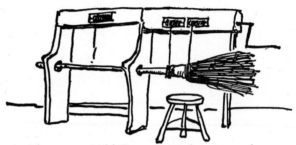

Remnant of old Connecticut broom machine
Not entirely understood

"A wooden roller, turned by a crank for winding on the cord. One hand holds the broom handle, and while winding on the twine, the brush is supplied with the other. The machine has a bench and a rag-wheel to hold the cord when wound on the roller. One man can make from five to eight dozen brooms a day." This sounds like real output, and while the description seems to call for three hands, it was doubtless skill which was substituted for the third one. The word machine seems almost too grand for the plain little rough contraption the broom-corn maker really was. Made of unpainted boards it had to fulfill a few certain requirements,—it must hold a spindle of twine, it must have a support in which the handle could turn about easily, and it must have either foot or hand power. Even this simplicity was simplified when the broom handle was held on the knees and a flat and solid vise held the corn while the broom-maker fastened the one to the other with no revolving conveniences, and then perhaps sewed the new brush across farther down from the handle to make the finished product more flat.

The accompanying sketch shows an old broom-corn machine still to be found in Connecticut, although no longer doing business. The machine itself looks like a low bookcase with a hole in each side at about the center point through which the broomhandle passes. The broom-maker sits at the right of the machine so that the handle and broom-corn lie on his knees. Projecting from the top of the machine is a wooden arm in which two wooden spools turn when the broom-maker turns it with a crank. With his left hand he guides the twine or wire which fastens the two parts together.

There were many devices, many kinds of power which included hand cranks, and barred cylinders which the foot kept in motion, and many kinds of vises for holding the corn when the binding was done entirely by hand. One simple device was two wooden drums beneath the insteps of the workman, joined with a smaller roller or bar upon which the twine was coiled, so that it could be drawn off and pulled up between the knees.

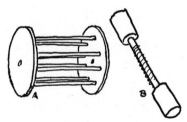

A. Foot power for broom-corn machine
B. Rollers held beneath insteps — center for reeling
off twine or wire

~~~~~~

⊷ IX ⊱

"I ain't no five or ten dollar man, holdin' out for no great
price, one way or t'other."
— *Florida Cracker*

~~~~~~

Behind the Counter

THERE came a time when the little home shops had produced more than the home needs, and more than the neighbors' needs, and more even than could be peddled by foot or
horseback. A little shop on the Street of the nearest town
became then not only a possibility but the one outlet for
over-production of busy winter months. Those who worked
in their shops the year round had unconsciously set themselves up as shopmen, although to their neighbors they were
still only "Henry, the cooper," or "Jock, what makes the
chears," or "Old Hollis, the smith." Along seacoast and
inland the little shops grew.

Shop of John Ward house, Salem, Mass. 1684

298

OUTLET SHOPS

No more perfect physical example of these little old shops in the rear of the home could be found than that which still clings to the old John Ward house at Salem, Massachusetts, built in 1684. In this case the house was an old saltbox with the shop in its original tail, with a door scarcely twenty inches wide leading into it from one of the large front rooms. Here one might mind the baby in her cradle, sand the kitchen floor, and almost keep the wool wheel turning, and yet be deep in the commercial stream of the town. There were many "she merchants" in the early days.

The first of our output shops where things were exchanged but not produced, was the old trading post, where the first comers stood under a tree or other shelter and bartered knives and beads with the Indians for their pelts of bear and beaver. Even the trading post was a part of the home, for if one building were actually achieved there need be no more. They were placed along an Indian trail which would in time be also the trail of the white man. There is an old trading post still pointed out in the basement of an ancient house in Catskill, New York, which was built in 1690, and it is to this period that we look for old trading posts; and yet at Brattleboro, Vermont, settled in the early 1800s, there was one which bartered in farm produce for goods brought up the Connecticut from the cities below. This brings the trading post rather close, or to within a hundred years.

Street Cries

There was still another place for bartering goods and that was in the open air upon the streets and sidewalks of our towns and cities. Naturally, being in the open, one cried one's wares aloud. The street crier who traveled up and down the streets became a familiar figure, sold almost anything

from the handwhittled splinter of a match to the black coal
for the grate, and his cries have been included among the
classics of early American song and story. Books of street cries
have been published and drawings made of the old street
criers.

> Right fresh good Oysters, hardly dead,
>   As sure as you are born!
> I took them up from their hard bed
>   This very blessed morn.

In 1771, New York City had twenty-six peddlers on its
streets, licensed variously for "on foot," and "with one
horse," and "with a cart and one horse." Exactly a hundred
years ago, zigzagging its way up Manhattan Island from the
old Battery, was a scene of amazing activity and one which
might have been mistaken for a cross section of a farmyard.
There were by this time, to be sure, real sidewalks slightly
raised above the cobbles but because so many creatures,
human and otherwise, strolled through the streets, posts
still stood before the shops, some of them rising to the height
of the second story windows, and with rods running along
their tops, from which wares swung in bold array. Wood-
cutters made no bones about setting up their woodyards in
the road itself, where with their bucksaws and sawbucks,
they cut wood to order in length and size and quantity. If
a horse came by drawing its cart the woodcutter went on with
his work undisturbed while the driver of the cart pulled out
and went around him. Men passed up and down the sidewalks, carrying long poles with shoes hanging from them,
as reminders. Old women sat in their chairs at the edge of
the gutter, with their benches before them holding the

candles which they had made at home and came forth to the highway mart to sell for a few pennies. "Horse and Carriage Markets" elbowed with trim little "Curl and Wig Stores," and "School Book Emporiums," while the walks were cluttered to the gutter with merchandise according to its shop.

Also the auction, or public vendue, or "outcry," was held in the street, or on the sidewalk, with rows of pants and jackets hanging from long poles from end to end of the premises.

Street Stalls

We have already seen the "dame shops" in a corner room of a dwelling, but there was another shop which grew up in the home which did business without violating the sanctity of this stronghold of privacy. The "stall" was little more than a booth, and a booth which was never entered by the customer, because across its front was the forbidding and defending counter over which goods were passed and paid for from the flagging without. Surely this must have been the original "shoplet" of which we read. We are familiar with the bookstall of this and other countries, and one wonders why the word stall lingered in connection with books, occasionally with cobblers, but passed for all else. Some of the early definitions of the word "shop," are "porch" and "vestibule" and "leanto" and even "shed," showing that our places of trade and barter were often merely the excrescences or outside edges of dwellings, there being no money for building better. In the most exact sense these house stalls were street stalls, the road running from house front to house front. There were walkers and footmen, but no pedestrians until after the Revolution, and sidewalks were often forgotten, the highway being good enough for all. The "high-way" was the "great road" or "public path," and it was along these public paths that men and women went for their trading. Philadelphia's famous Market Street was rightly first called "High Street," for a short time.

Along the high street the little stall was conspicuous for its numbers but not for its location, being a mere slit in the wall, perhaps no more than the width of the Dutch door, which could be swung open at the top and left closed at the bottom against stray pigs and dogs. The top of the lower part might serve as a counter, with or without broadening, but there was usually a "counter," or obstacle to progress which could be hooked up at night and dropped in the morning for business.

~~~~~~

Markets

~~~~~~

Slave and Otherwise

One old type of market there is which stands out in sombre colors, that one wherein men, women and children were sold like livestock. New York City had her first public slave market in 1709 and it stood at the foot of Wall Street until 1762, and was used during its latter years as the Meal Market. There are a few of these old slave markets left, the best known being those at St. Augustine, erected sometime between 1690 and 1765, one at Charleston, South Carolina, one at Fayetteville, North Carolina, and the one at Louisville, Georgia, which was built in 1758; here and there an old stone block stands on the border of a city square or at a corner, which is remembered as the "old slave block," and at Fredericksburg, Virginia, there is one remaining.

Market held here 1765, in 1598 slave market. Later, public auction. Still standing at St. Augustine, Florida

HANDWROUGHT ANCESTORS

Although the slave market has little to do with the output of the old workshop directly, it has its place in the sequence of markets and retail shops in general, and in nearly all cases became in time a general market where produce as well as slaves was sold in the open, until the time when the colored man was freed. Naturally the market place was in the center of the settlement, and the market at Louisville, after nearly two hundred years still stands supreme, all traffic reverencing its dimensions and having to "go round"— a great border of concrete assisting in this reverence. In 1758 it stood at the junction of the Georgetown and Savannah Trails serving as an Indian trading post and here slave traders going from up-country to the rice fields farther south, stopped and sold their slaves. In the center hangs the old French bell, cast in New Orleans in 1772, and decorated with medallions and inscriptions. Topped by a lovely slender iron and glass lamp, the sturdy old structure of weathered hewn timbers is a proud possession of the town.

Old slave market, built in 1758, still standing in Louisville, Georgia

For magnificence of architecture the old market at Fayetteville quite overrides the others. It straddles the earth like a great octopus, with its long arms reaching out to clutch

to itself the most of the public square, and doing it in graceful curves and pointed arches, both on its broad base, beneath
which roadways run, and on its turretlike second story. It
is a mighty, white memorial to the old days.

*Fayetteville, North Carolina, market — from a
passing car. With apologies to a unique structure*

"Market Place," and "Market Square," made up the
center of many but not all old towns. New York City was
late in establishing a real public market, apparently, the
famous old Fly Market not arriving until the latter part of
the 1600s. Its name evolved curiously. Smith's Vlei, in
Dutch, meant Smith's Valley in English, and in this vlei
the market spread along the center of Maiden Lane for three
of its short blocks, from Pearl to the waterfront. Not a nice
suggestion with reference to a center of open-air food, but in
time the English made over the Dutch names as they made
over the Dutch government of the town, and "Fly Market"
was among us. "Old Washington Market" still doing business, had its beginnings about 1738, being called at first the
"Oswego Market," and presuming to clutter up the center

305

of Broadway. In 1771 it was removed and a market erected
on the North River at Meiser's Dock. This was known as
the Bear Market until 1814, and upon this site the then
new, but now old, Washington Market began.

Philadelphia lost no time in arranging for her market-
place, for a year after the new name and new buildings had
changed the earlier settlement into a city in 1682, the
butchers were boasting of their movable stalls. Severe laws
were made concerning this market which stood close to the
pillory and other aids to human growth. It was to be open on
Wednesdays and Saturdays, and nothing might be sold until the ringing of the town bell from six to seven o'clock of a
summer morning, or an hour later in the winter. By 1706
the market had its own bell. Any one selling goods in any
other part of the town had to forfeit their goods or barter,
the half of which went to the poor and the other half to the
clerk of the market.

The outgrowths of these first markets became established
institutions throughout the southern part of the country, the
climate making open-air selling possible, but so late an opening as six o'clock was abandoned in favor of an hour or two
earlier. Pennsylvania has had her roads lined with farmers
bringing in their produce throughout the night for a dawn
opening of their booths or stalls. One of the advantages of
these outdoor markets was that they soon led to the smoothing of the streets where they were held, to graveling, and in
time to traffic regulations. Today the Southern markets in
full swing before breakfast are a sight worth seeing, with
flowers and fruits and vegetables mingled under the open
sky or some rough sheltering roof.

OUTLET SHOPS

Weight to pull the door "to"

Exteriors

So many kinds of little dame-shops there were, and thread-and-needle shops, and penny-shops where women tended; and there was the early soda-water and ice-cream parlor (but oh, what soda) sometimes called the "Magnesian Shop" because of the ingredients of this forerunner of present joy; there was the coffee shop, one of these doing a big business along the waterfront in Charleston, South Carolina, in the 1690s, and also the "Sop Shop" where one might drop in and sop his bread in his liquor and break no rules of etiquette; there was even the "Banker's Shop" well enough for those times of smaller fortunes. While in the lane of small industries a shop became symbolic of handwork and manual labor, in the lane of commercialism the word shop stood for business in the large. In time, the penny-shops stood side by

307

side with the shops where shoes were not only sold but made, and wine shops and chandler, cabinet-makers' and money-lenders' shops rubbed elbows all down the street.

Shop Windows

There was something about the little shop window which catches at one's devotion, making one's eyes and feet draw nearer, not because of the displays therein but because the window itself is generally so inviting in line. Take a country road today, or some old alley in a city which has traveled far since this alley was first trodden out, and there will be old windows of diminutive size to catch our glances. Perhaps it is because they lean out in a beckoning way, perhaps because the muntins of their tiny panes of glass crisscross what is behind them to entice us to a closer look, perhaps it is because the long flat line of buildings fall into such monotonous uniformity that these little bulbous watchtowers become the real points of individuality for the whole street.

Shop window angles

The House of the Seven Gables at Salem, Massachusetts, still retains its old shop, perhaps changed from its original condition, but still with its little show window overhanging the sidewalk a few inches, its smaller casement window on the other side of the door, and the door itself having down one side a movable piece of woodwork which in the old days was taken out to admit large sized barrels. Old Salem abounded in the little shops kept in the saltbox tail, or the leanto, or linter, at the rear of the home, and this rear was directly upon the street since the houses were generally placed with their sides to the public and their entrances within the more private side dooryards which were well fenced.

Old shop and post office, with granite hitching posts in front. Stoddard, New Hampshire

One might say that shop windows were applique work, patched on like baskets of grapes to a patchwork quilt, not part of the beam and timber of the house itself. Thus they might take on any form which the shopkeeper desired. The little window measuring only four or five feet from side to side, and eight inches from front to back, glazed with tiny panes, are as beautiful as any. Then there was the even narrower window which blossomed further over the sidewalk and in shape a cylinder cut in two from top to bottom. In order to use glass—which was then always in straight sheets — and make it fit into this extreme curve, some of these windows had as many as eight lines of glass running from top to bottom, and such a window still lasted on Pearl Street, New York City, in the 1830s. One such window became so shallow in its curve that it was a mere wave-like swell, holding twenty-four panes within its miniature size. Regardless of the style, the old projecting shop window was small.

Even after the flat insertion of a window was resorted to, the size was kept small, for glass cost money, and the smaller pieces cost less. Although it lacked the lines of the standout window, the flush window with its great wooden shutters which must be set up at night and taken down each morning, and locked with a great iron bar and a bolt running through into the house, had their own charm. One shop-pad took down this great bar one day as it hung through the day at the side of the window and had a blacksmith put a screwhead in place of the solid head and then, unobserved, hung it back again. That night after it had been run through the wall, and supposedly fastened, he unscrewed the head, opened the shutter and entered as the "pad" that he was. The small panes of course helped in attractiveness and the little shelves which were set across them inside, lined with bottles and all sorts of things, seemed to be peeking out at the passerby. Pennsylvania is rather rich in her left-over shop windows from the past.

As in the stall, the shop door was often a divided one, the bottom of which would keep out straying animals while the top let in the air and showed that business was being carried on. Many an old house as though fearful lest its domestic appearance fail to attract the buying mind, ran out a tiny cube at one end, just large enough for a small counter and a few shelves, and then raised a great square false front of boards utterly unadorned except for its little sign and a lot of bleak grandeur. While the North generally finished up its old church benches in country stores and shops beside the warm chunk stove, the South ran planks from outside pole to pole where its hangers-on might hope to keep cool under a wooden awning.

One can never be thankful enough for the heat of the Southern sun which has brought into being those many wooden shelters which at all angles delight the eye of the passerby. Since no foundation raises the shops from the ground, the ground serves as a porch floor and vines and palm leaves, covering post and slanting roof, lend their shade to idlers of all colors. Because of their sidewalk displays as well, old shops took on an artistic note not common to ordinary houses. New England in the late 1600s used the second story overhang; New Orleans slanted her story-and-a-half shop roofs out over the sidewalk; Pennsylvania tied a penthouse about her shop and thereby turned the sun's rays; while New York and New Jersey stuck a sort of wooden awning over door and window or across the front of the shop.

Shop window in New Orleans last half of 1700s
Dutch shop door, New Amsterdam

The log building has been resorted to for many purposes, for the hog-pen and the barn as well as for house and store and these last bore the name of "log-pen stores." St. Augustine has her inimitable coquina walls with the shop windows flush with them, since the narrow streets can admit of no overhanging ones, and her enticing balconies and hipt roofs, and best of all her little gardens hidden at the rear. New Orleans has painted and repainted her plaster exteriors through the years until the walls of her little shops glow with a brilliance which only her climate can achieve. Dashed across these brilliant surfaces and the ever-green shutters, are signs of every sort, running riot over wood and plaster, picking out old handwrought irons which clothe door and shutter and window.

While our famous and well known and oft-described country store is seldom called a shop, it should be mentioned here, since many of them were for years the outlet for much of the handwork done by our handwrought grandmothers. One of the oldest of these buildings still doing business stands at Ralston, New Jersey. Although the sign of GEN-ERAL STORE is still in place above its door, it is now the village Post Office. Built before the Revolution began, the old building is still in good condition, and under its ancient overhung porch — a part of the original timber construction — two great windows appear. In each of them there are thirty-five panes of oblong glass of a generous size, twenty in the upper sash and fifteen in the lower, bringing the joining below the eye as was usual, and wise, in the old days. There is no overlapping of the wall boards as with clapboards, but a tight joining which has proved weather-worthy for over one hundred and sixty years, as though the little store might have been built to be launched upon a wet sea. Two little windows in each end peak look off across the beautiful valley of its birth. Could its first owner, Mr. Peter De Mott come back and find it still in place, what stories he could tell us of the life of the valley at that venturesome period.

Old store built before the Revolution at Ralston, New Jersey — still in good condition

Interiors

The little door opens directly from the street, up a few steps if in the North, on a level with the ground if in the South. A bell may announce a customer, one hanging overhead and at the end of a long wire, or a cowbell fastened at the right height from the ceiling to hit the top of the door. The North will have its central stove for heating and spitting at when time hangs heavy in the winter, and the South will be without it. Both will have its loafing idlers who seem to fill a needed place in the world. Both will have shelves and goods upon them, and both will have festoons from the ceiling, in the North of dried and salted fish, in the South of dried and salt fat-meat, with cobwebs in both. There was no celophane to cherish, no laws to cover exposed food; jerked meat and bacon sides were allowed to swing free for

313

man and insect, and rope and pails, and boots and overalls
went unsweetened by the proximity of sweetbough, or sour-
bough, or gravenstone apples, or their ilk. Battledore and shut-
tlecock and Medford Rum knew each other in those days
from close association, onions and blue drilling found something in common, and inkpots and hickory shirts never
quarreled of themselves. The sandy South needed a drinking well close by and thatched this haven of coolness with
great leaves and kept the fleas away from the store's vicinity
by spreading black walnut branches about the ground. Both
North and South needed hitching posts or railings to tether
the oxen or the horses or the mules or the cows in their
various riggin's. We all know these country stores, if not
from personal visits at least from literature where they have
run wild.

An old gentleman who kept a country store for many
years in New York's rural parts recalls the days of the 1870s:
"We had to tie everything up in brown paper, for there were
no paper bags or sacks. A little later we did get a small
quantity of white paper to tie up some of the smaller things.
Yes, it wasn't easy to use flat paper for everything. Take
sugar, now. We'd scoop the sugar out of the barrel and put
it, scoop and all, on the steelyards to weigh it,— yes, we
knew how much the scoop weighed — and then pour it out
onto the brown paper. Oh, we learned to manage it, so we
could keep it from coming out all around. For little quantities like pepper and such we made cornucopias out of paper
and turned over the top and pinched the bottom.

"Another thing we did with the brown paper was to put
it into the vinegar to make it stronger, to make the Mother
form. What was it made of? Why, straw. And do you know
that brown sugar sometimes got so hard we'd use a cooper's

adz on it to break it. You could even rub it round and make the sparks fly."

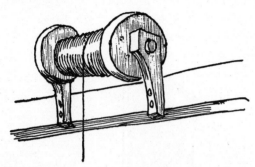

Rough twine holder fastened to cross beam

Bench and Board

Within most of the little shops where things were made, the "bench" was the piece de resistance among the furnishings, and the "workman at his bench" was the symbolic figure of industry. However, in the shop of the taylor, or tailour, or tailor — still where things were made — we find the bench becoming the "shopboard," upon which the tailor sat crosslegged as he snipped and plied his needle. Within those little shops where things were sold we find this word "shop board" quite universally among the early words synonomous with our word "counter," and achieving the name quite naturally as did the dining table of feudal days, when the "board" and "sideboard" were simply huge planks or boards so great that no others were needed to lay beside it for the required width. The counter was also the "shop stall," which seems strange, and as we have already seen, the word "counter" itself grew out of the need of something to go counter to the desire of the public to come too close while buying, first used to keep them out of the little stall, then out of the rich stores of supply, and especially as a deterrent to the shop-pad or thief.

A shop balcony. St. Augustine

Whether bench, shop-board, stall or counter, this wall of defense built up by the shop-rid tradesman, seems to have been used quite as much for a place of lounging and rest, for reclining and sleep, as for its original purpose. Both customer and shop-keeper indulged themselves upon its restful bosom, and many a man going in for a jug of molasses or seventeen nails found the shopkeeper lying full length upon his counter. Sometimes he found it fringed with dangling legs of those who had arrived too late for the benches and cask tops. One old country storekeeper remembers as one of his special trials the row of loungers who sat along his counter to be near the stove, and, helping themselves to peanuts on the sly, hid the shells in the receptacles for new nails, and that he had to pick them out — the shells — one by one before he closed the store for the night. The old counters were always made to slant back under a little, perhaps so that one standing in front of it would not stub his toes, perhaps so that those sitting on it could swing their legs with greater freedom.

The little old shops for work have become the factories of today, while the little old shops for sales have grown into our vast department stores, and many of both kinds cover acres of land which once blew to buttercups.

∾∾∾∾∾∾∾∾∾∾∾∾∾∾∾∾∾∾

⤜§ X §⤛

"A penny saved is a penny earned."

∾∾∾∾∾∾∾∾∾∾∾∾∾∾∾∾∾∾

Account Books

WE might say that their account books were as hand-wrought as the ancestors themselves. A stump of dirty chalk often represented the whole desk equipment of the man with the small shop. Sometimes the wall was all that he had for his figgerin'.

"Want I should set it down or will you settle for it?"

"What do you prize it fer?"

"Two shillin'."

"You best score it, this time."

"Jes'y' say. I'll set it down 'fore it gits cold," and a chalk mark on the wall would be all that was needed. The system was easy,— four vertical marks stood for four bags or bushels or four hens, while the fifth was slanted across the four to make adding easy. These old hieroglyphics keep popping up in all sorts of places. One pleasant bed-room door has fading marks of some such transaction where the score was not set-tled until five slant lines had been swept across — probably "set down" on the door while the house was building and the lumber and nails were being reckoned up. They fig-gered on everything handy, including wall-maps, family-trees and cuffs. A grocer in Pensacola chalked his accounts on the floor under his bed, which was a safe enough place until his wife mopped the floor one day. Another Florida shopkeeper kept his accounts by drawing pictures of the things purchased and charged. One day he reminded a man that he owed him for a whole cheese. The man denied the charge and then remembered that he did owe for a grindstone. "That's so," the shopman said, "I forgot to draw a hole in the middle." Apparently men have always been hard up for money to buy the things they have needed, for back in the 1600s our forebears were "scoring for quarts and bushels."

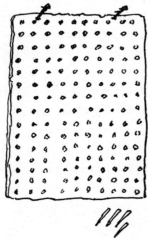

Old Pennsylvania "shop-book" — a hole-and-peg "score board" for keeping individual accounts in rows 16 x 12 feet — 150 holes

The shopbook might have leaves and a wooden cover, but it might also be a long slab of wood hung on the wall by a trunnel, with holes bored up and down it in rows, into which pegs were stuck for keeping separate accounts of different purchasers. A name to a row. Barter has been with us always, and of all sorts. "Barter: Maple sugar, cordwood, geese feathers, butter, fowl, cheese, cider, etc." In 1754 a Boston shopkeeper was advertising goods to be sold "for Indian Corn, Maryland Pork, Bacon, Myrtle Wax, Hogshead and Barrell Staves." Living with our ancestors we would not have had to "go without" for want of certain pieces of round metal curiously stamped. John Locke, in 1704, wrote: "He also bartered away plums that would have rotted in a week, for nuts that would last good . . . a whole year."

"Ready Pay. One price store," was another sign which one ran into many times, which brings us to the fact that it is only about a century ago that stores had as many prices for their goods as they had purchasers, or might have. One paid for his appearance, that is, a shop-keeper fixed upon the price which he thought the man would pay. A group of worthwhile men finally took a stand on this matter, and after working on the reform for some time, won the decent shop-keepers over to the habit of marking one price and keeping to it. This put an end to much of the old and expected chaffering, higgling and bargaining which had been going on for centuries.

Subtle Appeals

Quarter Day, Pray
Gentlemen Pay.

This couplet was the legend on a shaving mug with a Dutch background, a century or two ago, and gives us the name for that day of settling accounts which in some places came four times a year. *The Ulster County Gazette,* published at Warsink, January the fourth, 1800, carried this broad hint:

BARTER AND SCORE

Luther Andres and Company have this day
Been opening goods both fresh and gay.
He has receiv'd near every kind,
That you in any store can find,
I am determined to retail,
For Ready Pay a little lower
Than ever have been had before.
I with my brethren mean to live;
But as for Credit shall not give.
I would not live to rouse your passions,
For credit here is out of fashion.
My friends and buyers one and all
It will pay you well to give a call.
You always may find me by the sign,
A few rods from the house divine.

The following articles will be received in payment.
Wheat, Rye, Buck-wheat, Oats, Corn, Butter, Flax,
Ashes and Raw Hides. These articles will be taken in
at the Esopus prices. Cash will not be refused.

In a Southern city this sign hangs upon the wall of a
little shop on a side street:

I may have a big ♡
And you may have a big ◊
But there's always a man with a big ♠
Ready to dig my grave
If I trust behind the Counter.
So I keep
A little ♣ for anybody who
Asks for credit.

"You see," said the kind shopkeeper, "it means playin'
cards. That's pretty good, don' you 'low?"

321

HANDWROUGHT ANCESTORS

Strong Boxes

In order to make money out of barter the shopkeeper must of course dispose of it, and much barter was shipped to the city from the country stores as soon as the snow made good sleddin'. Raw materials were often the barter received and these were never difficult of disposal. Carried to New York or Boston, they brought back the much wanted "Ready Cash."

"My grandfather Cole carried produce down to Boston and brought back goods for his store. A week for a trip. I used to see the chest with lock and key which the driver used for a seat, and all of the best small things were kept safe under his boots. He had his food and other things he needed in the box too. This box always sat in the counting room when it wasn't traveling back and forth to Boston. There was a little recess in the brick wall covered by an iron door with a staple and lock. This was the first safe we ever had in the village."

A woman in one New Hampshire store who had to have all of her goods teamed in over the hills, always mourned when her stock was selling, because more would have to be sent for. One spring she made a break in custom and sent for some bananas. The result was horrifying. Every boy for miles around wanted one at once, and before the evening was over they were all gone. She tried it once or twice more and then gave up in disgust. "What's the use of buying them if they're sold so fast I can't keep any in stock?" Her strong box was an old "Post Office," a high desk of home-made build which had a slit in one side for the occasional mailed letter, and a top which went up when unlocked. It might have been called a Uriah Heep desk, but that was not the right name, it must always be called the Post Office.

Along the coast, strongboxes or safes were more numerous,

322

for here the produce and imports were brought in many ships, and custom houses with their secret, strong holds were necessary. At Kennebunkport, Maine, the old "safe" where both precious cargo and money were kept, is a great closet off what was once the custom house office. This closet is lined with great slabs of stone, ceiling, sides and floor, and the lock upon the door is a work of art and ingenuity. Virginia still has some of her ancient custom-houses, perhaps the very oldest in the country.

Buildings of America's oldest custom house at Yorktown, Virginia, 1715

The usual strongbox for the small shop-keeper, whether he made or sold goods, was the plain wooden chest, or the "fur trunk," both of which took on the name of "till" as soon as they became repositories of wealth. In each wooden till was usually a smaller wooden pocket built in close to the top, where sometimes secret drawers and cubby-holes were hidden away, and this was the "till" par excellence, a till within a till.

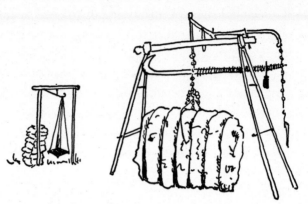

Modern scales in a cotton warehouse. S. C.
Old sidewalk scales of early New York City

Weights and Measures

The steelyard was the usual "scales" for getting a record of weight, and these old steelyards were homemade tools, forged, marked and fashioned by hand, with a great rough chunk of iron for the paez, or balance weight. The great scales which stood always on the sidewalk in the cities, were nothing more than a great steelyard with a wooden platform tied on with rope or chain for holding the article to be weighed. The "ell" rather than the "yard" was the popular measure for cloth, the former measuring a yard and a quarter. "Give him an inch and he'll take an ell."

The Pinch Fist

Not a nice name to apply to either man or woman, but some of them were so called, and even "pinch penny." This sort of person had many ways of slicing a little off the under side of the pound of butter between weighing and wrapping, and helping the weight with his fat hand or his heavy foot, and asking for the bean pods back again for the hogs after

BARTER AND SCORE

the buyer had shelled them. One shopman stooped at nothing short of the courts to collect the smallest sums. As one of his old neighbors tells it: "Sure, he'd get body judgment against a man for some triflin' amount — he'd take a man's carcass — and laugh." If it had not been for the forefather who never remembered to set down any of his charges and never under any circumstances asked a neighbor to pay up, we should have been a sad race. "The devil to pay and no pitch hot."

A familiar signature on receipted scores at 34-35 Partition Street, from 1806 until 1854 "Duncan Fife, the joiner," in 1793

325

❧ XI ❧

"Humpff! Call that a rain? T'was only a gutter-washer and chunk-floater."

— *Kentucky*

A country doctor's shop near the Helderbergs, New York — "Where he done his tinkerin'."

More Little Shops

AS we look back at those tiny buildings which have been scattered over the country ever since our ancestors felt their first material needs in everyday living, they do indeed seem like little more than the inconsequential rains of the South which descend quickly in volume, float the stray chunks of wood for a brief ride, and then are gone. The real historian of the growth of America will however see in them the seedlings of our great industries and fortunes, and, on the side, will love them for all those devices, tricks and tools which they brought into being during their years of tenure. Only ten or twelve feet square, some of them, and yet they shod a large countryside; boasting of but one narrow window, perhaps, through which the sunlight fell upon the bent workman, they were yet the place from which came the rigging to tie a cart to a horse, the pounded herb to save a sick man's life, or perhaps the birthplace of great anchors to save a ship at sea.

This story of the handwork of our forebears has traveled so swiftly over some of these little four-walls-and-a-roof,— touching them scarcely long enough to learn their ways and often passing on before their secrets have been discovered — that the picture has been almost kaleidoscopic. There is a temptation to go on and on and let the light fall, if only for a moment, on all of those old centers of handwrought skill which might be dug up and brought back, if not to memory, at least into recognition before it is too late. Some of them must be mentioned if only by name and a few more given at least a chance to make a hurried bow. Here are a few of the hitherto unmentioned articles which deserved and won their own shops: horse-collars, hat-blocks, cut files, horse-hair "sives," wooden piggins for milkpails, wooden decoy ducks, hobby-horses, wooden noggins for dippers, cards for carding wool, cages, traps, patterns for woodworking, "drawed wyre," wooden spoons, silver of all sorts, watches and clocks, pewter ware, keys and locks and guns, jugs, tinware, anchors, and so one might go on for a long time, and with years of research never hope to discover what was made in some of the old shops, because we do not know the full run of needs of those early days.

Wooden pigin used for milking pail

BREVITIES ON – LITTLE, BUT OH MY!

༄ᝰᗕᝰᗕᝰᗕᝰᗕᝰᗕᝰᗕᝰᗕᝰᗕᝰᗕᝰᗕᝰᗕ

THE CHANDLER SHOP

"Yei shul bene at ye chaundelers by pryme of ye day." 1389

༄ᝰᗕᝰᗕᝰᗕᝰᗕᝰᗕᝰᗕᝰᗕᝰᗕᝰᗕᝰᗕᝰᗕ

If one of us had arisen at dawn to meet this appointment we should have found ourselves in a candle-maker's shop, perhaps. We might have been in the shop of a man who had charge of the lighting of some master's hall, for they bore the same name, or of a "petty shopkeeper," or a "corn chandler," or of a dealer in small wares, for the original candlemaker came in time to be a dealer in all sorts of goods. As he is best remembered today he was the keeper of those shops along the waterfronts where everything which a sea-faring man might want, might be found. "The Chandler's Shop" came to smack of the sea, and the memory of a little handmade candle had long ago smoked itself out.

Back in his original reason for being, the chandler was an important man, even though for the farm folks who made their own candles, he scarcely existed. For the wealthy planter or city-dweller, the situation was different. We have this from the diary of Colonel Landon Carter, of South Carolina, in 1770:

> "March 24. I can borrow no candles at Beverley's and if Thompson's purchase from Norfolk don't come up soon, we must be content to sit in the dark, which I get by lending candles myself. Mr. Carter of Corotoman had two boxes containing better than 5 gross. Mr. Parker had some dozens, but these are gentlemen who only think of favors when they want them."

HANDWROUGHT ANCESTORS

The South says: "He couldn't hold a light to him."

The North says: "He couldn't hold a candle to him."
Both sayings mean that someone is inferior to some one else.
The original of these sayings comes to light as "He can't
hold a candle to him. Not even to hold a light for his work."
How many of us have thought that hours were spent in just
holding a light for some other man to work by?

BREVITIES ON – LITTLE, BUT OH MY!

THE CLAY PIPE SHOP

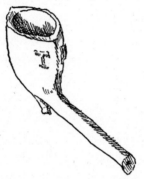

The "TD" clay pipe, or "nose toaster." 1700-1800s

The name of Timothy Dexter stands for leather-dressing, amassing of great wealth, the assuming of high sounding titles, and the making of the little old "nose toaster." On each of the little clay pipes which for years were sold over shop counters in New England and farther afield, the initials "T. D." carried the great and the foolish Dexter's fame. He called himself "Lord Timothy Dexter of Newburyport, Earl of Chester, first in the East, first in the West, and the greatest philosopher in all the known world," and yet he had arrived in town with eight dollars and forty cents in his pocket and a "bundel" over his shoulder.

Dexter was born in 1747 and those who write of him tell of his wealth and his "pallaces," but the men and women of New England — or some of them — knew him only by his pipes. A clay pipe is a perishable thing, and the slender stem was always getting snapped off at the slightest provocation. Very soon these pipes had worn their stems down until they were little more than a stub and the bowls therefore came so close to the smoker's face, that they were dubbed "nose-toasters." Some people speak of the old clay pipe as "those cutty clay pipes."

At "Wiggins Old Tavern" in Northampton, Massachusetts, there is an old clay-pipe mould which gives us an idea of what went on in a pipe shop when the pipe was in the making. The mould frame is of oak and the forms are of pewter. The clay was poured into the bowl forms and then slender forms of pewter were stuck in at the side to form the stem.

The tobacco dealers of Philadelphia in 1739, called themselves "Tobacconists to Women and Men."

Oldest tobacco store in America founded by Christopher Demuth, Lancaster, Pa., 1770. Original sign in use today in shop on same site, run by same family. Goods sold through window for fear of Indians. Figure sign run out each morning on little platform; holds a snuff-box and a hand of tobacco and was carved by the son of the proprietor

BREVITIES ON – LITTLE, BUT OH MY!

THAT WOODEN INJUN

"As silent as an Indian chief."

A Pennsylvania wooden Indian peddling cigars

The "wooden injun" was a usual sight before the shops of the tobacconists until a quarter of a century ago, and now they are as scarce as hen's teeth, and hiding away from searchers for them as their flesh and blood forebears did centuries ago. They are said to have begun their silent but appealing existence back in the time of Queen Anne, but their greatest vogue in this country was in the third quarter of the 1800s, after which they began their silent and gliding exits until no longer were there bright feathers and high cheekbones and an outstretched handful of cigars to beguile the passerby. Sometimes the Indian was given the go-by and

333

HANDWROUGHT ANCESTORS

Sir Walter Raleigh, or some grand old gentleman, or even an appealing lady, or a befringed trapper took his place. But they never won our hearts. What is considered the oldest of our wooden Indians had his place in Lancaster, Pennsylvania, and was made in 1770.

The wooden Indian has a double reason for mention in this list, for he not only acted as a sign before a shop door, but was created in a shop of his own. It is believed that as the demand for figureheads for sailing vessels declined, some of the Swiss carvers of the seagoing figures turned their eyes inland and seized upon the red savage as their next piece de resistance. Some of the best of our wooden Indians were carved in Detroit. Someone who knew this work well has given us this description:

> "The wood used was white pine bought at the spar yards. Paper patterns guided the workers for the first rough outlines. Then the log was blocked out with an ax into spaces for the head, to the waist, to the knee, and for the legs, — these were at once divided. Only a native feeling for form made the work possible. A hole was then bored in each end of the prepared log, about five inches deep. An iron bolt was placed in each and the ends rested on supports. The body hangs free. The workman chips with a chisel and finishes with finer tools. The hand and arms were made separately and joined to the figure with screws. The finished chief with the cigars in his outstretched hand was then fastened upon a square standard which moved upon ignominious wheels."

Such figures, hewn and chiseled out by a master hand, are claimed among our examples of American art today; but those Indians, which looked like lady barrels on parade and were turned out on a lathe like a porch post, and painted up to seem like Indians, made no donation to our art trends.

BREVITIES ON – LITTLE, BUT OH MY!

THE PRINT SHOP

The first of these most important shops was established at Harvard College in 1639; in Virginia, John Buckner printed — alas, without a license — the "laws of 1680," and was reproved by Governor Lord Culpepper and had all later printing prohibited; in 1685 William Bradford, according to some authorities, set up his press in Philadelphia and started with an almanack, while according to others he started his paper making in Philadelphia in the late 1600s and went into New Jersey shortly after to start the first printing there; at Ephrata, Pennsylvania, Conrad Beitzel and his celibates soon had a printing press running and turned out the Christopher Saur Bible in 1743; and in 1749 Isaiah Thomas was born and through a long life made a real advance for all print shops and books in America; in this same year of 1749 James Davis set up at New Bern, the first printing press in the state of North Carolina.

Print shop of B. Franklin

The little shop of B. FRANKLIN PRINTER was perhaps the most famous of all. Franklin not only printed but

made a hand press for printing which was so good that it
was still in use in New York City in 1859.

*The well-worn door under the chained wooden
awning of "The Bookery," Winter Park, Florida*

BOOK BINDERIES

Book press in the Conrad Beitzel Community, in
1730, Ephrata, Pennsylvania

Last of all the many kinds of shops chosen for mention herein is that one which made the work of the printer permanent and carried "learning" to the most isolated farms, that little shop where books were bound. The first man to own such a shop in America was John Ratcliffe, and in 1663 he was commissioned to bind Eliot's "Indian Bible." His orders were to "take care for the binding of two hundred of them strongly and as speedily as may bee with leather, or as may bee most serviceable for the Indians." On the thirtieth of August he sent word to the Commissioners of New England that he was not satisfied with the prices paid for the binding, and that three shilling fourpence or three shilling sixpence was the lowest price for which he could do the binding.

337

HANDWROUGHT ANCESTORS

Many of our old books show the crude split oaken covers over which was wrapped home cured rawhide or sheepskin for a fine finish. We find the current newssheets of the day cut and pressed into service as a sort of reinforcing lining and some of the news proves interesting reading. In 1823 an advertisement appeared in a Hamilton, New York, newspaper:

> "The highest price in Books and Stationery will be paid for good tanned Sheepskins, suitable for book binding at this office."

In the tanning of leather for these purposes the sumach seems to have been the preferred ingredient for proper curing and results. Even paper covered books must be bound and we find this work starting off strongly in the Connecticut Valley, a chain of independent shops developing as able apprentices learned their trade and started in for themselves in shops farther up the river. The sewing and careful stretching of leather for full and half bindings of calf, and the change from wood to what was known as "mill-board," or a stout pasteboard, for the inner part of the cover, would make a full book in themselves. We are here only taking off our hat to one of the most interesting and important of all those little shops in which our forebears, in the making of many handwrought things, wrought most capably and satisfactorily upon themselves and gave us our much treasured handwrought ancestors.

Old store, Glenriddle, Pa.
"Rest awhile"

LIST OF ILLUSTRATIONS

341

LIST OF ILLUSTRATIONS

LIST OF ILLUSTRATIONS

LIST OF ILLUSTRATIONS

344

LIST OF ILLUSTRATIONS

345

LIST OF ILLUSTRATIONS

LIST OF ILLUSTRATIONS

LIST OF ILLUSTRATIONS

348

LIST OF ILLUSTRATIONS

LIST OF ILLUSTRATIONS

LIST OF ILLUSTRATIONS

351

LIST OF ILLUSTRATIONS

LIST OF ILLUSTRATIONS

LIST OF ILLUSTRATIONS

354

LIST OF ILLUSTRATIONS

355

LIST OF ILLUSTRATIONS

LIST OF ILLUSTRATIONS

357

LIST OF ILLUSTRATIONS

358

INDEX

359

INDEX

INDEX

INDEX

362

INDEX

363

INDEX

INDEX

INDEX